CW00420554

EMIGRANT SHIPS

The vessels which carried migrants
across the world, 1946–1972

Anthony Cooke

Published by
Carmania Press
Unit 224, Station House, 49, Greenwich High Road, London SE10 8JL

Contents

Inside cover: The *Australis* at Southampton in November, 1973. This large ex-American is said to have carried more than a quarter of a million passengers in Chandris's very profitable Australian service. *R. Bruce Grice*

Front cover top: The world famous *Achille Lauro* at Southampton in November, 1979. *R. Bruce Grice*

Front cover bottom: Two ships owned by the Mogul Line, an Indian company owned by P&O made individual migrant voyages from the Mediterranean. The *Mohammedi* is here seen during her acceptance trials on the Clyde. *P&O Archives*

Back cover: The *Britanis*, is one of a number of former American liners which Chandris bought for their Australian service. Now sailing as a very popular cruise ship, she is dated back to 1932. *Steffen Weirauch collection*

ISBN 0 9518656 0 9

British Library Cataloguing-in-Publication Data. A catalogue record for this book is available from the British Library.

© Anthony Cooke & Carmania Press

Production by Waterfront Publications, Poole, Dorset.
Typeset by PageMerger, Southampton.
Printed by Amadeus Press, Huddersfield, Yorks.

Chapter One
Who Were the Emigrants?

The Second World War devastated the passenger ship fleets. Taking only the figures for vessels over 10,000 gross tons, the scale of the destruction is horrifying. At the beginning of the War there were 368 such ships. Only 196 survived and some of those did not return to commercial service, either because they had become unfit for it or because they were never released from government hands. Many of those which did come back were not available to their owners for several years after the end of hostilities – they could not be spared immediately and they needed lengthy refits. Compounding the problem was the delay of two or three years before new passenger ships began to enter service. War had taken its toll of the shipyards and there was a dearth of steel and other materials. It is hard now to imagine just how short Europe was of most of the necessities.

At the same time, there was an enormous need for passenger ships. Quite apart from the six or seven years backlog of traffic which the liner companies were eager to catch up with, there was a vast migration from Europe – fully on the scale of the flood which had left in the years around the turn of the century. In particular, there were the displaced persons, as they were bureaucratically called. There were fourteen million refugees of whom a million or more were unable to return to their native countries – and, indeed, in some cases had no countries to return to. They had to be re-settled elsewhere. As late as the twelve month period to June, 1950 the International Refugee Organisation (the I.R.O.) was planning to carry 285,500 displaced persons overseas, in addition to those it hoped to settle in Western Europe.

There were others, too, who wished to leave the Old World. Thousands felt that they and their families deserved greater opportunities and a better life than Britain, tired after the War and suffering the rigours of austerity, could apparently offer. They had their counterparts in other countries and often they were encouraged to go. The governments of Holland and Italy, for instance, saw over-population as one of the causes of their economic problems. Fortunately, Canada, Australia, New Zealand and, briefly, South Africa were crying out for able-bodied and skilled people. All sought to attract British immigrants

Migrants taking Assisted Passages from Britain to Australia (£10, one way), could expect clean but stark quarters aboard elderly liners. Here we see an eight-berth cabin on P&O's *Chitral*.   *P&O Archives*

with free or assisted passages. British settlers were, for instance, encouraged to travel to Australia at a cost of just £10 for the one-way voyage. Australia also relaxed its attitude towards the natives of other countries and attracted vast numbers of Greeks, Italians, Yugoslavs and others. In addition, some of the more prosperous Latin American countries were still taking in immigrants by the thousand. The delusion that South America was on the brink of enormous prosperity, which had sucked in men and money from Europe for several generations, had yet to be shattered.

In retrospect, the number of people requiring long distance transport at that time seems enormous. To those struggling with the problem it must have seemed overwhelming. There were no jet aeroplanes capable of whisking the emigrants to their new countries. Even a fast sea voyage to Australia was likely to take thirty days – many took considerably longer. The number of ships required, therefore, was staggering.

Somehow they were found. Gradually the liner companies resumed their peacetime business and they were joined by new and enterprising shipowners, often operating under flags of convenience. There were various government-sponsored programmes. There were the operations of the International Refugee Organisation.

The I.R.O. was a United Nations Agency formed in 1947 and based in Geneva. The size of the task which it faced has already been indicated. It used a varied fleet of vessels to carry displaced persons, mainly from German and Mediterranean ports. They flew the I.R.O.'s blue flag with a green and white lifebuoy device. The programme started with American army transports and in the months of July, August and September, 1949, for instance, no less than 22 of these vessels sailed into New York carrying 51,906 displaced persons in addition to 19,518 military personnel. It proved necessary to supplement the efforts of the troopships by time-chartering a number of commercial vessels and booking space in others. In the early stages the Salén company of Sweden was much involved in the organisation of the fleet. (It was reported at the time that it had previously been employed by the International Red Cross in carrying 16 million gift parcels to Allied prisoners of war.)

Most of the passengers on the I.R.O.'s chartered ships were housed in dormitories, often with the men accommodated separately in the forepart of the ship and the women and children in the afterpart. Contemporary reports made great mention of the medical facilities which were provided and it was stated that the *Skaugum*, for instance, had workrooms where her passengers could occupy themselves with dressmaking, tailoring, ironing, shoe-repairing and carpentry. Despite these facilities, however, it is probable that most of the ships employed by the I.R.O. carried their passengers in extremely stark conditions.

The shortage of passenger tonnage forced the I.R.O. to charter some very odd ships indeed. Their owners were not invariably reliable. The story of the *San Francisco*, told in a later chapter, does not show either the honesty of the 'owners' or the business sense of the I.R.O. officials concerned in a good light. Somehow, however, a most varied and often extraordinary fleet was assembled to cope with the traffic.

As time went on new ships were brought into the trade which were much more comfortable, even luxurious – particularly on the Australian run. Even so, emigration remained a daunting step to take. For some it no longer had the finality which it had in earlier years, but many were still unlikely to see their homeland, their family or their friends ever again. It was a step into the unknown and, although the dangers of sea travel were less, things could still go wrong. There was the pathetic case in the early 'seventies of the passengers who arrived in Australia on a rather elderly liner and were told that a sewage pipe running through one of the holds had been leaking. The authorities condemned the entire contents of the hold to be destroyed. They were the belongings which the migrants had brought with them to start their new life. There was a near-riot on the quayside.

This book is an attempt to make a record of the ships, ranging from the most antiquated 'rust-buckets' to sleek modern liners, which carried the migrants across the world.

The Smoke Room on *Chitral*.   *P&O Archives*

4

Chapter Two

The British Ships

The British contrived on the whole to use old liners to carry their migrants. Many well-known British ships had, of course, been tragically lost but quite a few survived the War, albeit in a somewhat worn state. An early post-War task for several famous Cunarders was transporting war brides and their babies to their husbands' countries across the Atlantic. The veteran *Aquitania* (1914/45,547 gross tons) made several voyages to Canada although she was now in a fairly frail state. The *Queen Mary*, no less, (1936/81,235 gross tons) carried G.I. brides and their children to the United States in 1946. (G.I. brides were British girls who had married American servicemen. There were stories current at the time of girls who had extravagant expectations of the American way of life and who received an unpleasant surprise when they found that home was to be an isolated farm in Idaho or a tenement in Chicago.) The *Queen Mary* made thirteen such voyages, carrying a total of 22,000 passengers before being taken in hand by her builders, John Brown of Clydebank, for restoration to her luxurious pre-war state.

Union-Castle Line

The Union-Castle Line's *Arundel Castle* (1921/19,118 gross tons), *Carnarvon Castle* (1926/20,123 gross tons) and *Winchester Castle* (1930/20,012 gross tons) also had their refurbishments postponed in order that they might be made available to carry various migrants to Southern Africa. In January, 1947 a piece in 'The Times' contrasted conditions on the *Capetown Castle*, newly restored to pre-war Union-Castle standards, with those on the *Carnarvon Castle*. Both ships were lying at Southampton at the time. It stated that the *Carnarvon Castle* accommodated 1,200 passengers 'in conditions reminiscent of those in which troops were carried'. Men were berthed in dormitories, 'to some of which more than 100 are assigned'. The women were carried in rooms accommodating perhaps 12 each. 'Before travelling in ships like this, which have not been re-conditioned, all passengers are asked to sign a statement that they are aware of the conditions of austerity. So great is the demand for passages that such vessels carry large numbers of passengers

The famous Cunard–White Star express liner, the *Aquitania*, made unglamorous austerity voyages in the late 1940s. Here she is seen at Southampton.
Steffen Weirauch collection

on every voyage.' In all, the three Union-Castle 'austerity' ships carried over 30,000 passengers before the service was closed in mid-1949.

This did not mark the end of the line's interest in the emigrant trade, however. A new motor ship was built specifically to carry migrants not only to South Africa but also to the East African territories. The *Bloemfontein Castle* (1950/18,400 gross tons) had a recognisably Union-Castle profile but unlike the company's other major liners she carried no first-class passengers. Unfortunately, the anticipated migrant boom did not develop on the route, partly owing to the political changes beginning to take place in South Africa. Also the collapse of the 'Groundnut Scheme' early in 1951 robbed the ship of an important source of traffic. (This was a grandiose, and eventually notorious, project set up by the British government to use enormous tracts of land in southern Tanganyika for the cultivation of groundnuts.) As a result, the *Bloemfontein Castle* was not a successful ship and after only nine years she was sold to Chandris for their new Australian service.

Ministry of Transport Ships

Australia almost certainly absorbed more migrants than any other country after the War and her government was particularly vociferous in its demands for more ships to be provided to supplement the regular liner sailings from Britain which P&O, Orient, Aberdeen & Commonwealth and Shaw, Savill & Albion were gradually reinstating. At one time there was even a suggestion that the Australian administration should itself acquire vessels to carry migrants, but this option was not pursued. Perhaps the memory was too vivid of the financial and other disasters which had attended their previous attempt, after the First World War (the Commonwealth Government Line which was ultimately sold off to become the Aberdeen & Commonwealth Line.) In the event, the British Ministry of Transport gathered together a group of elderly liners to carry migrants who were mainly travelling under the assisted passage scheme. Some of these ships it chartered, others it actually owned. The first to go into service, in October 1947, was the Orient Steam Navigation Company's *Ormonde* (1917/15,047 gross tons) whose passenger capacity had been increased from the pre-War figure of 777 to 1,070. The following year two Peninsular & Oriental ships, the *Ranchi* (1925/16,974 gross tons) and the *Chitral* (1925/15,555 gross tons) were also taken on charter after being refitted.

These three vessels sailed regularly from London, but the Bibby liners *Somersetshire* (1921/9,787 gross tons), *Dorsetshire* (1920/9,789 gross tons) and *Cheshire* (1927/10,623 gross tons), which joined the Ministry of Transport fleet under charter in 1948 and 1949, sailed from their home port of Liverpool. All three had already had interesting careers. The *Somersetshire* and the *Dorsetshire* were the largest motor ships afloat when they were built. Originally they were cargo ships, designed to carry lead ore from Burmese mines but the mining company started its own smelter, thus doing away with the need to ship ore overseas. The two new ships, therefore, spent much of their time on charter to other owners. However, when Bibby's trooping contract came up for renewal in 1927, the sisters were converted into troopships in order to fulfil the new contract which the company was awarded. While serving as a hospital ship during the War the *Somersetshire* was torpedoed and evacuated. However, she stayed afloat and her crew boarded her again and brought her into port. The third Bibby ship to be placed on the Australian run, the *Cheshire*, had been built for the line's passenger and cargo service to Ceylon and Burma. She too was fortunate to survive the War, having been torpedoed twice. In the late 'forties, political developments in Burma leading up to the country's independence killed off much of Bibby's regular trade and left them as one of the few lines with surplus passenger tonnage.

The final chartered liner recruited to the Ministry's Australian service was the Anchor Line's *Cameronia* (1921/16,584 gross tons). The sole survivor of the company's Atlantic passenger fleet, she required so much restoration after her War service[1] that her future seemed doubtful, particularly as the Anchor Line decided that fully-fledged passenger liners were no longer a viable proposition on their historic Glasgow–New York route. However, after a £½ million refit the Ministry of Transport took her on charter with an option to purchase at a later date. Her voyages to Australia commenced at Glasgow and on several occasions she, and some other migrant ships, sailed home via the East Indies to help in the repatriation of the many Dutchmen who were forced to leave during the emergence of the new state of Indonesia.

Of the ships actually owned by the Ministry of Transport which appeared on the Australian emigrant run, three might well have been discarded as beyond repair in less straitened times. All had been notable liners in their day. The *Georgic* (1932/27,469 gross tons) was the last vessel to be laid down for the White Star Line. She retained the old company's livery, even though White Star was soon absorbed by Cunard as a quid pro quo for government aid in financing the completion of the *Queen Mary*. With her squat but well-balanced appearance, the *Georgic* had been typical of the many motor liners built by Harland & Wolff for the constituent companies of Lord Kylsant's mighty but insecurely financed empire. However, her looks had changed for the worse. In 1941, she had been bombed and set on fire near Suez. Somehow she was patched up and survived the long and perilous tow to Karachi. She was re-built, initially as a troopship. Of her two short motor-ship funnels, the forward one had been a dummy and it was not thought necessary to replace it. Similarly, she now sported just one very stumpy mast. The result was a singularly ill-proportioned vessel, but a serviceable one – she was even chartered by the Cunard–White Star Line for use in their less glamorous North Atlantic services during several summers in the 'fifties.

---

1   During the War she had steamed over 321,000 miles and carried 167,600 troops and other personnel, taking part in the North African, Italian, Normandy and South of France landings. During the North African campaign she was seriously damaged in an attack by torpedo-carrying aircraft but managed to reach safety.

Chitral's dining room may look rather bare, but the tables are set for a six-course meal – quite a change for migrants leaving a Britain still enduring food-rationing.
P&O Archives

The *Asturias* (1926/22,608 gross tons) had been another of the large Harland & Wolff – Kylsant motor-ships. Belonging to the Royal Mail Line, she had been converted to steam turbine propulsion in order to increase her speed and make her more competitive with the Germans, Italians and French on the South American route. While being fitted out for War service she too had her forward funnel removed. She was badly damaged in a torpedo attack and, although saved, was written off as a total loss. However, the shortage of ships was so severe that the government eventually had her reconstructed as a trooper and later as an emigrant-carrier. As usual with Ministry of Transport ships, she was placed under the management of her former owners.

The *New Australia* (1931/20,256 gross tons) was the ugliest of them all. She had been the luxurious *Monarch of Bermuda* on the Furness Bermuda Line's weekly cruising service between New York and the island from which she took her name. The ships of some companies seem particularly prone to fire – the French lines were a case in point and Furness Bermuda was another. While being refitted to resume her regular service after the War the turbo-electric *Monarch of Bermuda* suffered a blaze which caused severe damage, although her machinery escaped the

worst effects. The hulk was bought by the Ministry of Transport and was re-built as an emigrant ship at a cost of well over £2 million. In her new form she could accommodate no less than 1,593 passengers. She retained just one of her three funnels, although she also exhausted smoke through a curious twin uptake arrangement which also served as a mast. It is said that her relatively shallow draught, dictated by the requirements of the Bermudan ports for which she was built, made her unsteady while crossing long expanses of open ocean. She was placed under the management of Shaw, Savill & Albion, a Furness Withy subsidiary with great experience of the Antipodean trades.

These vessels maintained the Ministry's service with occasional help from others, including the Australian coastal liner *Kanimbla* (1936/10,985 gross tons), a notable motor ship belonging to McIlwraith McEacharn. In 1948 she brought over the crew of a new aircraft carrier which was being built in Britain for the Royal Australian Navy. On her return trip she carried a full load of emigrants. 1951-52 was the peak period of the assisted passage scheme. Thereafter numbers declined and, increasingly, the commercial liner services were able to accommodate much of the traffic. By 1957 all the vessels employed by the Ministry on the Australian route had either been transferred to troopship service or had been scrapped, with the exception of the *New Australia* which was sold to the Greek Line and became their *Arkadia*. The Australian government had awarded contracts to the Sitmar Line to bring their migrants from Britain and Sitmar retained this trade until being replaced as the official carrier by the Chandris group in 1970.

P&O

Mention should also be made of those ships which the regular liner companies on the Australian route devoted more or less specifically to the carriage of emigrants on their outward voyages. The P&O Line (The Peninsular & Oriental Steam Navigation Company[1]) refitted the sisters *Maloja* (1923/21,036 gross tons) and *Mooltan* (1923/21,039 gross tons) on their return from government duties and in 1948 the pair re-entered the Australian service with accommodation for 1,030 migrant passengers (or tourist class in the euphemism of the time), compared with the 656 in two classes which they had carried before the War. When the *Maloja* and *Mooltan* were withdrawn for scrapping in 1954 they were replaced as the company's one-class ships by the *Strathnaver* (1931/22,270 gross tons) and *Strathaird* (1932/22,568 gross tons) which were refitted accordingly. These two had been the first members of the prestigious 'Strath' class of stately white liners with which P&O had up-graded their Australian service in the 1930s. Originally they had three funnels but when they were returned to commercial service after the War the first and third, which had been dummies, were dispensed with, thus bringing the ships into line with the later members of the class.

The *Strathnaver* and the *Strathaird* spent their declining years in the one-class service until they in turn were replaced in 1961. Their successors were their near-sisters *Strathmore* (1935/23,580 gross tons) and *Stratheden* (1937/23,732 gross tons). This pair differed from their immediate predecessors not only in the number of funnels with which they had originally been endowed, but also in being propelled by conventional geared turbines rather than turbo-electric machinery. They did not remain long in the tourist class-only service, being withdrawn in 1963. One problem with them had been that their lack of complete air-conditioning made them uncompetitive with the new ships which had been introduced onto the emigrant run by other lines, notably the Italians. Unusually for P&O liners, the *Strathmore* and the *Stratheden* were sold for further trading rather than for scrap. (Although their subsequent careers were not relevant to the present subject, they were sufficiently unusual to merit some note here. They were sold to the Greek shipping and oil magnate John S. Latsis, who chartered them out annually to Arab governments to carry their Hajj pilgrims to Mecca – or, more precisely, to Jeddah from where the pilgrims made their way overland. Mr. Latsis appears to have been quite content to employ most of his passenger ships in this way for just the six or

seven weeks of the pilgrim season and then leave them idle until the following year. The former *Strathmore* and *Stratheden* became the *Marianna Latsi* and *Henrietta Latsi* but, in a confusing move, exchanged names after a few years. They were almost certainly the largest pilgrim ships ever, sometimes accommodating as many as 4,000 passengers at a time. Many of these were, as was customary in pilgrim ships, merely provided with a small rectangle of deck space on which they placed the roll of bedding they had brought with them. The *Marianna Latsi* and the *Henrietta Latsi* were almost entirely employed in carrying the annual quota of pilgrims from the Libyan ports, although in 1965 and 1966 they also made voyages from Algeria, Morocco and Senegal. The closure of the Suez Canal in 1967 brought to an end the pilgrim traffic from the countries of North and West Africa and thus finished the careers of these once-notable liners.)

Subsequently, P&O devoted the *Himalaya* (1949/27,989 gross tons) to their single-class service on the Australian route but with Sitmar (and later Chandris) vessels acting as the official migrant-carriers and the jet aeroplane cutting a swathe through the shipping companies' lists of port-to-port passengers, she became as much a tourist ship as an emigrant vessel.

Orient Line

Like P&O, the Orient Line devoted several of their older liners to the migrant trade in the post-War years. There had, as a matter of fact, been financial links between the two companies since 1919. In the 1940s and 1950s, though, the Orient Steam Navigation Company, managed by the Anderson family, still had very much more than a nominal independence. It was not until the 1960s that the sprawling P&O empire was re-shaped into a more compact organisation – much to the regret of the traditionalists who were sad to see many famous companies subsumed. (However, old loyalties died hard – even on the board of directors where, it was said, strong rivalries persisted between the Orient Line faction and the former British India people.)

In 1949 the *Otranto* (1925/20,051 gross tons) returned to commercial service by the Orient Line as a one-class ship carrying mainly assisted passage migrants on her outward voyages but operating in the normal commercial market on the return journeys. In 1953 she was joined by the *Orontes* (1929/20,186 gross tons) whose place in the more prestigious main service was about to be assumed by a new vessel. Both the *Otranto* and the *Orontes* were recognisably members of a family of vessels stretching back to the *Ormonde*, already mentioned, which – although not completed until 1917 – had been laid down in 1913. Their two narrow funnels capped by Admiralty cowls must by the 1950s have given them a rather antique appearance. But then, the Orient Line would seem not to have been greatly concerned with convention in the external appearance of its ships. (Some of its post-War vessels verged on the eccentric.)

The sale for scrapping of the *Otranto* in 1957 led to

---

1   Note the spelling of the word Peninsular – in this case it is an adjective rather than a noun. The peninsula referred to is, of course, the Iberian.

the substitution of the *Orion* (1935/23,696 gross tons). When built, the *Orion* had represented a considerable break in tradition. With her single funnel, single mast profile; her new, lighter livery; and her contemporary interior decor, she was as big an innovation for the Orient Line as the 'Strath' class had been for P&O. Indeed, her hull design is said to have borne a strong resemblance to that of the 'Straths'.

The *Orontes* was withdrawn in 1962 and the *Orion* in 1963. Thereafter the *Orcades* (1948/28,472 gross tons) assumed the role of a one-class tourist ship in which form she could accommodate 1,635 passengers. By now, she and her fleet-mates had been transferred to full P&O ownership and were operating under the name P&O–Orient Lines.

Aberdeen & Commonwealth and Shaw, Savill & Albion

The third British company on the Australian route via the Suez Canal was the Aberdeen & Commonwealth Line. Its ships had the traditional dark green hulls of George Thompson's Aberdeen Line which had carried passengers to Australia via the Cape since 1846. However, the line itself had originated much more recently as the Commonwealth Government Line, set up by the Australian authorities during the First World War and which in 1921 and 1922 had taken delivery of the five 'Bay' steamers.

These vessels, each named after an Australian bay, had passenger accommodation designed to house migrants in moderate comfort rather than luxury. Like most liners of the day, the ships also had considerable cargo space – much of which, as usual on the Australian run, was refrigerated. The new line had been beset by almost every conceivable problem and had been sold off to Lord Kylsant's Royal Mail Steam Packet Company group in 1928. Although the shareholders and creditors of that group later complained that he had paid too much (£1,900,000), opinion in Australia seems to have been that the government had struck a poor bargain. The ships were transferred to the British register (not without incident) and were placed under the management of George Thompson & Co., also a member of the Kylsant group. In recognition of their new managers' long-standing connections they henceforth ran as the Aberdeen & Commonwealth Line. During the financial re-arrangements which followed the crash of the Kylsant group in 1930-31, ownership of the line passed to a group of British shipping companies of which Shaw, Savill and P&O were predominant. Management was placed in the hands of Shaw, Savill and by the early 1950s they had become the sole owners.

After the War, the Aberdeen & Commonwealth Line resumed its service in October, 1947 but by then the five 'Bays' had been reduced to three. The original *Esperance Bay* had been transferred to Shaw, Savill in 1936 but her

The 'Bay' liners had always been large carriers of migrants on their outward voyages to Australia. The *Largs Bay* made the Aberdeen & Commonwealth Line's final sailing in 1957.   *World Ship Society*

The *Queen Mary* at New York in 1946, with her hull still painted in war-time grey but with Cunard colours restored to her funnels. Note the degaussing strip along her side.
Southampton City Museums

name had been assumed by the former *Hobsons Bay* since the *Esperance Bay* had built up some following as a summer cruise liner. The *Jervis Bay* had been lost in one of the most gallant and famous episodes of the War. The post-War fleet therefore consisted of the *Moreton Bay* (1921/14,376 gross tons) which had been refitted by Cammell Laird; the *Largs Bay* (1921/14,362 gross tons), refitted by Harland & Wolff's Glasgow yard; and the second *Esperance Bay* (1922/14,343 gross tons) refitted by Swan Hunter & Wigham Richardson. In order to compete with the superior type of tourist class accommodation being provided on the more modern P&O and Orient Line ships, the 'Bay' liners had long since been modified to carry rather fewer than their original 700-odd passengers in somewhat better conditions. Now the figure was again cut, this time to 514 in each ship. On her first post-War voyage, in February, 1949, about half of the *Largs Bay*'s passengers were travelling under Australian Government settlement schemes and this may well have been the pattern on subsequent trips. On that occasion and on a number of others, 'Bay' liners proceeded to New Zealand after making their customary Australian calls at Fremantle, Adelaide, Melbourne and Sydney. These occasional extended voyages were presumably made partly under the aegis of the Shaw, Savill & Albion company. The British ports were London (for cargo) and Southampton (for passengers).

By 1955 the three sisters were nearing the end of their useful lives and the parent Shaw, Savill & Albion company was introducing the superior new *Southern Cross* on a round-the-world tourist class service which took in both Australian and New Zealand ports. It was no surprise, therefore, when it was announced that the *Esperance Bay* was to be withdrawn in mid-1955. The Suez crisis in 1956 caused the two remaining Aberdeen & Commonwealth ships (and also the P&O and Orient vessels) to be diverted to the route round the Cape. The *Moreton Bay* and *Largs Bay* were finally withdrawn and sold for scrap in 1957 by which time they had both achieved nearly 2 million miles of commercial service, carrying over a million tons of cargo each and about 70,000 passengers. The final voyage of the *Largs Bay* (and of the Aberdeen & Commonwealth Line) was a sad affair. The ship was not in a good condition. She suffered a fire while in Australian waters and there were problems with generators and other equipment. On the return leg she limped into Durban and her passengers were sent on to Britain by other means. She remained in Durban for a month before being able to resume her last voyage to London.

The old Aberdeen Line's traditional service to Australia via the Cape had passed to Shaw, Savill & Albion in the 1930s. After the War it was maintained by the *Arawa* (1922/14,491 gross tons), but now from London rather than Liverpool which had been the British terminus in the immediate pre-War years. Another difference was that many voyages now continued to New Zealand. The *Arawa* had been the original *Esperance Bay* before her transfer to Shaw, Savill, but since then she had provided accommodation for many fewer passengers than her sisters, as befitted a vessel primarily serving the less populous dominion of New Zealand. In her post-War guise she could carry 274 in tourist class. With the advent of the *Southern Cross* she too went to the scrapyard in 1955.

The Shaw, Savill & Albion company also ran several tourist or cabin class-only vessels on their main route from London to New Zealand via the Panama Canal in the late 1940s and the early 1950s. Once again there was a strong Aberdeen Line connection since, with the dismemberment of that company in the 1920s and 1930s, several of its ships had been used to re-vitalise the antique but still profitable Shaw, Savill fleet. Now as the *Akaroa* (1914/15,320 gross tons), the *Mataroa* (1922/12,369 gross tons) and th e *Tamaroa* (1922/12,375 gross tons), they carried 190 cabin class, 372 tourist and 372 tourist passengers respectively. First class travellers patronised the company's smart new generation of combined passenger and cargo ships.

M.o.T. Ships to New Zealand

The Ministry of Transport was also represented on the route to New Zealand via the Panama Canal. In 1948 they chartered their *Atlantis* (1913/15,363 gross tons) to the government of the dominion. Built as the *Andes* for the Royal Mail Steam Packet Company's service to the east coast of South America, she was a typical Harland & Wolff product of the period both in appearance, with her smartly raked masts and funnel, and in her form of propulsion (triple-expansion engines driving two propellers and a low pressure turbine driving a third). In 1930 she had been refitted as a splendid cruising liner, sporting a new name and a white hull. She was bought by the government at the outbreak of the War in which she served as a hospital ship. Refitted as an emigrant steamer she remained on the New Zealand route until 1952.

She was then replaced by two ships. The *Empire Brent* (1925/13,876 gross tons) had originally been the *Letitia* of the Anchor-Donaldson and later the Donaldson Atlantic Line. Since the War she had been used by the Ministry on the Canadian and Australian routes. Now, after a refit by Barclay Curle and suitably re-named as the *Captain Cook*, she was placed in emigrant service from Glasgow to New Zealand together with another formerly Scottish-owned ship, the *Captain Hobson* (ex-*Amarapoora*, 1920/9,306 gross tons). The *Amarapoora* had belonged in pre-War days to the Henderson Line, Bibby's great rivals in the Burma trade. Since passing into government hands she too had been employed on the Australian run, but under charter to the International Refugee Organisation. As usual in these cases, both ships remained under their former management: Donaldson Bros. & Black and P. Henderson & Co., respectively. The *Captain Hobson* was mainly used as a troopship after 1954 but the *Captain Cook* remained on the New Zealand route for much of the time until withdrawn for scrapping in 1960.

Cunard and Others

The *Amarapoora* was not alone among British ships in being chartered for a time to the I.R.O. The Bibby Line's old *Oxfordshire* (1912/8,648 gross tons), which had served as a hospital ship in both wars, was employed as a migrant ship by the organisation from 1948 to 1951. Despite her age, Bibby then sold her to the Pan-Islamic Steamship Company of Pakistan who used her as a pilgrim-carrier, finally selling her for scrap in 1958. The *Dundalk Bay* (1936/7,105 gross tons) belonging to the Irish Bay Line of Henry P. Lenaghan & Co. of Belfast was also chartered to

Shaw Savill & Albion's *Akaroa*, dating back to 1914. Like most liners on the New Zealand route she had considerable space for refrigerated cargo.
World Ship Society

the organisation for about two years and was mainly used on the Australian run. She was one of a number of former German vessels which were seized by the allies and re-emerged as emigrant-carriers. She had been Norddeutscher Lloyd's *Nürnberg* and after her I.R.O. service she reverted to a purely cargo-carrying role.

Although not chartered outright by the I.R.O., two Cunard intermediate liners were used in a service between Cuxhaven and Canadian ports on which the I.R.O. made block bookings of berths on the outward voyages. The service lasted for something over a year from late-1948 onwards. The two vessels were the *Samaria* (1921/19,602 gross tons) and the *Scythia* (1921/19,730 gross tons). The late Captain Donald Sorrell was master of the *Samaria* during this period. He described her as a very happy ship. The crew were ordered to treat their refugee passengers with as much kindness and compassion as possible, and they did. Language problems made communication difficult, however. Captain Sorrell recounted how one old lady lay in her bunk for days, refusing all food despite the encouragement of the stewards, yet the doctor could find little wrong with her apart from malnutrition. The voyage was nearly over before it emerged that she was desperately hungry but, unable to understand what the stewards were trying to say to her, she had not realised that the food was free. Having no money, she had been afraid to eat. At the end of one voyage Captain Sorrell was presented by two migrants with a beautifully carved wooden box which they had made during the voyage. It bore the inscription 'To the Captain of Ship Samaria from Ukrainian emigrants, October 21st–November 1st 1948'. It was 'one of the most moving tributes I ever received.'

(Captain Sorrell, incidentally, later became something of a public figure as master of the *Caronia* and the *Queen Mary* – particularly after docking the *Queen Mary* at New York without either tugs or a pilot during a strike. Even the strikers cheered.)

Another Cunarder, the *Ascania* (1925/14,013 gross tons) made a series of 'austerity' voyages between Liverpool and Canadian ports from late 1947 to 1949, before being refitted as a two-class ship once again. Of the six A-class steamers which had maintained Cunard–White Star's pre-War Canadian services, she was the only one to return to civilian duties after the War.

Canadian Pacific, too, involved itself in the emigrant trade to Canada. They used another former German vessel, the *Beaverbrae* (1939/9,034 gross tons) which had been the Hamburg–America Line's *Huascaran*, a diesel-electric cargo ship with limited passenger accommodation which had been briefly employed on the route from Hamburg to the west coast of South America before the outbreak of hostilities changed her career. After the War she was handed over to the Canadian government who eventually sold her to Canadian Pacific. Between 1948 and 1954 they ran her between the north German ports and Canada carrying emigrants in fairly basic accommodation on the westward leg and returning as a purely cargo vessel. We shall meet her again in Chapter Four as the Italian *Aurelia*. Later still, she became the well-known Chandris cruise ship *Romanza*. Now (1991), at the age of 52, she has passed to Cypriot owners for further service.

FLEET LIST

Akaroa

15,320 gross tons, triple screw, triple expansion engines plus a low pressure turbine, 15 knots. Built, 1914, by Harland & Wolff, Belfast as *Euripides* for Aberdeen Line (Geo. Thompson & Co.). 1914: taken up as a troop transport. 1920: returned to her owners' service. 1925: laid up for a short period. 1925: Aberdeen Line's service to Australia via the Cape was integrated into a White Star–Blue Funnel–Aberdeen Joint Service. 1926: with the acquisition of the Aberdeen Line's parent company, White Star, by

A boat deck view of Cunard's *Ascania* taken in 1955, towards the end of her career on the Canadian run. The tall funnel, steam whistles and large ventilators are redolent of an era which was already passing. *Steffen Weirauch collection*

Lord Kylsant's Royal Mail Steam Packet Co., the line became part of the Royal Mail group. 1928: management of the line transferred to White Star and the British terminal port changed from London to Liverpool. 1931: briefly laid up again. 1932: ownership transferred to Shaw, Savill & Albion, whereupon she was refitted for that company's New Zealand service via the Panama Canal and given the name *Akaroa*. Remained on the New Zealand route during the War, but under government control. 1946: after a refit, returned to Shaw, Savill's control and continued on the New Zealand run, but with London and Southampton as the British ports. 1954: sold for scrapping at Antwerp.

Amarapoora

9,342 gross tons, single screw, triple expansion, 13 knots. Built, 1920, by William Denny, Dumbarton for the Henderson Line's service from Glasgow to Burma. 1939: converted into a hospital ship. 1946: bought by the Ministry of Transport and chartered to the International Refugee Organisation, but remained under the management of P. Henderson & Co. 1951-2: refitted as an emigrant ship for the New Zealand service – still under Henderson management, but with Shaw, Savill & Albion assuming responsibility in the Antipodes. Now 9,306 gross tons, re-named *Captain Hobson*. Also used for trooping. 1957: towed into Auckland (5 days) after breaking down. 1958: laid up at Bombay and sold for scrapping at Osaka the following year.

Aquitania

45,647 gross tons, quadruple screw, turbine, 23 knots. Built, 1914, by John Brown, Clydebank for the Cunard Line as a running-mate for the *Mauretania* and the *Lusitania* on the line's express service to New York. 1914: taken up as an auxiliary merchant cruiser, but later in the First World War was mainly used as a troopship and a hospital ship. 1919: returned to commercial service. In that year she was converted to oil-firing, an operation which most major liners underwent at this time. 1934: passed to the Cunard–White Star Line. 1939 onwards: served as a troop transport during the Second World War. 1948: started a series of austerity voyages between Southampton and Canada. 1949: retired, and sold for scrapping at Faslane the following year. In her prime she had been a notably economical ship for a luxury, express liner.

Arawa

14,491 gross tons, twin screw, geared turbine, 15 knots. Built, 1922, by William Beardmore, Glasgow as the *Esperance Bay* for the Commonwealth Government Line's new emigrant service between London and Australian ports. 1923: owners re-organised as the Australian Commonwealth Line. 1928: line acquired by the Royal Mail group and placed under the management of Geo. Thompson & Co. under the name Aberdeen & Commonwealth Line. The ships continued to sail via the Suez Canal despite the new managers' previous connection with the Cape route. 1933: with a change in the ownership of the Aberdeen & Commonwealth Line, management passed to Shaw, Savill & Albion. 1936: the *Esperance Bay* was sold to Shaw, Savill & Albion and re-named *Arawa*. After a refit which reduced her passenger capacity and increased her

refrigerated cargo space, she was placed in her new owners' New Zealand trade via Panama. 1939: taken up as an Armed Merchant Cruiser. 1941: changed to a troopship. 1946: returned to Shaw, Savill's service. 1955: broken up at Newport.

Once a stately four-funnelled liner, Union-Castle's *Arundel Castle* acquired a rather racier look in the 'thirties. In the early post-War years she participated in the emigrant service.

A. Duncan

Arundel Castle

19,118 gross tons, twin screw, geared turbine, 20 knots. Laid down, 1915. Completed, 1921, by Harland & Wolff, Belfast, as a four-funnelled express liner for the Union-Castle Line's mail service. 1937: as part of Union–Castle's programme to accelerate the mail service the *Arundel Castle* was re-built by Harland & Wolff. She now sported two, more modern funnels and a lengthened bow; and new turbines gave her 3 extra knots of service speed. 1939: taken up as a troop transport. 1947: started a series of voyages in connection with the South African government's immigration programme. 1949: taken in hand for a thorough refit and returned to the mail service the following year. 1958: sold for scrapping at Kowloon. She had steamed 2,850,000 miles in commercial service and 625,000 as a trooper.

Ascania

14,013 gross tons, twin screw, geared turbine, 15 knots. Built, 1925, by Armstrong Whitworth, Newcastle as one of six sisters for the Cunard Line's Canadian services. 1939: taken up as an Armed Merchant Cruiser. 1943: became a troopship. 1947: commenced 'austerity' sailings between Liverpool and Canadian ports. 1949: refitted for normal two-class service. 1957: scrapped at Newport.

Asturias

22,445 gross tons, twin screw, geared turbine, 18 knots. Built, 1926, by Harland & Wolff, Belfast as a motor liner for the Royal Mail Steam Packet Company's South American service. 1934: converted to turbine propulsion partly to increase her speed. 1939: commissioned as an Armed Merchant Cruiser, her conversion involving the removal of the forward funnel. 1943: torpedoed and rendered unmanoeuvrable by an Italian submarine. Laid up in her damaged state at Freetown. 1945: although written off as a total loss, she was bought by the British government and repaired by her builders, being converted into a troopship and placed under the management of Royal Mail Lines. 1949: transferred to the Australian emigrant service. 1953: reverted to trooping. 1957: scrapped at Faslane.

The *Asturias* was one of three badly damaged liners which the Ministry of Transport bought and converted into emigrant ships. *World Ship Society*

Atlantis

15,363 gross tons, triple screw, triple expansion plus low pressure turbine, 15 knots. Built, 1913, as *Andes* for the Royal Mail Steam Packet Co. by Harland & Wolff, Belfast. 1915: taken up as an auxiliary cruiser. 1916: with her sister, *Alcantara* she was involved in a battle with the German auxiliary cruiser *Greif* in the North Sea. Both the *Alcantara* and the *Greif* were sunk. 1919: resumed civilian service. 1930: converted into a luxury cruise liner and renamed *Atlantis*. 1939: sold to the British government for use as a hospital ship, remaining under Royal Mail management. 1948: refitted for the New Zealand emigrant trade. 1952: scrapped at Faslane.

Beaverbrae

9,034 gross tons, single screw, diesel-electric, 17 knots. Built, 1939, as *Huascaran*, a Hamburg America Line cargo vessel with limited passenger accommodation for the service to the west coast of South America. Builders, Blohm & Voss. 1940: became a German Navy repair ship. 1945: allocated to the Canadian government for whom she was managed by the Park Steamship Co. 1947: bought by Canadian Pacific Steamships and converted to a migrant carrier, entering service in 1948 as the *Beaverbrae*. Route: Bremen–Canada. 1954: after 51 round voyages for Canadian Pacific she was sold to Cia. Genovese di Armamento (the Cogedar Line). 1955: after a substantial re-building, she entered the Australian emigrant service from Italy as the *Aurelia*. 1958: re-engined. 1968: Cogedar absorbed by Linea "C,, (Costa) and the *Aurelia* had a brief and unsuccessful stint on cruise service from Southampton to Madeira. 1970: sold to the Chandris family who renamed her *Romanza* and placed her in Mediterranean cruise service. 1977-78: Chartered to Lloyd Brasileiro. 1991: sold to Cypriot owners and re-named *Romantica*.

Bloemfontein Castle

18,400 gross tons, twin screw, diesel, 18½ knots. Built, 1950, by Harland & Wolff, Belfast as a one-class ship for the Union–Castle Line and placed in service between London and South and East Africa. 1959: sold to the Chandris group and renamed *Patris* after a substantial extension of her accommodation which increased her passenger capacity from 721 to 1,036. Initially used in a service between the Mediterranean and Australia, but by the early 1970s mainly employed in cruising from Australian ports. 1976: converted into a side-loading car ferry with capacity for 1,000 passengers. Placed on routes between Italy and Greece. 1979: on the withdrawal of Chandris from the ferry market, sold to Michael Karageorgis and renamed *Mediterranean Island*. Continued in service between Venice and Patras. 1981: renamed *Mediterranean Star*. 1986: after a period of lay-up, chartered to the Star Navigation Company for an unsuccessful service between Piraeus and Alexandria which closed after a few months. 1987: scrapped at Gadani Beach.

The *Bloemfontein Castle* was a new motor liner which Union-Castle introduced on a one-class service to South and East Africa which lasted just nine years. *World Ship Society*

Cameronia

16,584 gross tons, twin screw, geared turbine, 16½

The *Cameronia* at Malta during her charter to the Ministry of Transport. Unrelieved white paint did not flatter her appearance. *World Ship Society*

knots. Built, 1921, by William Beardmore, Glasgow for the Anchor Line's Atlantic service. 1934: laid up. 1935: Anchor Line, hitherto a Cunard subsidiary, became insolvent and a new company, controlled by the Runciman group, took over the undertaking and its ships. 1935: *Cameronia* brought back into operation on a trooping contract. 1936: returned to the Glasgow–New York service. 1937: chartered by the government as a floating grandstand for the Coronation Naval Review at Spithead. 1940: requisitioned as a troopship. 1942: damaged by an aerial torpedo during the North African landings but managed to reach safety. Repaired. 1947: laid up. 1948: chartered to the Ministry of Transport and converted into an emigrant-carrier at a cost of £½ million. Placed on the Australian run from Glasgow. 1953: the Ministry exercised its option to purchase the vessel (at £41,000) and refitted her as the troop transport *Empire Clyde*, still under the management of the Anchor Line. 1958: scrapped at Newport.

The Ministry of Transport's *Captain Hobson* divided her time between the New Zealand emigrant trade and trooping.
World Ship Society

The Ministry of Transport's *Captain Cook* was managed by her former owners, Donaldson, whose funnel colours she still wore. Also in this picture is the *Monowai* of the Union S.S. Co. of New Zealand. *Steffen Weirauch*

Captain Cook
(See *Empire Brent*).

Captain Hobson
(See *Amarapoora*).

Carnarvon Castle
20,123 gross tons, twin screw, diesel, 20 knots. Built, 1926, by Harland & Wolff, Belfast for the Union–Castle mailship service between Southampton and Cape Town. 1938: re-entered service after being rebuilt to fit her for the accelerated, 14-day run to Cape Town required by the company's new mail contract. New engines increased her service speed from 16½ knots to 20; she was also lengthened and her two funnels were replaced by one of a streamlined design. 1939: converted into an Armed Merchant Cruiser. 1940: severely damaged in an encounter with the German raider *Thor* in the South Atlantic, but made safety. 1944: refitted as a troopship. 1947: returned

to her owners and used initially as an emigrant-carrier with accommodation for 1,283 passengers. 1950: with the emigrant service being run down, she was returned to the mailship service after a refit. 1962: scrapped at Mihara in Japan.

Cheshire

10,623 gross tons, twin screw, diesel, 15½ knots. Built, 1927, by Fairfield, Glasgow for Bibby Line and used on their Liverpool–Rangoon service. 1939: commissioned as an Armed Merchant Cruiser. 1940: torpedoed off the Irish coast, but reached port. 1942: again torpedoed, this time in the Atlantic, but again reached safety. 1943: converted into a troop transport. 1948: returned to Bibby. Three of her four masts removed during her refit. 1949: commenced service for the Ministry of Transport on the Australian emigrant run. 1953: reverted to trooping. 1957: scrapped at Newport.

Before the War the *Cheshire* had the traditional Bibby Line four-masted profile. However, this had changed by 1949 when she was chartered to the Ministry of Transport for the Australian emigrant run. *World Ship Society*

Chitral

15,555 gross tons, twin screw, quadruple expansion engines with additional low pressure turbines, 17 knots. Built, 1925, for the Peninsular & Oriental Steam Navigation Co.'s Australian route by Alexander Stephen, Glasgow. 1930: the original engines were supplemented by low pressure turbines. 1939: commissioned as an Armed Merchant Cruiser. 1944: became a troopship. 1948: after being returned to P&O in 1947, she was converted into an emigrant-carrier for charter to the Ministry of Transport who used her on the Australian route. 1953: scrapped at Dalmuir.

Dorsetshire

9,789 gross tons, twin screw, diesel, 12 knots. Built, 1920, by Harland & Wolff, Belfast as a cargo ship for the Bibby Line. Spent time on charter to Brocklebanks and others. 1927: converted into a troopship, but during the War she served as a hospital ship. Bombed twice, at Tobruk and later off Sicily. 1948: refitted as an emigrant-carrier and chartered to the Ministry of Transport for the Australian service. 1952: served as an accommodation ship at an oil refinery at Aden. 1953: briefly returned to trooping. 1954: scrapped at Newport.

Dundalk Bay

7,105 gross tons, single screw, diesel. Built, 1936, by Bremer Vulkan, Vegesak as *Nürnberg*, a cargo vessel for the Norddeutscher Lloyd. 1945: seized by the British forces and used as a depot ship. 1948: became the *Dundalk Bay* of H.P. Lenaghan's Bay Line and chartered to the I.R.O. as an emigrant ship. 1951: reverted to a purely cargo-carrying role (5,579 gross tons). 1957: sold to Duff, Herbert & Mitchell (Billmeir group) and renamed *Westbay*. 1962: scrapped at Hamburg.

An ex-German, the *Dundalk Bay* was chartered by her new owners, Lenaghan's, to the I.R.O. in 1948. For most of her career, however, she was purely a cargo ship, in which form we see her here. *World Ship Society*

Empire Brent

13,475 gross tons, twin screw, geared turbine, 15 knots. Built, 1925, as *Letitia* for the Anchor–Donaldson Line's Glasgow–Canada service by Fairfield, Glasgow. 1935: transferred to the Donaldson Atlantic Line, remaining on the same route. 1939: taken up for service as an Armed Merchant Cruiser, later becoming a troopship and later still a Canadian hospital ship. 1946: sold to the Ministry of Transport and renamed *Empire Brent*, still managed by Donaldson Bros. & Black. At first used as a troopship but later for emigrant sailings. 1951: refitted for the New Zealand emigrant trade and renamed *Captain Cook*, 13,876 gross tons. 1955: chartered by the Donaldson Line for an unsuccessful attempt to revive their pre-War Canadian service, thereafter returning to the Ministry's New Zealand run. 1960: scrapped at Inverkeithing.

Esperance Bay

14,343 gross tons, twin screw, geared turbine, 15 knots. Built, 1922, by Vickers, Barrow as the Commonwealth Government Line's *Hobsons Bay*. 1923: owners became the Australian Commonwealth Line. 1928: the line was acquired by the Royal Mail group who allocated the management to Geo. Thompson & Co. and renamed it the Aberdeen & Commonwealth Line. 1933: management passed to Shaw, Savill & Albion who became part-owners of the line together with several other leading British shipping companies. 1936: with the sale of the original *Esperance Bay*, the *Hobsons Bay* assumed her name. 1939: commissioned as an Armed Merchant Cruiser. 1941: became a troop transport. 1948: returned to the Aberdeen &

The post-War *Himalaya* replaced the 'Straths' in P&O's one-class service when they began to lose out to the Italians and others.

P&O Archives

Commonwealth London and Southampton to Australia service via Suez. 1955: scrapped at Faslane.

Georgic

27,469 gross tons, twin screw, diesel, 18 knots. Built, 1932, by Harland & Wolff, Belfast for the White Star Line. 1934: White Star amalgamated into the new Cunard–White Star Line. 1940: taken up as a troopship. 1941: very seriously damaged in an air raid near Suez. 1942: towed to Karachi for repairs. 1943: returned to Britain and fitted out as a troopship. In the process the forward funnel and the mainmast were removed. Now owned by the Ministry of Transport and managed by Cunard–White Star. 1949: began sailing as an emigrant ship on the Australian route. 1950-1954: chartered by Cunard for North Atlantic sailings each summer. 1956: scrapped at Faslane.

Himalaya

27,989 gross tons, twin screw, geared turbine, 22 knots. Built, 1949, by Vickers-Armstrongs, Barrow-in-Furness for the P&O Line, their first post-War passenger liner. 1963: refitted as a one-class ship. 1974: scrapped at Kaohsiung.

Kanimbla

10,985 gross tons, twin screw, diesel, 17 knots. Built, 1936, by Harland & Wolff, Belfast for the Australian coastal service of McIlwraith, McEacharn of Melbourne. 1939: taken up by the Royal Australian Navy as an Armed Merchant Cruiser. 1949: returned to her owners after a long period of repatriation voyages and one emigrant sailing from Great Britain. 1961: bought by Pacific Transport Co., a Panamanian associate of the Toyo Yusen Kaisha concern of Japan, and renamed *Oriental Queen*. She was chartered to the Indonesians but, contrary to some reports, for local services and not for the pilgrim trade. 1964: commenced cruising from Australia and New Zealand. 1968: cruising from Japan, now under the direct ownership of Toyo Yusen Kaisha. 1973: scrapped at Kaohsiung.

Largs Bay

14,362 gross tons, twin screw, geared turbine, 15 knots. Built, 1921, by William Beardmore, Glasgow for the Commonwealth Government Line. 1923: owners reorganised as the Australian Commonwealth Line. 1928: the line acquired by the Royal Mail Steam Packet group and renamed Aberdeen & Commonwealth Line. 1933: further change of ownership but still operated under the name

The *Mataroa*, a typical Harland & Wolff product of the 1920s, sailed on for Shaw, Savill & Albion in their service to New Zealand via Panama until the mid-'fifties.   *A. Duncan*

Aberdeen & Commonwealth. 1941: taken up as a troopship. 1944: struck a mine but only slightly damaged. 1949: re-entered the Australian service after a refit. 1949: damaged by fire. 1956: diverted via the Cape owing to the Suez crisis. 1957: scrapped at Barrow-in-Furness. Her final round voyage had been beset by troubles. With her withdrawal the historic Aberdeen flag and livery which had been familiar on the Australian routes since 1846, disappeared finally. The 'Bay' liners had assumed these colours when management was taken over by Geo. Thompson & Co. in 1928.

Maloja

21,036 gross tons, twin screw, quadruple expansion (a system to which her owners remained faithful rather longer than most) plus auxiliary low pressure turbines, 17 knots. Built, 1923, one of a pair by Harland & Wolff, Belfast for P&O's Australian service. 1929: low pressure turbines installed. 1939: became an Armed Merchant Cruiser. 1941: troopship. 1947: returned to P&O and, the following year, re-entered the Australian service, but now as a one-class ship. 1954: scrapped at Inverkeithing.

Mataroa

12,369 gross tons, twin screw, geared turbines, 15 knots. Built, 1922, by Harland & Wolff, Belfast as the *Diogenes* for the Aberdeen Line. 1926: with the Aberdeen Line suffering difficult trading conditions and Shaw, Savill & Albion needing to replace some of the older units of its fleet, the *Diogenes* and her sister were chartered to Shaw, Savill. *Diogenes* became the *Mataroa*. 1932: ownership transferred to Shaw, Savill. 1940: became a troopship. 1948: resumed her owners' service to New Zealand via Panama. 1957: scrapped at Faslane.

Mooltan

21,039 gross tons, twin screw, quadruple expansion with auxiliary turbo-electric sets, 17 knots. Built, 1923, by Harland & Wolff, Belfast for the P&O Line. 1929: speed increased by coupling the original engines to turbo-electric machinery, as opposed to the method employed in her sister *Maloja* where auxiliary low pressure turbines were installed. 1939: commissioned as an Armed Merchant Cruiser. 1941: became a troop transport. 1947: returned to P&O and refitted as a tourist class-only ship, entering service the following year. 1954: scrapped at Faslane.

Moreton Bay

14,376 gross tons, twin screw, geared turbine, 15 knots. Built, 1921, by Vickers, Barrow-in-Furness as the first of the Commonwealth Government Line's five 'Bay' liners. 1923: Australian Commonwealth Line. 1928: Aberdeen & Commonwealth Line. 1933: management assumed by Shaw, Savill & Albion. 1939: became an Armed Merchant Cruiser. 1941: converted to a troopship. 1948: returned to the Aberdeen & Commonwealth Line's Australian service after a refit. (She and her sisters had already made a number of voyages to the Antipodes while under requisition.) 1957: scrapped at Barrow-in-Furness.

The *Mooltan* opened P&O's post-War one-class service to Australia together with her near-sister *Maloja*.
Steffen Weirauch collection

The Ministry of Transport's *New Australia* bore little resemblance to her former self as the luxurious *Monarch of Bermuda*. Note the unusual combined mast and funnel abaft the bridge.
Steffen Weirauch collection

New Australia

20,256 gross tons, quadruple screw, turbo-electric, 19½ knots. Built, 1931, by Vickers-Armstrongs, Newcastle for Furness Withy's New York–Bermuda cruise service and named *Monarch of Bermuda*. 1939: taken up as a troop transport. 1947: partly destroyed by fire while being restored for civilian service. The remains were bought by the Ministry of Transport and used as the basis of an emigrant-carrier, *New Australia*. 1950: entered the Australian service under Shaw, Savill & Albion management. 1953: used for a few trooping voyages. 1958: bought by the Greek Line who further rebuilt her and renamed her *Arkadia*. 1966: scrapped at Valencia.

Orcades

28,472 gross tons, twin screw, geared turbine, 22 knots. Built, 1948, by Vickers–Armstrongs, Barrow-in-Furness for the Orient Line. 1960: passed to P&O–Orient Lines. 1964: refitted as a one-class ship. 1966: P&O became the sole owners. 1973: scrapped at Kaohsiung.

Orion

23,696 gross tons, twin screw, geared turbine, 20 knots. Built, 1935, by Vickers–Armstrongs, Barrow-in-Furness for the Orient Steam Navigation Co. 1939: taken as a troop transport. 1947: resumed civilian service on the Orient Line route to Australia. 1958: switched to the tourist class service, although retaining some cabin class accommodation. 1960: passed to P&O–Orient Lines and became a one class ship. 1963: after being withdrawn from the Australian route, was chartered out for a few months as a hotel ship at Hamburg. 1963: broken up at Tamise.

Ormonde

15,047 gross tons, twin screw, geared turbine, 18 knots. Laid down for the Orient Line by John Brown, Clydebank in 1913 but not launched until 1917. Initially used as a troop transport. 1919: began her career as a passenger liner on the Australian route. 1939: taken up again as a troop transport.

The *Orion* was a very innovative ship when the Orient Line introduced her in 1935. She spent much of the late 'fifties and early 'sixties as a mainly tourist class vessel.
P&O Archives

1947: returned to the Orient Steam Navigation Co. and chartered to the Ministry of Transport for their Australian emigrant service. 1952: scrapped at Dalmuir.

Orontes

20,186 gross tons, twin screw, geared turbine, 20 knots. Built, 1929, by Vickers–Armstrongs, Barrow-in-Furness for the Orient Line. 1940: taken up as a troopship. 1948: after a refit, returned to her owners' Australian service. 1953: converted to a single class ship accommodating 1,410 passengers as against her previous figure of 1,112. 1962: scrapped at Valencia.

Otranto

20,051 gross tons, twin screw, geared turbine, 20 knots. Built, 1925, for the Orient Line by Vickers, Barrow-in-Furness. 1926: ran aground off the Greek coast. 1939: taken up as a troop transport. 1948: returned to her owners and reverted to commercial service the following year, thus initiating the company's post-War single class service. 1957: scrapped at Faslane.

Oxfordshire

8,648 gross tons, twin screw, quadruple expansion, 15 knots. Built, 1912, by Harland & Wolff, Belfast for the

The *Otranto* (Orient Line) is seen here at Fremantle in June, 1954. The company's older ships continued to have their hulls painted black after the War. *Steffen Weirauch collection*

Like many Bibby Line ships, the *Oxfordshire* had four masts. Built in 1912, she survived until 1958, latterly as a Pakistani pilgrim ship. *World Ship Society*

In this view, taken in March 1958, a typical pre-War Orient liner, the *Orontes*, invites comparison with the post-War *Orsova*. By then the *Orontes* was operating as a one-class ship. *P&O Archives*

The Ministry of Transport chartered several ageing British liners for its migrant service to Australia. P&O's *Ranchi* now sported only one funnel instead of her original two.

Bibby Line. Served as a hospital ship in both World Wars. 1949: chartered to the I.R.O. as an emigrant-carrier. 1950: used briefly as a troopship. 1951: sold to the Pan-Islamic Steamship Co. of Karachi and renamed *Safina-E-Arab* for their seasonal pilgrim service to Jeddah. 1958: scrapped at Karachi.

Queen Mary

81,235 gross tons, quadruple screw, geared turbine, 29 knots. Laid down, 1930, by John Brown, Clydebank for the Cunard Line. 1931: construction halted because the economic recession had adversely affected Cunard's finances. 1934: work resumed with financial encouragement from the British government following agreement to merge Cunard with the White Star Line. 1936: completed. There was some controversy as to whether she or her great rival, the *Normandie* of the French Line, was the largest ship in the world. Later that year the *Queen Mary* won the Blue Riband for the fastest crossings of the Atlantic (an average of 30.14 knots for crossings in both directions). The *Normandie* regained the honour the following year, but in 1938

The Cunard intermediate liner *Samaria* carried large numbers of refugees from Germany to Canada in the late 'forties.

the *Queen Mary* clinched the matter with an average of 31.34 knots, a record which remained until 1952. 1939: laid up at the outbreak of the War. 1940: became a troop transport. During the War the *Queen Mary* and her running-mate, the *Queen Elizabeth*, carried no less than 1,622,054 passengers (mainly troops) and steamed 1,150,406 miles. 1942: in a collision with the cruiser *Curacoa*. The naval vessel was sliced in two and sank almost immediately with very heavy loss of life. 1946: repatriated American troops and, later, their British wives and children. 1947: returned to her normal three class service for the Cunard–White Star Line. 1967: sold to the municipality of Long Beach, California for conversion to a floating hotel and leisure centre (price £1.23 million). She has since changed hands several times and at the time of writing (1991) is operated by an off-shoot of the Walt Disney organisation.

Ranchi

16,974 gross tons, twin screw, quadruple expansion with low pressure turbines, 17 knots. Built, 1925, by Hawthorn Leslie, Newcastle for P&O's Indian service. A near-sister to the famous *Rawalpindi*. 1931: low pressure turbines fitted. 1939: taken up for conversion to an Armed Merchant Cruiser, involving the removal of one of her two funnels. 1943: became a troopship. 1947: returned to her owners and refitted as an emigrant-carrier for charter to the Ministry of Transport. Placed on the Australian route in 1948. 1953: scrapped at Newport.

Samaria

19,602 gross tons, twin screw, geared turbine, 16 knots. Built, 1921, by Cammell Laird, Birkenhead for the Cunard Steam Ship Co.'s Liverpool–Boston and New York service. 1934: Cunard–White Star Line formed. 1939: became a troopship. 1948: placed on a new Cunard–White Star service from Cuxhaven and Bremen to Canada which lasted for something over a year. 1950: returned to regular Cunard sailings. 1956: scrapped at Inverkeithing.

Scythia

19,730 gross tons, twin screw, geared turbine, 16 knots. Built, 1920, by Vickers, Barrow-in-Furness for the Cunard Line. Sister ship to the *Samaria*. 1934: on the amalgamation became a member of the Cunard–White Star fleet. 1939: taken up as a troop transport. 1948: returned to Cunard–White Star service as an emigrant ship on the Germany–Canada run. 1950: transferred to the company's regular service after a refit. 1958: scrapped at Inverkeithing.

Somersetshire

9,787 gross tons, twin screw, diesel, 12 knots. Built, 1921, as a cargo ship for the Bibby Line by Harland & Wolff, Belfast. Much employed on charter out. 1927: rebuilt as a troopship. 1939: taken up by the Admiralty and used as a hospital ship. 1942: torpedoed and abandoned but later boarded by her crew and saved. 1948: reconditioned as an emigrant-carrier. 1953: returned to trooping. 1954: scrapped at Barrow-in-Furness.

Strathaird

22,568 gross tons, twin screw, turbo-electric, 20 knots. Built, 1932, by Vickers–Armstrongs, Barrow-in-Furness for the P&O company's newly improved service to Australia. 1939: taken up as a troopship. 1946: reverted to her owners and refitted, now with one funnel only rather than three. 1954: refitted with increased accommodation in one class only. 1961: scrapped at Hong Kong.

Stratheden

23,732 gross tons, twin screw, geared turbine, 20 knots. Built, 1937, by Vickers–Armstrongs, Barrow-in-Furness for the P&O Line. 1939: taken up as a troopship. 1946: returned to her owners. 1950: chartered to Cunard for several voyages to New York. 1953: chartered to the Travel Savings Association for cruises. 1960: P&O and Orient Lines integrated. 1961: switched to the tourist class-only service. 1963: sold to John S. Latsis and renamed *Henrietta Latsi* and employed for a few weeks per year in the pilgrim trade, mainly from Libya. 1966: exchanged names with her sister *Marianna Latsi*. 1967: laid up. 1969: scrapped at La Spezia.

Strathmore

23,580 gross tons, twin screw, geared turbine, 20 knots. Built, 1935, by Vickers–Armstrongs, Barrow-in-Furness for P&O. 1939: became a troopship. 1948: reverted to her owners and refitted. 1960: P&O–Orient Lines. 1961: became a one class ship. 1963: sold to John S. Latsis and used as the pilgrim ship *Marianna Latsi*. 1967: renamed *Henrietta Latsi*. 1967: laid up when the closure of the Suez Canal brought her trade to an end. 1969: scrapped at La Spezia.

Strathaird, one of P&O's famous White Sisters, is here seen at the end of her career flying her paying-off pennant.

P&O Archives

Strathnaver

22,270 gross tons, twin screw, turbo-electric, 20 knots. Built, 1931, by Vickers–Armstrongs, Barrow-in-Furness as the first of P&O's 'Strath' liners. 1939: became a troop transport. 1948: released to her owners and refitted, re-entering the Australian service in 1950. 1954: converted into a single class ship. 1962: scrapped at Hong Kong.

Tamaroa

12,375 gross tons, twin screw, geared turbine, 15 knots. Built, 1922, by Harland & Wolff, Belfast as the *Sophocles* for the Aberdeen Line. 1926: chartered to the Shaw, Savill & Albion Line for their New Zealand service via Panama and renamed *Tamaroa*. 1932: ownership trans-

After a distinguished career on P&O's express service between Britain and Australia, the *Strathnaver* was converted into a one-class ship in 1954. *P&O Archives*

Three 'Straths' are lined up at Tilbury in April, 1948. The *Strathmore*, still in grey, awaits restoration after her War. The *Strathaird* is already back in civilian service, now with only one funnel instead of her original three. The *Strathnaver*, still with three funnels, remains in government service.

ferred to Shaw, Savill & Albion. 1940: taken as a troop transport. 1948: returned to her owners' New Zealand service after being refitted as a tourist class vessel. 1957: scrapped at Blyth.

Below: Before being restored as a luxurious express liner, Union-Castle's *Winchester Castle* operated as an emigrant carrier on the South African route in 1948. *A. Duncan*

Winchester Castle

20,012 gross tons, twin screw, diesel, 20 knots. Built, 1930, by Harland & Wolff, Belfast for the Union-Castle Line's mailship service to South Africa. 1938: rebuilt with more powerful engines and with one funnel replacing her previous two, giving her what became the characteristic Union–Castle profile. 1940: taken as a troopship. 1941: converted to a Landing Ship (Infantry) – L.S.(I). 1947: released for civilian service and temporarily used in the emigrant service to South Africa. 1948: refitted for the mailship service. 1960: scrapped at Mihara.

Chapter Three
The Charlton Sisters

The passenger activities of the Charlton Steam Shipping Co. Ltd. were omitted from the previous chapter – partly because although British-registered the firm was Greek-owned. Also, however, it is sufficiently interesting to deserve closer study on its own.

The Charlton ships were the precursors of the extensive Chandris passenger fleets of later years. Their operations give us an insight into the opportunities and problems which presented themselves to shipowners in the difficult period after the Second World War. The emigrant business was not the Charlton company's only interest. Like several of the owners whose activities are covered in this book it also hired its ships out for trooping. In fact, it had considerably more success as a troopship operator than with its activities in the emigrant trade.

Charlton was already an old-established concern when it passed into Chandris hands. It had been formed in June 1892, one of the many small cargo ship companies then based in Newcastle upon Tyne. By 1945 its assets consisted mainly of investments and a claim for government compensation for war losses.

In April, 1945 the Chandris family and their associates acquired the company and transferred its headquarters to their own office in St. Helen's Place in the City of London. Demetrios John Chandris, whose nationality was rather picturesquely given as 'Hellene' in the company's official return, headed the new board of three directors and in due course he was joined by his brother, the young Anthony Chandris. In those days, the London–Greeks were an even more prominent part of the British shipping scene than they are today. Although the family was very active in building up its shipping interests in the years after the War, the Charlton company did not immediately figure in these plans. Instead it acquired the lease of a property near

A rare photograph of the *Charlton Monarch*. After a single disastrous and uncompleted voyage she was laid up in Barry Docks. In the top right-hand corner of this picture (taken from the photographer's bedroom window in 1950) we see her awaiting her fate.
G. Deighton

Regents Park and there was also a small engineering subsidiary, Huntsworth Equipment Co. Ltd.

However, towards the end of 1946 two ships were purchased from the Canadian War Assets Corporation. The *Prince David* and the *Prince Robert* were members of a trio of rather stubby-looking, three-funnelled passenger liners of just under 7,000 gross tons which had been built in 1930-31 for Canadian National Steamships. They were intended for a new 'Tri-City' service (Vancouver–Victoria–Seattle) in which they were to compete directly with the Canadian Pacific 'Princesses'. The new ships were very fast – capable of 23 knots – but not, it must be admitted, particularly successful. Canadian National was soon forced to abandon the service. No doubt the economic climate was unfavourable and the venture seems to have been unlucky from the outset. For instance, the specially constructed terminal at Vancouver was destroyed by fire a couple of days before the service was due to commence.

The three sisters may have been expensive to operate, being complicated and labour-intensive. John D. Henderson of Victoria, British Columbia knew them as an engineer later in their careers and describes them as 'a mass of boilers and pipes'. He quotes one crewman who, on seeing the *Prince David*'s boiler room for the first time, exclaimed 'It's just like a bowl of spaghetti'.

Nevertheless, the three 'Princes' do seem to have aroused much loyalty among Canadian ship enthusiasts despite the fact that they spent a relatively short time on the West Coast. As the 'thirties progressed, they all had periods in lay-up and were used for cruising from New York, Boston and other East Coast ports. In 1937 the *Prince Henry* was chartered out to the Clarke Steamship Co. for cruising service and they bought her outright in 1938. All three ships were very usefully busy during the War, at the end of which the *Prince Henry* was bought by the British Ministry of War Transport (as it was then called). Now renamed the *Empire Parkeston*, she operated on the shuttle service between Parkeston Quay and the Hook of Holland serving the British Army of Occupation on the Rhine (B.A.O.R.).

The *Prince David* and the *Prince Robert* had a period of lay-up at Vancouver but early in 1947, some months after buying them, Charlton brought them over to Southampton under their own power. Coincidentally, the *Prince Henry* was already lying in the port awaiting conversion. Post-War shortages and extremely strict government controls meant that it was some time before permission could be obtained for the *Prince David* and the *Prince Robert* to be refitted for their new role. Eventually however, they were sent to Antwerp where they were placed in the hands of Beliard Crighton, shiprepairers. The Charlton company's balance sheet for the 31st December, 1947 contained the item: Ships at cost £288,463.

In May, 1948 it was announced that the *Charlton Monarch* (ex-*Prince David*) and the *Charlton Sovereign* (ex-*Prince Robert*) had been time-chartered to the I.R.O. for one year with the option of a further year. As converted they each rated about 5,500 gross tons. For their naval service their three funnels had been reduced to two, with the first one containing two uptakes and consequently being much broader than the second. They – and the *Empire Parkeston* – retained this odd arrangement in their new guises. The two Charlton ships could now accommodate 750 passengers in 8-berth cabins and in dormitories for 20 to 40 people. The men were, as usual in I.R.O. ships, housed quite separately from the women and children.

John D. Henderson comments that the *Prince David* had been the 'bad luck ship' of the trio – four times aground (once so seriously as to be 'very close to becoming a total loss'); mined in the Aegean during the War; and on fire at Curacao during her delivery voyage from Vancouver to Southampton in 1947. She was also the hardest used of the three sisters. He remarks with some understatement that 'her life was not a bed of roses'. Alas, there was to be no change of fortune for her in her new career.

On 16th May, 1948 she departed Bremerhaven for Buenos Aires flying the British flag and bearing her new name, *Charlton Monarch*. The voyage proved to be a fiasco. She put in at St. Vincent with boiler trouble. Repairs were made but further problems arose as the voyage continued and on 11th June she was towed into Pernambuco. There was some suggestion that the damage had been caused by sabotage but this was never substantiated. By early July she was sufficiently repaired to undergo trials but the British Corporation surveyor declared her unfit to proceed. It was reported that by 9th July all her long-suffering passengers would have left the ship, presumably being taken on to their destination by other means. Attempts to rectify the problems continued but after further unsuccessful trials the *Charlton Monarch* left Pernambuco for the United Kingdom under tow by the tug *Zeelandia*. Even now her misfortunes were not at an end. The *Zeelandia* developed furnace trouble and, having struggled into Las Palmas, handed over the tow to another tug, the *Tyne*. At last, on 1st October, the *Charlton Monarch* was delivered to the Clyde. Five days later she arrived at Barry Docks in South Wales where she lay for the next three years. Here an attempt was made at repairs, but the ill-fortune which had dogged the ship held to the end and some of the workmen were asphyxiated.

All this was a costly misfortune for the Charlton company. The accounts for the period to 31st December, 1948 show that the *Charlton Monarch*'s operations had produced a net cost to the company of £88,366. In the following year expenditure related to the vessel amounted to a further £62,426. This figure included the net cost of an agreement with the I.R.O. regarding the charter of a substitute ship. Eventually, the company lodged a notice of abandonment with the insurance underwriters declaring that on 10th June, 1948 the *Charlton Monarch* had become a constructive total loss. They claimed £417,000 but evidently the underwriters disputed the claim. It would seem that in the end a compromise was reached and the company eventually received about £50,000. Even so, a few thousand pounds owed by foreign underwriters were never forthcoming. In October, 1951 the unhappy vessel, now the property of the underwriters, was towed away to a breaker's yard.

The *Charlton Sovereign* also suffered from boiler and machinery defects, no doubt due in part to intense wear and spasmodic maintenance during her War service. Unlike her sister, however, she remained in operation. It is not possible to deduce from the company's accounts whether she was profitable.

She first sailed from Bremerhaven for Australia on 4th August, 1948 calling at Rotterdam. Her voyage to Sydney took no less than 86 days. She had been delayed at Gibraltar for nearly a month with boiler troubles and then at Batavia with engine defects. Her second round voyage – from Bremerhaven to Rio de Janeiro – was also interrupted. On her return she spent nearly two months on the Tyne being repaired at Palmer's Dry Dock and by Hawthorn Leslie. Once back in service she performed more satisfactorily. She made a total of three round voyages from Naples to Rio de Janeiro, one from Naples to Halifax and one from Naples to Central America. This ended her employment by the I.R.O. which had lasted for almost eighteen months.

There followed a fallow period of almost six months during which she lay idle at Naples. She then sailed to Liverpool and finally, in August 1950, she proceeded to Bremerhaven. It was reported that she had been chartered to the Continental Shipping Co. of Bremen for an East Asian passenger service and would be the first British ship to have a German crew since 1939. The identity of the Continental Shipping Co. remains a mystery. At the time West German crews came rather more cheaply than those of many other nationalities and many concerns found it convenient to employ them. In the event, the *Charlton Sovereign* seems to have remained tied up at Bremerhaven for a year until she sailed in August, 1951 under the ownership of another Chandris company, the Cia. Panameña Europea Navigación Ltda. She made a pilgrim voyage from Oran, Algiers and Bone to Jeddah and then proceeded to Port Sudan. Compared with the freighters fitted out with the most temporary and primitive facilities which usually carried pilgrims in those days, she must have seemed almost luxurious. After returning to Oran she sailed for Genoa in October, 1951.

Perhaps surprisingly, she had been bought by the Fratelli Grimaldi. This Italian family habitually made cheap purchases of elderly passenger vessels but the 21-year-old *Charlton Sovereign* was somewhat younger than their other ships and they had rather higher ambitions for her. At any rate when she emerged from refitting as their *Lucania* she had become by far the sleekest and finest member of their distinctly utilitarian fleet.

The sale of the *Charlton Sovereign* in 1951 was not the end of the Charlton company's activities. By 1950 they had ordered two new tankers from Doxford's. Only one of these actually entered their service – the *Charlton Venus*, which was delivered in December, 1951.

More relevantly, from the point of view of this book, they purchased another passenger vessel early in 1950 – a brave act in view of their unfortunate experiences with the previous two ships.

This further vessel, a steamer of 8,178 gross tons, had started life in 1921 as the *Elisabethville* of the Cie. Belge Maritime, built for their colonial service to the Belgian Congo. Since 1947 she and her sister, the former *Thysville*, had been the troopships *Empire Bure* and *Empire Test* managed for the British Ministry of Transport by Lamport & Holt. The Charlton company sent the old *Empire Bure* to her previous home port of Antwerp for a refit and renamed her *Charlton Star*.

In the early 'fifties the world was beset by political and military disputes and the company found ready employment for the *Charlton Star* in her previous role as a troopship. It is worth recording her movements in some

detail as they give an indication of the extent of Britain's military commitments at that time and of the way in which the armed forces were dependent upon sea transport.

September 1950–April 1951:
Chartered to the Ministry of Transport for four voyages (two to Port Said, one to Malta and one to the Far East, presumably in connection with the Korean War.)
Laid up.
August 1951–October 1951:
Marseilles to Indo-China, presumably under charter to the French government.
November 1951–November 1952:
Ministry of Transport charter (a total of five voyages to Port Said; two spells on a Tilbury–Hook of Holland shuttle service, deputising for the Harwich–Hook steamer *Empire Parkeston* (ex-*Prince Henry*) which had been in collision with her running-mate the *Empire Wansbeck*; nearly thirty trips between Port Said and Cypriot ports ferrying troops for the security operations on that island; and also voyages to Tobruk and Trieste.)
Laid up.
August 1953–June 1954:
Ministry of Transport charter (eleven voyages between Suez and Mombasa in connection with the military operations in Kenya, calling additionally at Mauritius on one trip).
July 1954–November 1954:
French government charter (Marseilles–Colombo and Marseilles–Indo-China).
Laid up.
May 1955–September 1956:
Ministry of Transport charter (seven voyages Suez–Mombasa, one to Famagusta and two to the Seychelles and Mauritius; then Southampton via the Panama Canal to Christmas Island presumably in connection with the atomic tests there).

Laid up, having missed out on the surge of troop movements at the time of the Suez crisis.
March 1957–August 1957:
Chartered to Zim Israel Lines to carry Jewish migrants from Poland who were being allowed to leave for Israel (4½ round voyages Le Havre–Szcezcin; one voyage Szcezcin–Haifa; three voyages Genoa–Haifa).
August 1957–October 1957:
Nine voyages Marseilles–Algiers. (Whether commercial or for trooping is uncertain.)
(Some sources suggest that the *Charlton Star* also made a single transatlantic voyage, but I have been unable to trace this.)

By now there was less trooping work available. The British government had commissioned two large new troopships from the British India Steam Navigation Co. and the Bibby Line, the *Nevasa* and the *Oxfordshire*; and in any case the armed forces were increasingly being transported by air. In 1958 the *Charlton Star* was renamed *Maristrella* and ownership was transferred to another Chandris company, Maristrella Naviera S.A. under the

Liberian flag. She remained idle at La Spezia until May, 1959 when she undertook a pilgrim voyage from Casablanca to Jeddah and back. After a few months at Huelva she sailed to Osaka in Japan where in January 1960 she was broken up.

It is not possible to ascertain how good an investment she had been for the Charlton company since their accounts did not separate her operations from their other activities in the tanker and dry cargo markets. It can be said, however, that Charlton made a profit every year from 1952 to 1957, the best year being 1954 when a net surplus of £252,136 was achieved.

The transfer of the *Charlton Star* to the Liberian register marked the end of the company's passenger shipping activities. At one time, however, it had seemed possible that they would operate another passenger vessel. Early in 1954 the Ministry of Transport offered for sale the motorship *Empire Pride* (1941/9,248 gross tons). She had been built as a cargo vessel but was converted into a troopship and managed for the Ministry by the Bibby Line. In reply to a question in the House of Commons the Minister said that, although she was only thirteen years old, she had been taken out of trooping service because her accommodation fell 'far short of present-day trooping standards'. The ship was originally designed as a cargo vessel and, owing to her construction, it would be difficult and very costly to modernise her with satisfactory results. Despite this, there were suggestions when the Charlton company bought her in

April, 1954 that she was to continue as a trooper. In the event, when she emerged from the Lübecker Flenderwerke after conversion she had become a high-speed dry cargo vessel, the *Charlton Pride*. Later she was sold to the Donaldson Line for whom she ran as the *Calgaria*. Charlton subsequently acquired another dry cargo ship, the *Charlton Mira*.

The company's vessels often carried a variant of the famous Chandris X on their funnels – but not, it would seem, the *Charlton Monarch* or the *Charlton Sovereign*.

The Charlton Steam Shipping Company continued in business until 1969 when the shareholders voted for a voluntary winding-up. By the time the final repayment of capital had been made in 1975, they had received just over 125p in the pound on their shares.

FLEET LIST

Charlton Monarch

5,563 gross tons, twin screw, geared turbine, 20 knots. Built, 1930, by Cammell Laird, Birkenhead as *Prince David* for the West Coast services of Canadian National Steamships. From 1931 onwards: periods of lay-up and cruising. 1931: ran ashore off the coast of Washington. 1932: ran aground off the coast of Bermuda and seriously damaged. (John D. Henderson quotes a figure of no less than $1,247,222 as being paid by the underwriters for salvage and repairs.) 1936: again stranded off Bermuda but with

Unlike her two predecessors in the Charlton fleet, the *Charlton Star* bore the now familiar Chandris X on her funnel. She was a former Belgian liner.
World Ship Society

little damage. 1939: bought by the Royal Canadian Navy and converted into an Armed Merchant Cruiser. 1941: again touched bottom near Bermuda. 1943: converted into a Landing Ship and took part in landings in several areas. 1944: mined in the Aegean. 1945: laid up at Vancouver. 1946: sold to the Charlton Steam Shipping Co. 1947: converted into an emigrant ship and renamed *Charlton Monarch*. 1948: under charter to the I.R.O. made one voyage to South America which was curtailed by boiler trouble. 1948: laid up at Barry Docks. Abandoned to the underwriters as a constructive total loss. 1951: scrapped at Newport.

Charlton Sovereign

5,516 gross tons, twin screw, geared turbines, 20 knots. Built, 1931, by Cammell Laird, Birkenhead as *Prince Robert* for Canadian National Steamships. 1931 onwards: lengthy periods of lay-up and some cruising. 1939: bought by the Royal Canadian Navy and converted into an Armed Merchant Cruiser. 1943: converted into an anti-aircraft cruiser. 1945: repatriated prisoners-of-war from Hong Kong. 1945: laid up and offered for sale. 1946: bought by the Charlton Steam Shipping Co. 1947: converted into an emigrant-carrier, *Charlton Sovereign*. 1948: chartered to the I.R.O. 1949: laid up. 1950: chartered to Continental Shipping Co. but apparently not used. 1951: transferred to Cia. Panameña Europea Navegación Ltda. and used for one pilgrim voyage. 1951: sold to Fratelli Grimaldi and converted into the liner *Lucania* for their service to Central America. 1962: scrapped at Leghorn.

Charlton Star

8,178 gross tons, twin screw, quadruple expansion, 14 knots. Built, 1921, as *Elisabethville* by J. Cockerill, Hoboken for the Cie. Belge Maritime which later merged to become the Cie. Maritime Belge (Lloyd Royal). Allied troopship during the war. 1947: bought by the British Ministry of Transport and managed as the troopship *Empire Bure* by Lamport & Holt. 1950: purchased by the Charlton Steam Shipping Co., renamed *Charlton Star* and used for charter work, mainly trooping. 1957: began a long lay-up. 1958: transferred to Maristrella Naviera S.A. and renamed *Maristrella*. 1960: scrapped at Osaka.

Wartime reconstruction as armed merchant cruisers left the sisters with little superstructure and with two unequally-sized funnels. In this picture of the *Charlton Sovereign* we see that after her post-War conversion into an emigrant carrier she retained these features.

World Ship Society

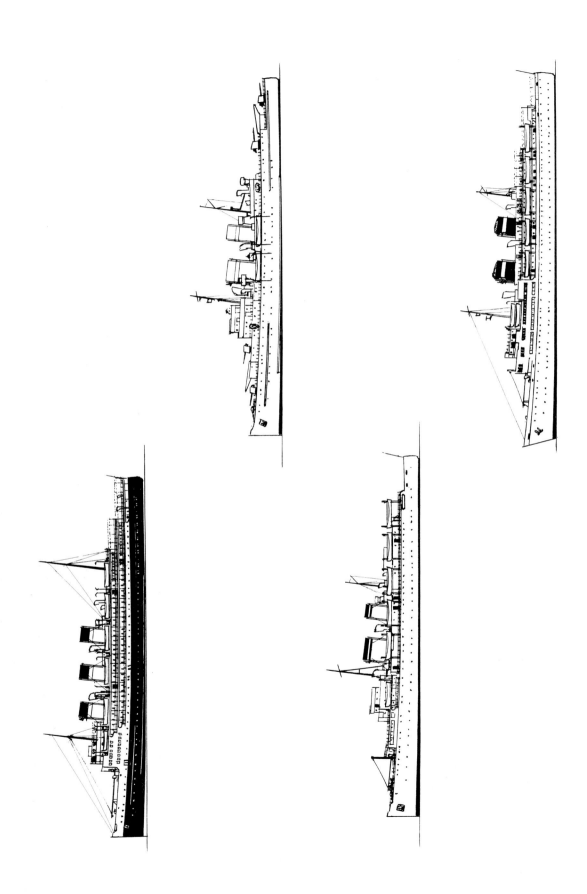

The *Charlton Monarch* and *Charlton Sovereign* had originally been Canadian National coastal liners. These drawings by the late Captain J.H. Isherwood show them, first, as completed in 1930-1. Then as armed merchant cruisers in the Canadian Navy. The third drawing shows the *Charlton Sovereign* as an emigrant carrier in the late 'forties. Finally, we see her as the Grimaldi Line's *Lucania*. (Note: the first two drawings are of the sister ship, *Prince Henry*.)   *The late Captain J.H. Isherwood, courtesy of Mrs Joan Sims*

Chapter Four
The Italian Renaissance

Before the War the Italians had one of the very finest passenger fleets. Italia[1] and Lloyd Triestino – two of the four state-aided companies which had each been allotted a sphere of influence by the Mussolini regime – had a number of elegant and prestigious liners noted for the exuberantly luxurious style of their first class accommodation and for the standard of service which they offered their more privileged passengers. But they were also important carriers of migrants. Ever since the mid-nineteenth century Italian ships had taken many thousands of their compatriots to new lives abroad, mainly to the United States and to South America, but also elsewhere – notably to Australia in the 'twenties.

Italia

The War played havoc with the Italian passenger fleet. True, the destruction was not as great as the almost total loss inflicted on the Japanese and the Germans. However, the Italians lost many vessels including their greatest, the *Rex* and the *Conte Di Savoia*. Had it not been for the generosity of the Americans they would have had virtually no liners at all. In 1946-47, having used them for their own purposes for a while, the Americans handed back four large vessels which had fallen into their hands. The *Saturnia* (1927/24,470 gross tons), *Vulcania* (1928/24,496 gross tons), *Conte Grande* (1928/23,842 gross tons) and *Conte Biancamano* (1925/23,562 gross tons) were not quite the largest of the pre-War Italian liners but they were very important ships nonetheless. They were passed to the Italia company and became for some years the mainstays of the services to New York (*Saturnia* and *Vulcania*) and to South America (the two *Conti*) which the company now resumed.

The *Saturnia* and *Vulcania* were massively squat-looking motorships which had been built in the 'twenties for the Cosulich Line. The Cosulichs were one of the best-known shipping families of the day and in addition to the line which bore their name they had interests in Lloyd Triestino and the Monfalcone shipyards. The Cosulich Line itself became part of the Italia combine in the 'thirties. Although the *Saturnia* and the *Vulcania* had previously sailed usually from Trieste (the family's base) they took over Italia's main service from Genoa to New York after the War, until displaced by a fine new generation of liners. They then reverted to their pre-War route. Their return to their home port and the reinstatement of a transatlantic service from the city provoked great celebration in Trieste. The two ships had always been large carriers of third class passengers, but in their post-War form this category, now called tourist class, became more preponderant (860, partly in dormitories, as against 240 first and 270 cabin class). Consequently, the pair was much involved with the migrant traffic of the early post-War years. They were both long-lived ships. Such vessels sometimes acquire a sentimental following among ship-lovers but are less fondly regarded by their passengers and by the people who have to keep them going. It would seem, however, that the *Saturnia* and *Vulcania* were widely liked even into old age. In 1965, after thirty-eight years of hard service, the *Vulcania* was still able to attract a buyer who wanted her for further trading. The Siosa Line ran her until 1972.

The steamers *Conte Grande* and *Conte Biancamano* had originated with another of Italia's constituent companies, the Lloyd Sabaudo. The Italian royal house had been involved in this concern's foundation and William Beardmore, the Scottish shipbuilder, was a director for a time. The *Conte Biancamano* was one of several ships which his yard produced for the line. In 1949 both liners resumed their civilian careers after lengthy refurbishment, having received new raked bows and, in the case of the *Conte Grande*, modified funnels of a more modern appearance. Internally, too, they were thoroughly updated. Like the former Cosulich ships, they carried large numbers of tourist class passengers. Both made voyages on the New York route but were usually employed on the South American run.

Before the two *Conti* arrived on the South American route in 1949 Italia had instituted a makeshift service mainly using a couple of much less grand vessels. The *San Giorgio* (1923/8,959 gross tons) had been built for Lloyd Sabaudo's attempt to break into the Australian trade. Towards the end of the War she was taken over by the British for use as a hospital ship but was soon returned to Italian ownership. Her running-mate was a hoary old veteran called the *Santa Cruz* (1903/15,511 gross tons) which Italia chartered from a Portuguese company, Tagus Navigation, who had already sent her on one voyage to the River Plate and one to the Caribbean. The *Santa Cruz* had, to put it mildly, been around a bit. She had belonged successively to the Pacific Mail, Atlantic Transport, American, Panama Pacific, Dollar and American President lines and had latterly been a U.S. Government transport, before being bought by the Portuguese. Built before the installation of turbines in ships of her size, she had quadruple expansion engines. In Italia service she accommodated 140 passengers in cabins and 1,050 in dormitories. (Incidentally, she had a sister ship which had a parallel career until 1940 and which will figure in Chapter Nine). Initially, Italia's South American sailings were co-ordinated with those of Dodero's converted 'Victory' ships *Tucuman, Mendoza, Buenos Aires* and *Santa Fe* (see Chapter Ten).

Two other vessels with which Italia eked out its services in these early years were the motor ship *Leme* (1925/8,059 gross tons) and the *Gerusalemme* (1920/8,052 gross tons). In her pre-War days with Navigazione Libera Triestina, *Leme* had been mainly a cargo vessel with accommodation for only about 40 passengers. Now owned by Italia, she could house 64 in cabins and 258 in dormitories. She, too, had fallen into British hands during the War but after

---

1   Better known in the English-speaking world as the Italian Line.

transfer to the Americans she was sold to Italy for a nominal sum. The *Gerusalemme* was a handsome steamer belonging to Lloyd Triestino which had been well-regarded on their African run before the War. After capture she had served as a British hospital ship. She ran to South America for Italia in the late 'forties before returning to her owners' service.

Surprisingly, perhaps, it was Italia's third service – that to Central America and then through the Panama Canal and down the west coast of South America – which received the company's first post-War passenger ships. Motor vessels of the 'Navigatori' class did make some voyages to the River Plate, latterly from Trieste, but mainly they were allocated to the route to the Venezuelan, Peruvian and Chilean ports. They had been ordered as freighters in the early days of the War and three of the six were launched during that period but their construction was delayed by sabotage and war damage. By the time they entered service they had acquired accommodation for about 500 tourist class passengers in addition to a limited number of cabin class. They had also been given new names, being now known as the *Ugolino Vivaldi* (1947/8,914 gross tons), *Sebastiano Caboto* (1947/8,967 gross tons), *Paolo Toscanelli* (1948/9,004 gross tons), *Marco Polo* (1948/8,949 gross tons), *Antoniotto Usodimare* (1949/9,715 gross tons) and *Amerigo Vespucci* (1949/9,774 gross tons).

It was in 1951, with the completion of the 27,000 gross ton *Giulio Cesare* that the Italians began the long series of splendid liners which fully restored their former position on the North and South Atlantic routes. These later vessels all carried tourist class passengers in large numbers, of course, but it is primarily as luxury liners, financed by the state to uphold the nation's prestige, that they are remembered.

Lloyd Triestino

Lloyd Triestino had also carried migrants before the War. In Mussolini's grand re-organisation of the shipping industry they had been allotted the Australian route, among others. Also, they took large numbers of settlers to Eritrea, then an Italian colony. (On a visit to Ethiopia many years later, I was surprised to find that despite the bitterness of the fighting during Mussolini's Abyssinian campaign, many Italians were still living there quite comfortably and happily.)

The company re-started its Australian service in 1948 with the *Toscana* (1923/9,442 gross tons), a rather staid ex-German. They also planned to bring the *Remo* back onto the run. She was the sole survivor in Italian hands of a class of motor ships which had maintained the service before the War. However, this plan was thwarted by a serious fire, possibly caused by arson. She did eventually sail again, but as a cargo vessel for other owners. In the event, the *Ugolino Vivaldi* and *Sebastiano Caboto* were briefly chartered from Italia to supplement the service and then, in 1952 the *Toscana* was joined for a while by the *San Giorgio* whose

The handsome *Oceania*, one of three new 12,000-tonners which made Lloyd Triestino a strong competitor on the Australian run in the 1950s.

A. Duncan

stint on Italia's River Plate service had recently ended. Both these ships were largely emigrant-carriers and made Trieste their home base. For historical reasons the pre-War service to Australia had run from Genoa and it was from this port that three new liners usually sailed from 1951 onwards, although the *Toscana* soldiered on out of Trieste and other Adriatic ports for a further decade.

The new vessels – *Australia* (1951/12,839 gross tons), *Oceania* (1951/12,839 gross tons) and *Neptunia* (1951/12,839 gross tons) were altogether better than anything the Italians had ever before had on the Australian run – smart motorships with a service speed of 18 knots and excellent air-conditioned accommodation. (Four very similar vessels for the African and Far Eastern services had much less third or tourist class capacity since their routes did not produce much in the way of migrant traffic.)

Twelve years later the *Australia*, *Oceania* and *Neptunia* were transferred to Italia and took over the service to the west coast of South America. In the Italia tradition they were named after great men, *Donizetti*, *Verdi* and *Rossini*. The move was prompted by Lloyd Triestino's introduction into the Australian service of two spectacular new liners. The *Galileo Galilei* (1963/27,888 gross tons) and *Guglielmo Marconi* (1963/27,905 gross tons) – Lloyd Triestino had caught Italia habits of nomenclature – were very definitely emigrant and tourist ships. 1,594 of their 1,750 passengers travelled in the tourist class, but in air-conditioned accommodation of a very high standard. With their sharply-raked bows and sleek superstructures well endowed with open deck space and swimming pools they were very characteristic Italian liners. With their service speed of 24 knots they cut the voyage time from Genoa to Sydney to 23 days.

Italia and Lloyd Triestino remained in the business of long-distance liner services longer than most companies, largely because they were by now effectively state-controlled through their parent organisation Finmare. Consequently, considerations of national prestige and pressure from the unions loomed large, keeping their big liners sailing long after competition from the airlines had destroyed their viability. In the 'seventies, however, economic realities asserted themselves. Of the major vessels in the two fleets only the *Galileo Galilei* and the *Guglielmo Marconi* remain in service. After a period in limbo they re-emerged as Chandris's *Galileo* and, following a $37 million rebuilding, Costa's *Costa Riviera*, both operating in the cruise market. *Galileo* has since undergone further rebuilding and is now the *Meridian*.

Costa Line

It was not only the state-controlled lines which revived Italian passenger shipping, however. There were also quite a few private shipowners who saw opportunities in the booming emigrant trade. Some, although established in the cargo business, did not survive long as passenger shipowners; others stayed the course and a few became major forces in the industry. Usually they started on the routes to Central or South America, although some later turned their attention to the Australian run. In the early post-War days they scoured the world for hulls in which they could install simple accommodation. Italian shipyards and ship-preparers became adept at conjuring passenger-carriers out of the most unlikely vessels. These skills of conversion

remain to this day – witness the efforts of the Mariotti company of Genoa who have to their credit a long list of notable transformations into cruise liners, including the French *Mermoz* and the *Costa Riviera*, already mentioned.

The Costa Line (or Linea "C,, – their ships to this day carry the letter "C,, in blue on their yellow funnels) was almost the archetypal Italian family business. Indeed, the family's influence is still very strong although their control has been somewhat diluted. They had gone into shipping in the 'twenties partly in order to transport the products of their olive oil business. After the War, they set about re-building their cargo trade and like many other shipowners were buyers of the surplus war tonnage which the American government was releasing. Also, however, they entered the passenger business.

Some of their freighters may already have been carrying a handful of passengers between Genoa and Buenos Aires, but their first true passenger liner was the *Anna C* (1929/11,736 gross tons). She had been one of a quartet of combination passenger and cargo ships belonging to the Prince Line, a Furness Withy subsidiary. They had been employed in the New York–River Plate trade but the Prince Line decided against restoring the passenger service after the War. Although the *Southern Prince*, as she had been called, was in a fairly worn state, Costa bought her and converted her into a full passenger ship with accommodation for 500. It has been claimed that she was Italy's first air-conditioned liner. The conversion was clearly a much more thorough job than the hasty installations which sufficed in some of the ships which eager owners rushed into the emigrant trades at that time. Over the years the *Anna C*'s accommodation was extended and improved several times – Costa have always tended to retain good ships, even into old age, and spend heavily on up-grading them periodically.

The *Anna C* was very quickly joined by the *Andrea C* (1942/8,604 gross tons), similarly converted from a standard American wartime freighter. The pair maintained a regular service to South America, helped out for a time by the *Giovanna C* (1919/6,475 gross tons), one of the company's cargo ships which was given extensive third class accommodation. Economic conditions in the Argentine and Brazil in the late 'forties caused some slackening in the flow of migrants. Also the Italian Line (Italia) had by now fully restored its South American service to its pre-War standard. As a result, several operators withdrew from the route, including Home Lines, but Costa remained.

In 1952 a further vessel was brought into the line's passenger service. The *Franca C* (1914/6,822 gross tons) has had a most remarkable history. For thirty five years she was a very ordinary American cargo steamer. Then in 1949 she was bought by the Cia. Naviera San Miguel, a Panamanian-registered but Italian-controlled concern which also had strong American connections. They had her converted into a passenger-carrier and renamed her *Roma*. Together with an old coal-burning steamer, the *Liguria* which was owned by an associated company, she was chartered out for several pilgrim voyages from America to Europe during Holy Year, 1950. There followed some Australian trips but, as with many of these old ships, mechanical problems developed. The Costa Line thought her worth buying, however, and installed diesel engines before placing her on the South American route as the *Franca C.* Later on, she and other Costa ships also ran to Central America. She remained with Costa until 1977, having been much rebuilt in 1959 and subsequently and receiving another set of new engines as late as 1970. By now, she had been transformed into a well-furnished cruise liner, becoming one of the pioneers of the Miami-based cruise industry. When Costa disposed of her at the age of sixty-three she presented a somewhat antiquated appearance, emphasised by her counter stern, but she was still very sound. She was bought by Operation Mobilisation, a missionary organisation, and has since sailed to ports in many parts of the world as the *Doulos*, a floating cultural centre and religious bookshop. Flying the Maltese flag, she is manned by volunteers. Said to be the oldest active deep-sea passenger vessel in the world, the *Doulos* is one of a number of extremely long-lived ships which have testified to the quality of American shipbuilding in the early decades of the century.[1]

To revert to the Costa Line, in 1957 they bought another elderly vessel with the announced intention of expanding her passenger capacity and using her as an emigrant-carrier. In fact, things turned out otherwise. Called the *Bianca C.*, she was a former Rotterdam Lloyd motorship whose passenger capacity had been reduced in favour of cargo space in the late 'forties. In 1956 she was bought for £200,000 by a Panamanian company managed by Fratelli Rizzuto of Genoa. Within months they had sold her on to Costa for £260,000. She made a few voyages on Costa's cargo route to the east coast of the USA on which she may have carried a few passengers but was then chartered to the Cogedar Line. They quickly sub-chartered her to Messageries Maritimes who placed her on their service from Marseilles to the French possessions in the South Seas and on to Australia. She acquired the French name of *Mélanésien* but retained a largely Italian crew. Such are the complications of the shipping business.

From 1958 onwards the Costa Line moved into a higher league. Over the next few years two large new liners were built, one of which – the *Eugenio C* – was generally considered the finest on the South American route. Other ships, bought secondhand or chartered in, were all of a high and often luxurious standard. Costa continued a regular, if ultimately diminishing, service to South America on which it still provided extensive tourist class accommodation but it was no longer primarily an emigrant line. At the same time it moved very successfully into the cruise market and was one of the pioneers of the fly-cruise concept. Its subsequent history lies outside the scope of this book.

Cogedar

Costa are said to have had a financial interest in another Genoese concern, the Cogedar Line. The name Cogedar was one of those acronyms beloved of Italian businessmen and stood for Compagnia Genovese di Armamento. The company's first fully-fledged passenger vessel[2] was the *Flaminia* (1922/8,779 gross tons) which had been one of the early funnel-less motorships. Starting as a cargo vessel with the American–Hawaiian Steamship Co., she had gone on to bear several British and Belgian names before passing into Cogedar's hands. They called her *Genova* at first and ran her to South America with fairly basic accommodation for 800 emigrants. In 1954-55 she was metamorphosed into a very presentable passenger-carrier on the Australian run, often starting her voyages from Trieste. On several occasions she returned via Saigon and North Africa, perhaps acting as a troopship for the French. It should be added that later still she was chartered to Zim Israel Lines and ended up as the *King Abdelaziz* carrying pilgrims for the Saudi Lines. She was a good example of the way in which the conditions on migrant ships were improved during the 'fifties. As the *Genova* she had accommodated her passengers in dormitories, but after she was thoroughly rebuilt as the *Flaminia* many travelled in air-conditioned cabins.

The company later acquired two further vessels. We have already met the *Aurelia* (1939/10,022 gross tons) in her previous guise as Canadian Pacific's *Beaverbrae* (see Chapter Two). Cogedar used her in their Australian service and also chartered her out for transatlantic student voyages in the summer months. She must have been something of a disappointment to them since, having spent heavily on extending her superstructure and installing fully air-conditioned accommodation for 1,124 tourist class passengers, they were fairly soon faced with the expense of re-engining her.

The other Cogedar passenger ship was the *Flavia* (1947/15,465 gross tons). She had been the *Media*, one of a pair of combination liners which Cunard placed in their New York service from Liverpool soon after the end of the War. After being bought by Cogedar in 1961 she underwent a drastic reconstruction from which she emerged quite unrecognisable as the former, rather foursquare Cunarder. With a new raked bow, extended superstructure, single streamlined mast and Italianate funnel – not to mention stabilisers – she now accommodated 1,224 tourist class passengers in almost luxurious conditions. All now travelled in cabins with private lavatories and showers. Not surprisingly, she was used for cruising as well as liner voyages.

Cogedar was one of several Mediterranean companies who extended their Australian services to Southampton and other northern European ports in the late 'fifties. Some voyages also became round-the-world, outwards via Panama and returning via Suez, partly to attract tourist passengers. Cogedar was finally absorbed by Costa in about 1968 after which the *Aurelia* was sold to Chandris for

---

1   Under the title 'Worse Things Happen At Sea', her former navigating officer, Clive Langmead, has written a most entertaining and thought-provoking account of her early years in her missionary role. (Lion Publishing, 1984.)

2   However, one of Cogedar's earlier ships, the *Philippa*, an elderly ex-American, may have carried migrants from Genoa to South America in 1947-8. Then in 1949, she was chartered by a short-lived venture called Compagnia di Navigazione 'La Fortuna', also for a South American service. In the words of one Italian source this concern 'collapsed clamorously' after a few months.

The *Ascania* of the Siosa Line (part of the Grimaldi group) brought many West Indian migrants to Britain. Grimaldi tended to give their second-hand purchases less fundamental refits than some Italian owners.   *A. Duncan*

roughly £1 million, it was said. The *Flavia* joined her new owners' cruising fleet.

Grimaldi-Siosa

A third Genoese concern also became prominent in the emigrant trades. The Grimaldi family group are now well-known operators of car-carriers, freight ferries and dry cargo ships whose main passenger interest is a share in the solitary cruise ship *Ausonia*. From the late 'forties, however, the Fratelli Grimaldi maintained a passenger line from Genoa to the Central American and Caribbean ports. Initially their ships were also liable to turn up in other parts of the world carrying loads of emigrants. It has to be said that Grimaldi vessels tended to be distinctly elderly and were consequently bought quite cheaply.

The first purchase was a former New Zealand Shipping Company liner, the *Ruahine*, already forty years old when Grimaldi bought her in 1949. She underwent a typical conversion – her considerable cargo spaces were largely turned into passenger quarters; the superstructure was extended; and the single, rather spindly funnel was replaced by a more modern-looking one. As the *Auriga* (1909/10,758 gross tons) she served Grimaldi for eight years until being scrapped in 1957. Not all her running-mates proved to be such long-term investments. The *Urania II* (1906/6,715 gross tons) had already spent forty three years on the Anchor Line's Indian service when she was bought by another Genoese company, Garibaldi (of which more later). She had sprung a bad leak on her final Anchor Line voyage and now she had a serious mechanical breakdown during her second for Garibaldi. Yet the Fratelli Grimaldi bought her and ran her for a further four years. Neither she nor the *Centauro* were thought worthy of very much in the way of cosmetic surgery. The *Centauro*

(1924/9,579 gross tons) had formerly been the *City of Hong Kong* belonging to Ellerman Lines. Apart from her regular voyages to Central America she is said to have carried displaced persons from Odessa to South America on one occasion. Her end was rather abrupt – after running aground in 1955 she was not considered worth repairing.

The company's rapid expansion continued with the purchase in 1951 of the Charlton Steam Shipping Company's *Charlton Sovereign* (see Chapter Three). Despite her rather chequered history she was singled out for a much more extensive and expensive refit than the existing members of the Grimaldi fleet. Pictures of her as the *Lucania* (1931/6,723 gross tons) show a well-proportioned, nicely raked and curved mini-liner, probably better-looking than at any time in her career. She may have been the first of the company's ships to make provision for first class passengers; and, although some of her tourist class customers were still housed in dormitories, the general standard of accommodation was almost certainly much higher than with this line hitherto. Grimaldi were, in fact, going through the same process of improvement which enabled several of the other opportunist companies to survive and flourish once the initial boom in emigrant transport had subsided.

In 1955 this process was carried further with the acquisition of the *Florida* and *Campana*, formerly the mainstays of the Marseilles–River Plate liner service of the Société Générale de Transports Maritimes. Always with an eye for a bargain, Grimaldi paid £380,000 for the pair. In view of their subsequent lengthy careers this does not seem an extortionate price. They were placed in the ownership of a new company, Sicula Oceanica SpA (the Siosa Line – another acronym) which the Grimaldi group set up in Palermo in order to take advantage of the financial incentives which the Italian government offered for investment in Sicily. Nevertheless the two ships customarily made Genoa their Italian home port. Henceforth the group's passenger operations carried the joint name Grimaldi–Siosa Lines until 1962 when, with the scrapping of the *Lucania*, the last of the old Grimaldi ships, the title became simply Siosa Line.

The two new purchases were renamed *Ascania* (1926/9,536 gross tons) and *Irpinia* (1929/12,279 gross tons) and their addition to the fleet brought about the group's entrance into other trades. In particular, a second service to Central America and the islands of the British West Indies was introduced from Southampton. This was unusual among migrant routes in carrying heavy traffic in both directions. Usually, the outward voyages of such services were heavily patronised but the return trips were relatively empty. In this case, however, the vessels called at Spanish and Portuguese ports on the westward leg in order to pick up migrants and seasonal workers going to the Latin countries of the Caribbean basin; and then visited several West Indian islands to embark heavy loads of migrants travelling to Britain. The Spanish Line also operated a similar service (see Chapter Six). Grimaldi-Siosa also entered the North Atlantic trades in a rather spasmodic way during several summer seasons from 1956 to 1961 but eventually withdrew, perhaps because these routes were already in decline.

The *Irpinia* was quickly modified and improved by Siosa. Before the *Ascania* was taken in hand, however, she made two West Indian voyages from Southampton and then spent several months trooping under charter to the French government, followed by a voyage for the International Red Cross at the time of the Suez crisis. Like the *Lucania*, the *Ascania* and *Irpinia* carried some first class passengers but they were primarily emigrant ships. Much of their accommodation was in cabins but they still had some berths in dormitories.

In 1956 they were joined by the *Venezuela* (1924/18,567 gross tons). For many years this ship had been the French Line's second rank Atlantic liner *De Grasse*; but she had then been bought by Canadian Pacific as a temporary replacement for their *Empress of Canada* which had been badly damaged by fire. In 1960 Siosa sent the *Venezuela* for a thorough modernisation. This included lengthening her with a new and exaggeratedly raked bow section which, from photographs, seems to have looked distinctly incongruous on a ship which otherwise had a profile typical of the 'twenties. She was not to display her new face for long. Early in 1962 she struck a rock near Cannes and was deemed beyond economic repair.

Three years later Siosa paid 776 million lire for yet another very elderly liner which they renamed *Caribia* (1928/24,496 gross tons). She was none other than Italia's motorship *Vulcania*, mentioned earlier in this chapter. For a while she operated on the Caribbean routes – not very profitably, it has been suggested – but by now Siosa were turning away from liner services and were concentrating on cruising. *Caribia* was advertised in Britain as 'The Big One' and continued to operate in the cruise market until she too met disaster on a rock near Cannes in 1972.

The later activities of the Siosa Line do not concern this book. It is worth mentioning, though, that the *Irpinia* – by now re-engined with diesels and much modernised both externally and internally – remained in service as a very successful cruise ship until Siosa were finally forced to retire her at the age of fifty one.

Flotta Lauro

Genoa was not the only Italian port whose shipowners went into the passenger trades after the War. At Naples there was the Flotta Lauro, the private shipping line of the formidable Achille Lauro who was also well-known as a right-wing politician. He too expanded out of cargo shipping into the emigrant business. As early as April, 1947 his motor ship *Ravello* (1941/8,806 gross tons) sailed for Rio de Janeiro, Santos, Montevideo and Buenos Aires and was joined in the new service a few months later by the Liberty ship *Olimpia* (1943/7,176 gross tons). Both were cargo vessels into which accommodation, presumably rather basic, had been hastily crammed for emigrant passengers. They may have been stopgaps, but the *Olimpia* was included in the list of vessels on whose regular line voyages the I.R.O. proposed to make block bookings in the year to July, 1950.

As with some other Italian owners, Lauro's interest in the South American run waned and he eventually concentrated on the Australian route and, until the mid-'sixties, the Central American run, with a few North Atlantic voyages as well (including several from Canada to Liverpool in 1953 – Coronation Year).

The first full-blown Lauro passenger ship was a prime example of the lengths to which some shipowners went in their quest for tonnage suitable for conversion. The *Napoli* (1940/8,082 gross tons) was built out of the remains of the Bank Line cargo vessel *Araybank* which had been abandoned after being very badly damaged by bombing off the island of Crete in 1941. Six years later she was salvaged and the remains were bought by Lauro who had them transformed into a serviceable ship with accommodation for 656 passengers of whom 480 slept in dormitories. She was placed in the Australian trade, usually from Genoa with a call at Naples, and when she arrived on her maiden voyage in September, 1948 she was said to be the first Italian passenger ship to call at an Australian port since the War. In 1949 she was joined by the *Surriento* (1928/10,699 gross tons), originally the Grace Line's *Santa Maria* and a somewhat superior ship with capacity for 187 first class passengers in addition to the 868 tourist class which formed the main part of her complement.

In 1951, with the advent of further tonnage both vessels were transferred to the Central American route which the line now established. Demand for passages to Australia was such, however, that the *Surriento* was for a while transferred back to that route. It was during this period that in 1956 her captain was fined for contravening safety regulations. The Australian authorities were becoming concerned about the condition of some of the vessels bringing migrants to their shores and there were a number of court cases. The masters of several ships were fined, including the Greek *Cyrenia* and the Egyptian *Gumhuryat Misr* (see later chapters).

The 'new' tonnage placed on the Australian run in 1951 consisted of two rather modern-looking vessels which had been created out of a pair of former escort carriers which Lauro had bought the previous year. There was a

The famous *Achille Lauro* at Southampton in November, 1979 after she had become a full-time cruise ship. Note the inward slope of her hull, known as tumblehome.
R. Bruce Grice

whole class of these vessels which had in many cases been laid down as standard C3 cargo ships but, with American involvement in the War, had been completed as aircraft-carriers. They had been handed over to the Royal Navy, but at the end of hostilities the British had returned them to America. In due course they were put up for sale and proved popular with shipowners searching for potential emigrant ships. The *Fairsea* and *Fairsky* of the Sitmar Line will be covered in the next chapter; and the Argentinian *Salta* and *Corrientes*, the *Anna Salén* of the Swedish Salén company and the Panamanian-flag *Nelly* of the Caribbean Land & Shipping Corporation (later the Europe–Canada Line's *Seven Seas*) will follow in subsequent chapters. The two Lauro ships became the *Roma* (1943/14,687 gross tons) and the *Sydney* (1942/14,708 gross tons).

In 1966 Lauro followed the example of the Lloyd Triestino and introduced two larger and vastly superior vessels into his Australian service. The displaced *Roma* and *Sydney* were briefly transferred to the Central American service but within a year this was closed down. The *Roma* was then scrapped, whereupon the *Sydney* assumed her name and was sent cruising. She was soon sold and spent the next five years staggering from one mishap to the next. She became notorious as Sovereign Cruises' *Galaxy Queen* and as the *Lady Dina* (or *Lady Tina*) belonging to a Mr. George Kotzovilis. Numerous mechanical failures; cancelled cruises; passenger complaints which received much publicity; seizure for debt; the arrest of some of her (allegedly unpaid) crew for theft and attempted smuggling; the arrest of her captain for failing to protect her stores from their depredations; the arrest of Mr. Kotzovilis; allegations (which were denied) that the ship had been sold for a nominal £1 in order to avoid settling an unpaid shipyard bill – in short she had become incident-prone.[1] A final attempt at respectability with new owners and under charter to the Siosa Line as the *Caribia 2* also proved unsuccessful.

---

1   A fuller account of this sorry saga is contained in the author's article, 'Cruising For The Masses' in the November, 1988 issue of Seascape.

To revert to the two fine liners which Lauro brought into his Australian service in 1966: his original intention had been that they should be new buildings. Indeed, as early as 1962 orders were said to have been placed with an Italian yard for two 30,000 tonners. Little seems to have happened until 1964, however, when these plans were superseded by the purchase of a pair of large Dutch motor liners. Since the collapse of the trade between Holland and the East Indies, the *Oranje* and the *Willem Ruys*, owned by the Nederland Line and Royal Rotterdam Lloyd respectively, had been operating a round-the-world service with rather moderate success. Lauro renamed them *Angelina Lauro* (1939/24,377 gross tons) and *Achille Lauro* (1947/23,629 gross tons) and sent them to yards in Genoa and Palermo for conversion. Their entry into this service was delayed by fires which damaged both vessels in August, 1965. Inevitably there was some suspicion of arson, perhaps prompted by Lauro's political activities. When they did at last go into operation they were hardly recognisable as their former selves. In addition to the alterations to bows and superstructure customary in such cases they had acquired unusually tall funnels topped by enormous smoke-deflectors. The *Angelina Lauro* had a single funnel but the *Achille Lauro* had two. They wore the striking livery of the Flotta Lauro – blue funnels bearing large white stars; and blue hulls. The *Angelina Lauro* now had capacity for 1,616 passengers and the *Achille Lauro* for 1,307, in both cases largely but not entirely in tourist class. Both were, of course, fully air-conditioned and carried their passengers in some comfort. They operated a route which had been extended at both ends, now starting at Bremerhaven and calling at Rotterdam, Southampton, Genoa, Naples and Messina before proceeding to Australia and then, after calls at Fremantle, Melbourne and Sydney, continuing across the Tasman Sea to Wellington. After the closure of the Suez Canal in 1967 the route became outward via the Cape and homeward via Panama or, on occasion, via the Straits of Magellan.

With hindsight it would seem that Lauro's large investment in fresh tonnage for the Australian route came rather late in the day. The emigrant trade was soon a mere shadow of what it had formerly been and there were too many competitors for the tourist trade. At any rate, after 1972 both ships were employed entirely in cruising. The subsequent careers of these vessels are well-known. The *Angelina* was destroyed by fire while on charter to the Costa Line and the *Achille Lauro* has suffered fire, arrest for debt and seizure by terrorists. It is sad to have to record that Achille Lauro himself lived long enough into his nineties to witness the collapse of the considerable shipping line which he had built up.

Other Italian Owners

Before leaving the Italian ships, mention must be made of the vessels of several owners whose involvement in the migrant trades was relatively short-lived. Ignazio Messina, for instance, operated two ships between the Mediterranean and South America between 1948 and 1955. One was the *Lugano* (1898/6,900 gross tons) which at one stage of her long career had been one of the early cargo ships owned by the forerunners of the present-day Blue Star Line. Messina acquired her, still as a cargo vessel, in 1936

and she was later renamed *Lugano* as a result of a war-time transfer to a Swiss concern. Her running-mate was the small *Pace* (1921/4,013 gross tons) which had been an American liner before Messina bought her.

The Società Anonima Cooperativa di Navigazione Garibaldi has already cropped up in connection with the Grimaldi Line's *Urania II*. She had briefly been Garibaldi's *Marengo* (1906/6,715 gross tons). She made two voyages to Central America for them in 1949 before engine troubles caused her withdrawal and sale to Grimaldi. At the same time Garibaldi were running a temporarily converted cargo ship on the Australian route. She was the *Luciano Manara* (1941/8,333 gross tons). The patriotically-named Garibaldi concern also had a fair fleet of cargo ships and at one time managed a few small vessels for the Italian Navy.

Sidarma, the Società Italiana di Armamento, used two modern freighters to carry migrants from Italy and Spain to South and Central America. They were the *Andrea Gritti* (1943/8,072 gross tons) and the *Francesco Morosini* (1948/8,678 gross tons). Italnavi, a similar company, operated the *Sestriere* (1943/8,652 gross tons) and the *Sises* (1949/9,177 gross tons) in conjunction with Sidarma.

Not all Italian-controlled vessels sailed under their country's flag. The registered owners of the *Roma* (1914/5,426 gross tons) and the *Liguria* (1917/7,474 gross tons) were Panamanian nominal companies, Compania Naviera San Miguel and Compania Naviera Baru. The address of the former was at one time given in Lloyd's Register as c/o Simpson, Space and Young of New York. The history of the *Roma* has already been outlined but her running-mate deserves further comment. The *Liguria* was built for the Woermann Line's service to South Africa and the German territories of East Africa. However, she never entered this service and at the end of the First World War was taken as a prize by the British. Eventually she passed to the Australian firm, Burns Philp who named her *Marella* and used her on their route to Singapore. By the end of the Second World War she was both worn and antiquated, being one of the few coal-burning passenger liners still in service and Burns Philp divested themselves of her as soon as they could find a replacement. However, in the climate of shortage which then existed it was possible to find buyers for even the most ramshackle vessels and the *Marella* was quickly bought by the Compania Naviera Baru. At first they named her *Captain Marcos*, but she soon became the *Liguria*. In 1949 she started her new career by carrying a full load of over 900 refugees from Genoa to Valparaiso where she was arrested presumably for debt. The following year she was used to take Holy Year pilgrims from New York to Europe in conjunction with the *Roma*. An attempt was then made to introduce her into the emigrant trade to Australia – but on her first voyage, from Bremerhaven, she took 78 days to reach Fremantle. She arrived on the end of a tow-rope, suffering from severe mechanical disorders and with her supplies of food and water running low. Unsettled debts kept her in Fremantle for eight months, after which she saw little useful service before being scrapped in 1954.

One more Italian-owned and Panmanian-flagged ship remains to be mentioned. The *Florentia* (1914/7,821 gross tons) was registered in the name of the Cia. de Navegación Florencia (note the different spelling). For forty five years she had been a stalwart of the Henderson Line fleet. For her new owners she ran consistently on the South American and, later, Australian routes. She was sold in 1953 to the Pan-Islamic Steamship Company who renamed her *Safina-E-Nusrat*. She maintained Pan-Islamic's pilgrim service in company with the even older *Safina-E-Arab* (ex-*Oxfordshire*) until finally being scrapped in 1958 at the age of fifty four.

A substantial amount of the emigrant traffic for the Italian, and indeed other, companies came from the Inter-Governmental Committee For European Migration, based in Geneva. It was said to be the world's biggest shipping customer and between 1952 and 1954 it shipped over 300,000 European migrants overseas at a cost of circa $57 million. In 1955 it planned to assist no less than 143,000 migrants.

FLEET LIST

Achille Lauro

23,629 gross tons, twin screw, diesel, 22 knots. Laid down in 1939 by De Schelde, Vlissingen for the Rotterdam Lloyd. Construction greatly slowed during the War. Completed, 1947, as the *Willem Ruys* and entered Rotterdam Lloyd's service from Rotterdam to the East Indies. 1958: after the cessation of the service to what was now Indonesia, she made several North Atlantic voyages including two from Bremen to Montreal under charter to the Europa-Kanada Line. 1959: following a refit was transferred to a new round-the-world service. 1964: sold to Achille Lauro and considerably rebuilt. Did not enter service until 1966, partly due to an explosion and fire while the work was in progress in 1965. Placed on a route from Northern Europe and the Mediterranean to Australia and New Zealand via Suez. 1967: on the closure of the Suez Canal the route became outward via the Cape and home via either Panama or the Straits of Magellan. 1972: full-time cruising. 1975: collision with a Lebanese vessel in which the latter sank. 1981: damaged by an electrical fire. 1982: seized for debt at Tenerife. Owing to the crisis in the affairs of the Lauro Line remained inactive after her eventual return to Genoa. 1983: used as temporary accommodation for earthquake victims in the Naples area. 1984: after a proposed charter for Australian cruises fell through, resumed Mediterranean cruising for the Lauro Line which was now in the process of re-organisation. 1985: while cruising under charter to Chandris was hi-jacked by terrorists near Port Said. One passenger was killed. 1987: a new Italian consortium, Starlauro, acquired the remains of the Lauro Line after several years in which it was effectively owned by the Italian government.

Amerigo Vespucci

9,774 gross tons, single screw, diesel, 15½ knots. Launched, 1942, by Ansaldo, Genoa. 1949: completed for Italia's service to the west coast of South America. Was originally to have been named *Giuseppe Majorana*. 1963: transferred to Lloyd Triestino and converted into a cargo vessel. 1978: scrapped at La Spezia.

Andrea C

Looking very unlike the standard War-time freighter she had originally been, the *Andrea C* is here seen as a cruise liner. In rather less reconstructed form she had been one of Costa's earliest passenger liners. *Lawrence Dunn collection*

8,604 gross tons, single screw, diesel, 15 knots. Built, 1942, by Permanente Metals Corporation, Richmond, California as the *Ocean Virtue*, a standard 'Ocean' class freighter and allotted to the British Ministry of War Transport (managers, Prince Line). 1946: bought by Giacomo Costa fu Andrea. 1948: entered service as the *Andrea C* following lengthening, the installation of passenger accommodation and conversion to diesel propulsion. 1971: switched to full-time cruising. 1981: scrapped at La Spezia.

Andrea Gritti

8,072 gross tons, single screw, diesel, 14½ knots. Built, 1943, by Cantieri Riuniti, Monfalcone as a freighter for Società Italiana di Armamento "Sidarma". 1946: converted into an emigrant-carrier. 1956: reverted to cargo only. 1967: sold to Vera Shipping Co. and renamed *Veritas* (Cypriot flag, but managed by Captain Luigi Monta of Genoa). 1970: now registered in the name of Veras Shipping Co. (note the apparently different spelling of the name), still Cypriot-flag but now managed by W.M. Caldeira and N. Tzivas of Brazil. 1971: scrapped at Kaohsiung.

Angelina Lauro

The *Angelina Lauro* was a radical conversion of the big Dutch motor liner *Oranje*. She entered the Australian trade rather too late to achieve great success. *Steffen Weirauch collection*

24,371 gross tons, twin screw, diesel, 21 knots. Built, 1939, by Nederlandsche S.B., Amsterdam as the *Oranje* of the 'Nederland' Line. Placed on the route between Amsterdam and the Dutch East Indies. War service as a hospital ship with the Royal Australian Navy. 1946: returned to the 'Nederland' Line. 1958: switched to an Amsterdam–Australia service via Suez. 1960: her Australian route was extended to become a round-the-world service. 1964: sold to Flotta Lauro and renamed *Angelina Lauro*. 1965: rebuilding delayed by a serious fire. 1966: entered Lauro's new service from northern and Mediterranean ports to Australia and New Zealand via Suez, with greatly enlarged passenger accommodation. 1967: route diverted via the Cape. 1971: now in round-the-world service. 1972: switched to cruising. 1978: chartered by Costa as the *Angelina*. 1979: destroyed by fire at St. Thomas.

Anna C

11,736 gross tons, twin screw, diesel, 16½ knots. Built, 1929, by Lithgows, Port Glasgow as *Southern Prince* for the Prince Line (Furness Withy), one of four passenger-cargo liners for their New York–South America service. 1940: became a troop transport. 1947: bought by Giacomo Costa fu Andrea and refitted to carry more passengers; named *Anna C*. 1948: started the Costa service between Genoa and the River Plate. Also used on the Central American route. 1952: re-engined, 18 knots. 1960: refitted and passenger accommodation extended. 1971: scrapped at La Spezia.

Costa's first passenger liner, the *Anna C*, a pre-War British vessel. Although an emigrant ship she was probably Italy's first air-conditioned liner. *Laurence Dunn collection*

Antoniotto Usodimare

9,715 gross tons, single screw, diesel, 15 knots. Launched, 1942, as the *Vittorio Moccagatta* for Italia by Ansaldo, Genoa but not completed until 1949 by which time she had become the *Antoniotto Usodimare*. 1963: transferred to Lloyd Triestino and converted into a freighter. 1978: scrapped at Trieste.

Ascania

9,536 gross tons, twin screw, geared turbine, 17 knots. Built, 1926, by Ateliers et Chantiers de la Loire, St. Nazaire as the *Florida* for the Soc. Générale de Transports Maritimes and placed on their Marseilles–River Plate run. 1931: collided with the aircraft carrier HMS *Glorious* off Gibraltar. 1942: sunk during an aircraft attack at Bone. 1944: refloated and restored. 1948: refitted and given one new funnel instead of the previous two. 1951: transferred to Chargeurs Réunis. 1955: sold to the Siosa Line and renamed *Ascania*. Early employment with Siosa included trooping for the French government. 1957: refitted. In addition to running on the line's regular services to Central America and the West Indies, also made several North Atlantic voyages between 1957 and 1960. 1966: switched to full-time cruising. 1968: scrapped at La Spezia.

Aurelia

Private Italian owners sometimes spent heavily on converting mainly cargo ships into comfortable emigrant carriers. Note the forward extension of the superstructure and the double-banked lifeboats of Cogedar's *Aurelia*.   *K. & D. Lane*

10,022 gross tons, single screw, diesel-electric, 17 knots. Built, 1939, as *Huascaran* by Blohm & Voss, Hamburg for the Hamburg–America Line's passenger-cargo service to the west coast of South America. 1940: became a German Navy repair ship. 1945: handed over to the Canadian government and managed on their behalf by the Park S.S. Co. 1947: bought by Canadian Pacific Steamships and converted into the migrant-carrier and cargo ship *Beaverbrae*. 1954: bought by the Cia. Genovese di Armamento (the Cogedar Line). 1955: after being substantially rebuilt, entered her new owners' emigrant service to Australia as the *Aurelia*. Initially she ran from Italy but after 1959 the service was extended to Bremerhaven. There were also some round-the-world voyages. 1959: re-engined. 1960 onwards: made regular summer season student voyages between Europe and New York under charter. 1968: transferred to the Costa Line and used briefly for cruising. 1970: bought by the Chandris Lines who renamed her *Romanza* and employed her in cruising. 1977-8: chartered to Lloyd Brasileiro. 1991: sold to Cypriot owners and named *Romantica*.

Auriga

10,758 gross tons, twin screw, triple-expansion, 14 knots. Built, 1909, by William Denny, Dumbarton as the *Ruahine* for the New Zealand Shipping Company. After 1938 confined to cargo service, but carried passengers again during the War. 1940: briefly became a troopship but soon reverted to sailings between Britain and New Zealand.

1949: bought by the Fratelli Grimaldi who renamed her *Auriga* and refitted her. Mainly employed on the Genoa–Central America service, but also made occasional voyages on other routes, including a period of charter to Chargeurs Réunis. 1957: scrapped at Savona.

Australia

12,839 gross tons, twin screw, diesel, 18 knots. Built, 1951, by Cantieri Riuniti dell'Adriatico, Trieste for Lloyd Triestino's Australian service. 1959: refitted to increase tourist class accommodation. 1963: transferred to Italia for their service to Central and South America under the name *Donizetti*. 1977: scrapped at La Spezia.

Captain Marcos

(see *Liguria*).

Caribia

(see *Vulcania*).

Centauro

9,579 gross tons, single screw, quadruple expansion, 15 knots. Built, 1924, by Earles, Hull as the *City of Hong Kong* for the Ellerman & Bucknall Lines' service from the UK to South Africa. 1936: transferred to the Ellerman group's City Line to India. 1940: became a transport in government service. Returned to the South African service after the War. 1951: bought by Fratelli Grimaldi and re-

named *Centauro*. Used on the Central American route and for voyages elsewhere. 1955: ran aground off Bermuda. 1955: scrapped at Savona.

The *Conte Biancamano*, one of the two big liners with which Italia maintained their South American service for some years.
A. Scrimali

Conte Biancamano

23,562 gross tons, twin screw, geared turbine, 20 knots. Built, 1925, by William Beardmore, Glasgow for the Lloyd Sabaudo Line's Genoa–New York service 1932:

Grimaldi's *Centauro*, once an Ellerman liner, proved mechanically troublesome. She is here seen laid up at Genoa.
Laurence Dunn collection

Looking very stylish after her post-War refit, Italia's *Conte Grande* carried many first and cabin class passengers as well as migrants.
A. Scrimali

This vessel started life as one of the early funnel-less motor ships. Rebuilt by Cogedar as the *Flaminia* in 1954, she now had a more conventional appearance.
World Ship Society

Lloyd Sabaudo amalgamated into the Italia combine. 1932: transferred to the new line's Genoa–River Plate service. 1937: transferred to Lloyd Triestino for their Genoa–Shanghai service. 1940: while on charter to Italia, took shelter at Cristobal when Italy entered the war. 1941: seized by the Americans, becoming the US Navy transport *Hermitage*. 1947: returned by the Americans to the Italian government who allotted her to Italia. Regained her old name of *Conte Biancamano* and thoroughly refitted. 1949: resumed service, this time on Italia's South American route; also ran regularly on the New York route during the summer months between 1950 and 1960. 1960: scrapped at La Spezia.

Conte Grande

23,842 gross tons, twin screw, geared turbine, 20 knots. Built, 1928, by Stabilimento Tecnico, Trieste for the Lloyd Sabaudo. 1932: Lloyd Sabaudo amalgamated into the new Italia concern (the Italian Line). 1933: transferred to the line's service to the River Plate, although made a few further voyages to New York. 1940: laid up in Brazil on Italy's entry into the war. 1941: seized by the Brazilian government. 1942: sold to the US government, who used her as the troop transport, *Monticello*. 1947: handed over to the Italian government, who allotted her to Italia via its parent company Finmare. She re-acquired the name *Conte Grande* and was heavily refitted. 1949: re-entered the South American service. 1956: briefly took part in the New York service as a replacement for the ill-fated *Andrea Doria*. 1960: withdrawn, but made one voyage to Australia under charter to Lloyd Triestino. 1961: scrapped at La Spezia.

Flaminia

8,779 gross tons, twin screw, diesel, 14½ knots. Built, 1922, by Merchant Ship Building Corporation, Chester, Pennsylvania as *Missourian*, a diesel freighter for the American–Hawaiian Steamship Co. 1940: bought by the British government (Ministry of War Transport) and renamed *Empire Swan*. 1942: Transferred to the Belgian government-in-exile and renamed *Belgian Freighter*, later being bought by her managers, Cie. Maritime Belge (Lloyd Royal). 1946: renamed *Capitaine Potie*. 1948: bought by Cia. Genovese di Armamento (i.e. the Cogedar Line) and converted into the cargo/emigrant vessel *Genova* (7,964 gross tons) which mainly operated to South America. 1954: reconstructed as the *Flaminia* with new diesel engines and with extended and improved accommodation. Placed on the Australian service usually from Trieste. 1958: made some sailings from Bremerhaven. 1962: chartered to Zim Israel Lines for use between Marseilles and Haifa. 1963: sold to Covena. 1964: sold to Saudi Lines (M.A. Bakhashab) and renamed *King Abdelaziz*. 1965: out of action for some months following a stranding. 1970: scrapped at Kaohsiung.

Flavia

15,465 gross tons, twin screw, geared turbine, 18 knots. Built, 1947, by John Brown, Clydebank as the *Media*, a combination passenger and cargo liner for the Cunard–White Star Line's Liverpool–New York service. 1961: bought by the Cogedar Line and rebuilt as a high-class emigrant ship under the name *Flavia*. 1962: entered

The *Flavia* of the Cogedar Line had been a Cunard combination liner. The Italians gave her a streamlined profile, stabilisers and new air-conditioned accommodation.

K. & D. Lane

service. Route usually from Bremerhaven and other northern ports to Australia via the Mediterranean and Suez. 1963: diverted to a round-the-world service. Also used for cruising from Australian ports. 1969: transferred to the Costa group who employed her as a full-time cruise ship, especially on short cruises between Miami and the Bahamas. 1982: sold to the Panamanian-flag Flavia Shipping S.A. and renamed *Flavian*, later *Lavian*. Laid up in Hong Kong. 1989: destroyed by fire.

The veteran *Florentia* displays her deeply curved counter stern in this photograph taken at Malta in the early 'fifties.

World Ship Society

Florentia

7,821 gross tons, single screw, triple expansion, 13 knots. Built, 1914, by William Denny, Dumbarton as the *Burma* for the Henderson Line. 1949: bought by the Cia. de Navegación Florencia (Panamanian-flag) for use as the emigrant steamer *Florentia*. 1953: bought by Pan-Islamic Steamship Co. for their pilgrim trade from Pakistan to Jeddah. Renamed *Safina-E-Nusrat*. 1958: scrapped at Karachi.

Franca C

6,822 gross tons, single screw, diesel, 14 knots. Built, 1914, as the cargo steamer *Medina* for Mallory Line by the

The extraordinarily long-lived *Franca C* has been often rebuilt and has had several careers. Here we see her as a typical 1950s emigrant carrier operated by the Costa Line.   *A. Duncan*

Newport News Shipbuilding & Dry Dock Co. 1928: transferred to the Clyde–Mallory Line within the Agwilines group. 1949: sold to the Cia. Naviera San Miguel and converted into a passenger steamer, *Roma*. 1950: chartered to the International Catholic Travel Committee and used for Holy Year voyages between America and Europe. Placed in the Australian emigrant trade but mechanical problems caused her withdrawal. 1951: bought by the Costa Line, re-engined with diesels and renamed *Franca C*. 1959: extensively refitted and thereafter mainly used as a cruise ship. 1970: again re-engined. 1977: sold to Operation Mobilisation, converted into a missionary ship and renamed *Doulos*, flying the Maltese flag.

Francesco Morosini

8,678 gross tons, single screw, diesel, 14½ knots. Built, 1948, by Cantieri Riuniti, Monfalcone for Società Italiana di Armamento "Sidarma" and employed on the South American emigrant run. 1955: became a purely cargo vessel. 1975: sold to Arnis Bulkcarriers Co. Ltd. (Cyprus-registered) and renamed *Arnis*. 1978: broken up at Shanghai.

Galileo Galilei

27,888 gross tons, twin screw, geared turbines, 24 knots. Built, 1963, by Cantieri Riuniti dell' Adriatico, Monfalcone for Lloyd Triestino's Australian service. 1977: conversion began for cruising. 1979: transferred to Italia Crociere Internazionale, an unsuccessful cruising venture set up by the Italian government. 1980: laid up. 1981: chartered to Chandris for cruising. Laid up at the end of the season. Remained idle with her sister *Guglielmo Marconi* while the Italian government negotiated with various shipowners, including Costa and Chandris. 1983: the *Galileo*, as she now became known, was bought by Chandris for $4.3 million and further rebuilt for cruising. 1984: commenced cruising from various American ports. 1989: $35 million refit for the inauguration of the new Chandris Celebrity Cruises operation in 1990. Renamed *Meridian*.

Genova
(see *Flaminia*).

Gerusalemme

8,052 gross tons, twin screw, geared turbine, 13½ knots. Built, 1920, by Cantieri San Rocco, San Rocco as *Cracovia* for Lloyd Triestino. 1934: renamed *Gerusalemme*. 1940: laid up at Maputo. 1943: seized by the British and used as a hospital ship. 1946: returned to the Italians. 1947: briefly ran to South America for Italia. 1948: resumed Lloyd Triestino's service to East and South Africa. 1952: scrapped at Savona.

Giovanna C

6,475 gross tons, twin screw, triple expansion, 12 knots. Built, 1919, by Ansana Shipbuilding, Tsurumi. In-

Showing off the shapely lines of her hull, typical of the big Italian liners of the 1960s, the *Galileo Galilei* carried her predominantly tourist class passengers to Australia in some luxury.
A. Scrimali

The *Irpinia* of the Siosa Line in Southampton Water. In much-modified form she went on to become a popular cruise ship.
Laurence Dunn collection

itially was the *Eastern Trader* of the US Shipping Board. 1923: became the *Horace Luckenbach* of the Luckenbach Steamship Co. 1946: bought by Giacomo Costa fu Andrea and renamed *Giovanna C.* She continued as a cargo vessel for her new owners for a few months, but was then converted into a temporary emigrant-carrier. 1953: scrapped.

Guglielmo Marconi

27,905 gross tons, twin screw, geared turbine, 24 knots. Built, 1963, by Cantieri Riuniti dell' Adriatico, Monfalcone for Lloyd Triestino's Australian service. 1976:

Lloyd Triestino's spectacular and speedy 27,000-ton *Guglielmo Marconi*. In this photograph her telescopic funnel cowl is fully extended. *Steffen Weirauch collection*

transferred to Italia's South American route for the final months of that historic service. 1977: laid up. 1978: transferred to Italia Crociere Internazionale for American cruises. 1980: laid up. 1983: sold to the Costa group, renamed *Costa Riviera* and greatly rebuilt at a cost of c.$37million. 1985: entered service in the American cruise market.

Irpinia

12,279 gross tons, twin screw, geared turbines, 17 knots. Built, 1929, by Swan, Hunter & Wigham Richardson, Newcastle upon Tyne for the Société Générale de Transports Maritimes who employed her in their service between Genoa and Marseilles and the River Plate as the *Campana.* 1940: laid up at Buenos Aires. 1943: seized by the Argentinian government and named *Rio Jachal.* 1946: returned to her owners and again placed on their South American service. 1951: with the advent of new tonnage she was transferred to the associated Chargeurs Réunis company. 1955: sold to Sicula Oceanica (the Siosa Line) and considerably modified. Operated in the Grimaldi-Siosa service between Italy and Central America. Also used in the Southampton–Central America and West Indies service; and made a number of North Atlantic voyages between 1956 and 1961. 1962: given a major refit together with the installation of new diesel engines. Her previous two funnels were replaced by one of more modern design. 1970: became a full-time cruise ship. 1975: took part in the British film 'Voyage of the Damned' for which she was

given two funnels in order to resemble the pre-War Hamburg–America liner *St Louis.* 1980: laid up. 1983: scrapped at La Spezia.

Leme

8,059 gross tons, twin screw, diesel, 14 knots. Built, 1925, by Stabilimento Tecnico, Trieste for Navigazione Libera Triestina as a cargo vessel with limited passenger accommodation. 1932: placed on the company's round-Africa route. 1937: the Libera Triestina company was taken over by Lloyd Triestino. 1938: re-engined. 1941: having fallen into American hands, she was renamed *Lowlander* and managed for the British Ministry of War Transport by the Port Line. 1947: returned to the Americans (U.S. Maritime Commission). 1948: handed back to the Italian government who allocated her to Italia. Passenger accommodation increased. circa 1961: scrapped.

The *Leme*, a former cargo vessel, was one of the stop-gaps used by Italia on their passenger services after the War. It is thought that in this view, taken about 1960, she is awaiting scrapping. *A. Scrimali*

Liguria

7,474 gross tons, twin screw, quadruple expansion, 14 knots. Launched, 1914, by Reiherstieg, Hamburg as the *Hilda Woermann* for the Woermann Line but not completed until 1917 when she was called *Wahehe.* 1918: seized by the British government and used for repatriating Australian

The *Liguria*, photographed at Dublin in 1950, gives ample evidence that she was then one of the few coal-burning passenger steamers still in service. *Walter Kennedy*

troops under Shaw, Savill & Albion management. 1920: bought by Burns Philp who renamed her *Marella* and placed her on their service between Australia and Singapore. 1941: taken up for trooping. 1946: handed back to Burns Philp who returned her temporarily to her old trade. 1948: sold to Cia. Navicra Baru of Panama who renamed her *Captain Marcos* and had her refitted as an emigrant steamer. 1950: renamed *Liguria* and chartered for voyages from New York to Europe for Holy Year. 1951: had a serious breakdown while on an emigrant voyage to Australia and had to be towed into Fremantle where repairs and debts detained her for eight months. 1951: renamed *Corsica*. 1952: laid up. 1954: scrapped at Ghent.

Lucania

6,723 gross tons, twin screw, geared turbines, 20 knots. Built, 1931, by Cammell Laird, Birkenhead as *Prince Robert* for Canadian National Steamships' West Coast services. 1931 onwards: periods of lay up and of cruising. 1939: bought by the Royal Canadian Navy and converted into an Armed Merchant Cruiser. 1943: converted into an anti-aircraft cruiser. 1945: repatriated prisoners-of-war from Hong Kong. 1945: laid up and offered for sale. 1946: bought by the Charlton Steam Shipping Co. (Chandris). 1947: converted into the emigrant-carrier *Charlton Sovereign*. 1949: laid up. 1950: chartered to Continental Shipping Co. of Bremen but apparently not used. 1951: transferred to Cia. Panameña Europea Navegación Ltda. and used for one pilgrim voyage. 1951: sold to Fratelli Grimaldi and rebuilt as the *Lucania*. Placed on their service to Central America. 1962: scrapped at Livorno.

A wide-angle photograph, perhaps intended for publicity purposes, makes the *Lucania* look much longer than she really was. *Laurence Dunn collection*

Luciano Manara

8,333 gross tons, single screw, diesel. Built, 1941, by Ansaldo, Genoa as a freighter. Post-war owners: Società Anonima Cooperativa di Navigazione Garibaldi who after 1948 used her as a migrant ship. 1953: rebuilt as a cargo vessel, the *Giuseppe Canera*. 1955: sold to the Polish government and renamed *Malcorzata Fornalska*. Later: sold to China. Said to have been named *Chung Ming* and later *Hong Qi*.

Lugano

6,942 gross tons, single screw, triple expansion. Built, 1898, by R. & W. Hawthorn Leslie, Newcastle upon Tyne as the cargo ship *Morayshire* for Elderslie Steamship Co. (Turnbull Martin, managers). 1910: transferred to the Scottish Shire Line (Turnbull Martin). 1916: bought by Brodlife Steamship Co. (Blue Star Line) and renamed *Brodlife*. 1920: transferred within the Vestey group to the Union Cold Storage Co. and renamed *Tuscanstar*. 1929: bought by Fratelli Rizzuto and renamed *Fortunstar*. 1936: bought by Ignazio Messina and renamed *Semien*. 1942: sold to Nautilus S.A. (Swiss Shipping Co.) and renamed *Lugano*. 1948: reverted to Ignazio Messina without change of name. Used on the South American run as an emigrant-carrier. 1952: scrapped at Savona.

Marco Polo

8,949 gross tons, single screw, diesel, 15½ knots. Launched, 1942, as the *Nicolo Giani* by Ansaldo, Genoa. 1948: completed as the *Marco Polo* for Italia's service to the west coast of South America. 1963: transferred to Lloyd Triestino and converted into a cargo vessel. 1978: scrapped at La Spezia.

Marengo

(see *Urania II*).

Lauro's *Napoli* had been a British cargo liner which became a war casualty. She was salvaged and Lauro had her converted into a serviceable emigrant ship. *A. Scrimali*

Napoli

8,082 gross tons, single screw, diesel, 14 knots. Built, 1940, by Harland & Wolff, Belfast as the Bank Line cargo vessel *Araybank*. 1941: bombed while in Cretan waters and abandoned. 1947: salvaged. Purchased by Achille Lauro and rebuilt as the emigrant-carrier *Napoli*. 1948: started operating between the Mediterranean and Australia. 1951 onwards: on the Central American route. 1960: converted into a freighter. 1971: scrapped at La Spezia.

Neptunia

12,838 gross tons, twin screw, diesel, 18 knots. Built, 1951, by Cantieri Riuniti dell'Adriatico, Trieste for Lloyd Triestino's Australian service. 1963: with the advent of new tonnage was transferred to Italia for their service to Central America and Valparaiso. Renamed *Rossini*. 1977: scrapped at La Spezia.

Oceania

12,839 gross tons, twin screw, diesel, 18 knots. Built, 1951, by Cantieri Riuniti dell'Adriatico, Trieste for the Australian route of Lloyd Triestino. 1963: transferred to Italia, renamed *Verdi* and placed in their service to Central America and the west coast of South America. 1977: scrapped at La Spezia.

Olimpia

7,716 gross tons, single screw, triple expansion. Built, 1943, by St. Johns River Shipbuilding, Jacksonville as the cargo ship *Shaula* for the US Maritime Commission, later renamed *James Screven*. 1947: purchased by Achille Lauro and renamed *Olimpia*. Temporarily used as an emigrant-carrier but reverted to cargo-only role in 1951. 1968: scrapped at La Spezia.

Olimpia was a Liberty ship in which Lauro installed very temporary passenger accommodation in about 1947. In 1951 she reverted to her former cargo-carrying role.

A. Scrimali collection

Pace

4,013 gross tons, twin screw, triple expansion, 17 knots. Built, 1921, by William Cramp, Philadelphia as *Cuba* for the Peninsular & Occidental Steamship Co. for their services from Tampa to Key West and Havana. 1942: taken up by the American government as a troop transport.

Ignazio Messina's *Pace* was a small, former American East Coast liner, very typical of her type.   *A. Scrimali*

1947: having been returned to Peninsular & Occidental, she was sold to Ignazio Messina and renamed *Pace*. 1948 onwards: carried emigrants to Central and South America but mainly operated on the Genoa–Marseilles–Haifa route with some voyages to East African ports. 1960: renamed *Sassari*. 1962: scrapped at La Spezia.

Paolo Toscanelli

9,004 gross tons, single screw, diesel, 15½ knots. Built, 1949, by Ansaldo, Genoa for Italia's west coast of South America service. 1963: transferred to Lloyd Triestino and converted into a cargo vessel. 1973: scrapped at La Spezia.

Soon after the War Italia restarted their service to the West coast of South America with six modestly-sized new motor ships which had originally been designed as cargo vessels. This is the *Paolo Toscanelli*.   *A. Duncan*

Ravello

8,806 gross tons, single screw, diesel, 16 knots. Built, 1941, by Cantiere Navale Riuniti, Genoa as a cargo ship for Achille Lauro. 1947: converted to emigrant-carrier, initially to South America and, from 1952, to Central America. 1960: reverted to a cargo carrier. 1971: scrapped at La Spezia.

(i) Roma

(see *Franca C*).

(ii) Roma

14,687 gross tons, geared turbine, single screw, 17 knots. Laid down as a C3 cargo vessel, 1942, by Seattle–Tacoma Shipbuilding Corporation, Tacoma. Launched as USS *Glacier*, an auxiliary aircraft-carrier. 1943: completed as HMS *Atheling* for the Royal Navy. 1946: returned to the US Navy. 1950: bought by Achille Lauro and rebuilt as the passenger vessel *Roma* for his Australian service. 1953-1956: made some summer sailings from Naples and Genoa to New York. 1966: displaced from the Australian service by the advent of the *Achille Lauro* and the *Angelina Lauro*. 1967: after a brief spell on the Central American route, scrapped at Savona.

San Giorgio

8,959 gross tons, twin screw, geared turbine, 13 knots. Built, 1923, by Cantiere Navale Franco Tosi, Taranto as the *Principessa Giovanna* for Lloyd Sabaudo and placed on the Australian route. 1932: Lloyd Sabaudo was taken over by Italia. 1944: taken by the British government as a hospital ship (managed by British India). 1946: returned to the Italians and allotted to Italia. Renamed *San Giorgio*. 1947: after a refit which included conversion to a two funnel configuration rather than one, was placed on the South American route, marking the Italia company's re-entry into the River Plate trade. 1952: transferred to Lloyd Triestino and briefly employed on the Australian run. 1953: scrapped at Savona.

Santa Cruz

15,511 gross tons, quadruple expansion, 16 knots. Built, 1903, by the New York Shipbuilding Corporation, Camden, New Jersey. Originally intended as the Atlantic Transport Line's *Minnekahda* but transferred to the Pacific Mail Line as their *Manchuria* and placed in the San Francisco–Hong Kong service. 1915: transferred to the Atlantic Transport Line for the New York–London run. 1918: taken up as an armed transport by the US Navy. 1919: returned to the International Mercantile Marine group and allocated to the American Line who used her in their service from New York to Hamburg. 1923: transferred to the New York–San Francisco service of the Panama Pacific Line. 1928: bought by the Dollar Line for their round-the-world route as the *President Johnson*. 1932: laid up. 1933: returned to service. 1936: laid up again. 1938: on the collapse of the Dollar Line, the US government was instrumental in the formation of the American President Lines which took over the Dollar ships and services. *President Johnson* remained in lay-up. 1941: re-activated as a US government transport. 1946: laid up. 1947: bought by Tagus Navigation Co. (F. Costa and A. Ribeiro) and renamed *Santa Cruz*. 1947: transferred from the Portuguese flag to the Panamanian and chartered to the Italia company for their South American service. 1952: scrapped at Savona.

Saturnia

24,470 gross tons, twin screw, diesel, 21 knots. Built, 1927, by Cantiere Navale Triestino, Monfalcone for the Cosulich Line's Trieste–New York service. 1932: the Cosulich Line became part of the Italia combine but retained a separate identity. 1935: fitted with new and more powerful engines. 1937: full merger consummated. 1940: laid up. 1943: seized by the American government for use as a transport. 1945: converted into the US hospital ship *Frances Y Slanger*. 1946: handed back to the Italian government by the Americans and returned to Italia, reassuming her old name, *Saturnia*. 1947: undertook the first post-War Italia sailing on the North Atlantic, re-establishing the Genoa–New York service. 1955: with her sister, *Vulcania*, was transferred to her original Trieste–New York route. 1965: withdrawn. 1966: scrapped at La Spezia.

Sebastiano Caboto

8,967 gross tons, single screw, diesel, 15½ knots. Built, 1947, by Ansaldo, Genoa for the west coast of South America service of Italia. 1963: transferred to Lloyd Triestino and converted into a cargo vessel. 1979: scrapped at Kaohsiung.

Sestriere

8,652 gross tons, single screw, diesel, 14 knots. Built, 1943, by Cantiere Navale Franco Tosi, Taranto. Post-War owners: "Italnavi" Soc. di Navigazione (managed in latter years by Carlo Cameli). 1948-1955: in emigrant service to South America. 1955: converted into a cargo ship. 1968: sold to Costa without change of name. 1970: scrapped at Vado.

Sises

9,177 gross tons, single screw, diesel, 17½ knots. Built, 1948, by Cantiere Navale di Taranto, Taranto for "Italnavi" Società di Navigazione (managed in latter years by Carlo Cameli). 1949: placed on the South American route. 1956: converted to a purely cargo ship. 1969: sold to Costa. 1978: scrapped at La Spezia.

Surriento

10,699 gross tons, twin screw, diesel, 17 knots. Built, 1928, by Furness Shipbuilding, Haverton Hill as the *Santa Maria* for the Grace Line. 1940: purchased by the US

Lauro's *Surriento* had been a well-known American liner. She is seen here at Genoa in May, 1960 in her final form, with one streamlined funnel. *A. Scrimali*

The big pre-War motor liners *Saturnia* (seen here) and *Vulcania* re-established Italia on the North Atlantic in the late 1940s. They were popular and long-lived ships. *A. Scrimali*

After her sale by Lauro, the *Sydney* became the notorious cruise ship *Galaxy Queen*. She is here seen at Malta in 1971.

Mark Banavage

government and renamed *Barnett*. 1946: laid up. 1948: bought by Achille Lauro and converted into the *Surriento* for his Australian service. 1951: switched to the Central American route but transferred back in 1953. 1957: finally returned to the Central American route. 1959: refitted. One funnel instead of two. 1965: chartered to Zim Israel Lines. 1966: scrapped at La Spezia.

Sydney

14,708 gross tons, single screw, geared turbine, 17 knots. Originally intended to be a C3-type cargo liner but actually laid down by Western Pipe & Steel Co., San Francisco as USS *Croatan*, an auxiliary aircraft-carrier for the US Navy; and completed, 1943, as HMS *Fencer* for the Royal Navy. 1946: handed back to the US Navy. 1950: bought by Achille Lauro and rebuilt as the passenger steamer *Sydney*. 1951: entered the Australian service. 1953: four voyages between Canada and Liverpool to catch the traffic generated by the Coronation of HM Queen Elizabeth II; then reverted to the Australian route. 1966: switched to the Central American route. 1967: devoted to cruising. Renamed *Roma* after her sister of that name was scrapped. 1969: sold to Aretusa SpA di Navigazione. 1970: bought by Sovereign Cruise Ships (Cyprus) Ltd. in conjunction with Cosmos Tours. Refitted and renamed *Galaxy Queen*. 1971: laid up after several months of troublesome service; sold to George Kotzovilis who renamed her *Lady Dina*. Arrested at Genoa. 1973: sold by the Italian authorities to Marimina Shipping Co. and renamed *Caribia 2* for a charter to the Siosa Line. The charter was terminated and she lay idle until being scrapped at La Spezia in 1975.

Toscana

9,442 gross tons, twin screw, triple expansion, 12 knots. Built, 1923, by A.G. Weser, Bremen as the *Saarbrücken* for Norddeutscher Lloyd. 1935: purchased by the Italian government and handed over to Italia who renamed her *Toscana*, subsequently being transferred to Lloyd Triestino. Served as a hospital ship during the War. 1948: reopened the line's Australian service, sailing from Trieste. 1962: scrapped at Genoa.

Although somewhat slow, Lloyd Triestino's *Toscana* plied between the Adriatic ports and Australia for 14 years.

A. Duncan

Ugolino Vivaldi

8,914 gross tons, single screw, diesel, 15½ knots. Launched in 1945 as the *Feruccio Buonapace* but completed, 1947, as the *Ugolino Vivaldi* by Ansaldo, Genoa for

Italia's service to Valparaiso. 1952: transferred to Lloyd Triestino and converted into a cargo vessel. 1978: scrapped at La Spezia.

Urania II

6,715 gross tons, single screw, triple expansion, 12½ knots. Built, 1906, as *Castalia* for the Anchor Line's Indian service by Barclay Curle, Glasgow. 1914: a brief period of trooping. 1916: survived a gunfire attack by a submarine. 1948: sprang a leak during her final Anchor Line voyage. 1949: bought by the Soc. Cooperativa di Navigazione Garibaldi and renamed *Marengo*. Fitted out as an emigrant ship. 1949: suffered a serious breakdown. Laid up. 1950: bought by Fratelli Grimaldi and renamed *Urania II*. 1954: scrapped at La Spezia.

Venezuela

18,567 gross tons, twin screw, geared turbine, 16 knots. Laid down for the French Line, 1920, by Cammell Laird, Birkenhead but not completed until 1924. Placed in the company's New York service as the cabin class liner *De Grasse*. 1940: laid up. Used by the Germans as an accommodation ship. 1944: sunk by the retreating German forces. 1945: raised and sent for refit. 1947: returned to service with one funnel instead of the previous two. 1952: transferred to the French Line's West Indian route. 1953: sold to Canadian Pacific to replace the fire-gutted *Empress of Canada* during Coronation Year. Renamed *Empress of Australia*. 1956: bought by Sicula Oceanica, the Siosa Line, and renamed *Venezuela* for their Central American service. 1960: refitted and given a new bow section. 1962: grounded near Cannes. Scrapped at La Spezia.

Vulcania

24,496 gross tons, twin screw, diesel, 19 knots. Built, 1928, by Cantiere Navale Triestino, Monfalcone for the Cosulich Line's Trieste–New York service. 1932: Cosulich became part of the Italia combine but did not lose its name. 1935: fitted with new engines. 1937: Cosulich finally lost its separate identity. 1941: laid up. 1943: became a US Army transport. 1946: was handed over to the Italian government who returned her to Italia. 1947: re-entered service, at first on the South American route, then in the Genoa–New York service. 1955: Trieste became her Italian terminus. 1965: sold to Sicula Oceanica and renamed *Caribia*. Used for the Southampton–West Indies service and for cruising. 1972: hit rocks near Cannes. Laid up. 1973: sold for scrapping at Barcelona, but re-sold to Taiwanese breakers. 1974: sank at Kaohsiung while awaiting demolition.

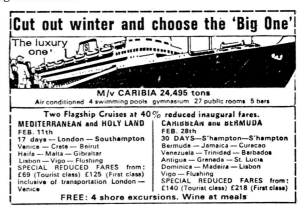

Siosa's *Venezuela* awaits her fate after being badly damaged when she ran aground in 1962. Just two years earlier she had been extensively rebuilt, acquiring a sharply raked new bow in the process.   *A. Scrimali*

Chapter Five

The Cosmopolitans

Forty years ago the Home Lines and Sitmar would both have been included in the previous chapter on Italian companies. Although their background was distinctly cosmopolitan, they were managed from Italy, their vessels sailed from Genoa and they were crewed by Italians. Many years later – when they had long since left behind their origins in the emigrant trades and had become very successful cruise lines based elsewhere – many of their customers must still have regarded them as Italian. The officers and stewards with whom passengers came into contact were still of that nationality and the Italian flair for catering was one of the attractions of their vessels.

There is a remarkable similarity in the histories of these two companies. Both were the creation of individuals who had interests in the freight trades but who saw an opportunity in the emigrant boom of the 'forties. Both went on to become respected liner companies and later switched decisively into the cruise market. After forty-odd years they were sold to larger companies at almost the same time. Presumably the charitable and family trusts which by now owned them felt unable to finance the scale of investment necessary if they were to hold their own against the massive, high-spending combines emerging from the 'big bang' which has re-shaped the cruise industry in the late 'eighties.

Home Lines

Study of Lloyd's Registers and other sources indicates that the accepted account of the formative years of the Home Lines is not entirely accurate. Home Lines was the trade name of two related concerns which came into being in 1946. On the one hand there was the Panamanian Navigation Company, registered in Panama but managed by Fratelli Cosulich of Trieste. This company purchased a Norwegian liner which it renamed *Argentina* and with which it entered the Genoa–River Plate trade early in 1947. Within about a year, this vessel had been transferred to Panamanian Lines Inc. and it may have been at this point that the Cosulich connection ceased. Panamanian Lines Inc. also owned the steamer *Protea* which was chartered out to the I.R.O., carrying displaced persons to Australia and elsewhere. The *Protea* has not usually been considered to have been connected with Home Lines and probably she did not trade under their name, but the evidence of common ownership is there.

Long before she joined the Home Lines fleet, the *Homeland* had been one of the pioneer turbine liners. Her career spanned nearly half a century.

Steffen Weirauch collection

Late in 1948 a third vessel, the *Atlantic* – a former American liner – was added to the Panamanian Lines fleet. Not long afterwards the three ships were transferred to Mediterranean Lines Inc., a Panamanian company with offices also in Genoa. In October, 1949 the *Protea* was sold for about $1 million. The buyers were described as Italian and the deal included the remainder of the vessel's charter to the I.R.O. until August, 1950.

Running in tandem with the Panamanian Navigation Co. and its successors was a concern called South Atlantic Lines Inc., also of Panama and Genoa. It was part-owned by the Swedish American Line which made something of a habit of spawning new shipping companies. (It later held a half-share in the Bremen–Atlantic Line with which the Norddeutscher Lloyd re-entered the North Atlantic passenger business in the 'fifties; and about the same time it was involved in the attempt to set up a Danish America Line.) South Atlantic Lines took over from the Swedes two of their pre-War vessels which they no longer required. They were renamed *Brasil* and *Italia*.

In 1951-2 the two South Atlantic Lines vessels were transferred to join their fleet mates in the ownership of Mediterranean Lines. It was probably at this time that Swedish American withdrew, leaving Mr. Eugen Eugenides in control of the combined group. A Greek, he had been the driving force behind Panamanian Lines Inc. Finally, in 1952-3 Mediterranean Lines officially became Home Lines Inc. It remains to be said that all the group's vessels flew the Panamanian flag.

The group had not remained long on the South American route. A decline in emigration to that continent – and probably the likelihood of stronger competition from Italia – had caused it to place the newly purchased *Atlantic* in the Genoa–New York trade in 1949. In that year, too, the *Italia* was transferred to the New York service and the *Argentina* was placed in the Central American trade where she remained until 1952. That left only the *Brasil* running to the River Plate and in 1950 she also was switched to the North Atlantic. At first she joined the other two on the Genoa–New York route and then, under the name *Homeland*, she initiated a new service from Hamburg to Halifax and New York via Southampton and Cherbourg. In the early 'fifties there was a considerable emigrant trade between the German ports and North America. Home Lines was one of a number of concerns which moved in to satisfy the demand in the absence of the traditional German lines which were still suffering the effects of their country's defeat.

Although the early Home Lines ships were secondhand and in two cases quite elderly, they were generally said to be a cut above most such vessels flying flags of convenience. In particular, after refits in 1950-51 the *Atlantic* and the *Italia*, now air-conditioned, were liners of some quality. When, in 1952, they were switched from the Mediterranean route to services from Southampton and Hamburg respectively, they competed effectively with the established Atlantic lines. The Hamburg America Line acted as the company's agents in West Germany and they would hardly have chosen to associate themselves with a cheap concern.

The *Argentina* (1913/11,015 gross tons) had been the *Bergensfjord*, one of a pair of liners with which the Norwegian America Line had commenced business shortly before the First World War. In the second conflict she served as a British trooper. In appearance she was very typical of her era with her tall masts, two pipe-stem funnels and deeply curved counter-stern. Carrying 969 tourist passengers and just 32 first class, she was emphatically an emigrant ship. By 1953, Home Lines had rather outgrown her. Although she was now forty years old she found a buyer, Zim Israel Lines, who used her to establish their new transatlantic service.

The first of the two ex-Swedish American vessels to enter Home Lines' service was the *Brasil* (1905/11,055 gross tons), a veteran of some historical note. She had been built as the Allan Line's *Virginian*, one of two sister ships which were the first turbine vessels on the Atlantic. She had passed to the Swedes in 1920, becoming their *Drottningholm* and making many voyages in the Second World War for the International Red Cross, carrying prisoners of war who were being exchanged between the two sides. As the *Homeland* she remained in Home Lines' service until 1954, by which time she was nearly fifty years old. The second ex-Swede, formerly the *Kungsholm* and now the *Italia* (1928/21,554 gross tons), was a notable motor liner – despite having two tall steamship-type funnels. Swedish American sold her to the American government during the war, in which she served as a troopship. The Americans sold her back in a fire-damaged condition in 1947, whereupon the Swedes passed her on to South Atlantic Lines (i.e. Home Lines) who took her to Genoa for repairs and refitting. She is said to have been very successful throughout her Home Lines career which culminated in her inaugurating in 1961 the cruising service between New York and the Bahamas which was to become one of the mainstays of the company's operations in later years. By then she had been so far refitted as to be suitably luxurious for her new trade.

Although originally intended to join her fleet mates on the South American run, the *Atlantic* (1927/15,602 gross tons) was, as we have already noted, used to initiate a new Genoa–New York service. She was the former *Malolo* (later *Matsonia*) – the first, and smallest, of a fine quartet of liners with which the Matson Line and its Oceanic Steam Ship subsidiary secured their position on the routes from San Francisco to Hawaii and to Australia between the wars. She had been a notably roomy ship so that when she was acquired by Home Lines it proved possible to increase her capacity from 693 first class passengers to a total of 1,242 (predominantly tourist class) without it being necessary to extend her superstructure.

At the end of 1954 Home Lines withdrew from the Mediterranean – nominally, at any rate. In fact, the *Atlantic* had been transferred to a new Greek-flag subsidiary, the National Hellenic American Line, and placed in a service from Piraeus to New York via southern Italian ports and Halifax. She was renamed *Vasilissa Freideriki* (or, more familiarly, *Queen Frederica*) and, with tourist class now accounting for 1,050 of her 1,240 passenger berths, she carried many migrants. A good proportion of these were bound for Canada and disembarked at Halifax. Home Lines had formed their new off-shoot with the encouragement of the Greek government. It was presumably not coincidental that just over a year previously there had been a squabble between the government and the Greek Line which resulted in that company's new flagship, the *Olympia*, sailing under the Liberian flag.

In 1958 Home Lines were also partly responsible for the formation of another new passenger shipping company, the Hamburg Atlantik Line which took over their Hamburg–New York route. Henceforth Home Lines concentrated on the routes to Canada. Then, in 1963, they quit the transatlantic trades altogether. The final severing of their links with the traditional liner trades came in 1965 when the National Hellenic American Line and its *Queen Frederica* were sold to Chandris. Age is no bar to activity in the Chandris fleet and she remained in service until 1973, by which time she was forty six years old.

Details of the career of the Panamanian Lines *Protea* will be found later in this chapter when we deal with her subsequent owners, the Arosa Line, for whom she sailed as the *Arosa Kulm*. Finally, mention should be made of the *Homeric* which had been another of the famous Matson quartet. She took over Home Lines' Southampton–Quebec run; but she was a genuine express liner and, although her accommodation was mainly tourist class, she can hardly be regarded as an emigrant ship.

Sitmar

What became known as the Sitmar Line sprang from the various shipping ventures of Alexandre Vlasov. A Russian émigré, he had before and during the War accumulated fleets of cargo vessels which he registered in Italy, Britain, Rumania, Greece, Panama and the Argentine. His Italian company was called Società Italiana Trasporti Marittimi – hence the acronymic name Sitmar which was used for his passenger operations. Until shortly before the line was sold to P&O in 1988, all Sitmar passenger ships carried a large blue letter V on their yellow funnels. Two of his early operating companies, Alva Steamship Co. of London and Alvion Steamship Corporation of Panama, presumably derived the first three letters of their titles from their owner's name.

Like many another shipowner, Vlasov restored his depleted fleet in the mid 'forties by buying some of the war-built standard cargo ships which the American authorities were making available. Among his purchases were two 'Victory' ships, *Wooster Victory* and *Vassar Victory*. It appears that, having been used as troopships, they already had the basis of some passenger accommodation. Accordingly, Vlasov chartered them to the I.R.O. and after brief refits they entered I.R.O. service carrying displaced persons to Australia and elsewhere. The *Vassar Victory*, having been allotted to the group's Italian company, was given the name *Castelbianco* (1945/7,604 gross tons). The *Wooster Victory* (1945/7,607 gross tons), on the other hand, retained her original name for a further three years until, shortly before being transferred to the Italian company, she became the *Castelverde*. By 1952 the I.R.O.'s Mass Resettlement Scheme was nearing completion and Vlasov began employing the pair mainly in a regular emigrant service from Genoa to Central America. Before embarking on this venture both ships were substantially re-built. They became quite unrecognisable as their former, very utilitarian selves. The *Castel Bianco*[1] (now 10,139 gross tons) now accommodated 1,200 passengers, rather more than the *Castel Verde* (now 9,008 gross tons) whose reconstructed superstructure was given one deck fewer than that of her sister. Sitmar withdrew from the Central American service in 1957. The *Castel Bianco* and *Castel Verde* were then sold to the Spanish Line, together fetching the very good price of $9½ million (£3,390,000).

Vlasov was a buyer not only of 'Victory' ships, but also of former C3 escort carriers (see the previous chapter). He seems to have been in the occasional habit of buying vessels and then leaving them fallow for long periods before deciding on their employment – an expensive form of investment, one would have thought. Having bought two ex-C3 carriers, he left one unreconstructed and idle for nine years. However, the other was soon rebuilt to carry 1,800 emigrants, mainly in dormitories, and pressed into service under charter to the I.R.O. She had been allocated to Alvion Steamship and was Panamanian-registered. She was called *Fairsea* (1942/11,678 gross tons) setting the future pattern for the naming of Vlasov group passenger ships. After her I.R.O. charter expired, the *Fairsea* was devoted mainly to the Australian run on which the group now began to operate a regular commercial service. She was, though, one of several Sitmar ships which made a few summertime crossings of the North Atlantic between 1953 and 1957; but the group was much less active in this trade than some of its contemporaries. In 1955 the *Fairsea*, by now a fully air-conditioned one-class liner, was given a long-term contract by the Australian government to carry migrants from Southampton. She was the first foreign-flag vessel to be employed in this way and the contract caused considerable anguish in the British shipping industry. After 1957 Sitmar concentrated almost entirely on the Australian run with its ships now sailing either from Bremerhaven or Southampton and sometime returning via the Panama Canal.

It was not until 1957 that a role was found for the other former escort carrier. She was rebuilt as a modern-looking liner with air-conditioned accommodation for 1,461 passengers and called the *Fairsky* (1942/12,464 gross tons)[2]. According to Laurence Dunn her medical facilities were particularly fine. Flying the Liberian flag, she entered the Australian service, also with a contract to carry migrants on her outward voyages from Southampton. Sitmar retained these contracts until the end of 1969, eventually employing four ships in this way. The loss of the migrant contracts to Chandris from 1970 onwards precipitated a sharp change of direction for Sitmar, with the Australian liner service being rapidly run down and the group seeking to establish itself as a major cruise company – successfully in the end. In the meantime *Fairsky* endured many months of lay-up. There was a plan to convert her into a passenger

---

1 From this time both vessels' names became two separate words.
2 Although the *Fairsea* and *Fairsky* were laid down as members of the same class, the former was a motor ship and the latter a steamer.

and car ferry for a service between Singapore and Fremantle but it came to nothing. In the end, she became a successful cruise ship based in Australia. This new career was cut short when in 1977 she struck a submerged wreck off Djakarta. Although sold for scrap, she was reprieved to serve as a floating hotel and casino at Manila. This twilight existence was brief – ended by a fire.

The other ships used by Sitmar on the Australian run were both of British origin. The *Castel Felice* (1930/12,150 gross tons) started life as the *Kenya*, a smart-looking British India liner built for the route between Bombay and the ports of East and South Africa. After War service, she was bought by the Ministry of Transport. In 1949 they sold her to Vlasov who registered her in the name of his Alva company in London. There followed a complicated series of name changes and two changes of flag before, as Sitmar's Italian-registered *Castel Felice*, she entered the Genoa–Australia service in 1952, having been refitted to carry no less than 1,540 passengers, many in dormitories. (Later her accommodation was improved.) She also made some North Atlantic voyages and some to South America in her early days with the company. She seems to have been a well-liked ship, despite being said to have a permanent list. Loss of its Australian migrant contracts caused Sitmar to sell her for scrap but it is probable that she would not have remained in service much longer in any case. She was a very hard-working ship, having made no fewer than 106 voyages to Australia in 19 years.

Sitmar's last emigrant ship – and the second of the two ex-Britons – was the large *Fairstar* (1957/21,619 gross tons). She had been constructed with the financial assistance of the British government as the Bibby Line's *Oxfordshire*, the last of the specially-built troopships. After six years the trooping contract was terminated following a decision that aircraft would be used for the purpose in future. Initially Sitmar merely chartered her from Bibby but they bought her outright before conversion was completed. The terms of the charter would have presented difficulties, particularly over the employment of a mixed crew of British, Italian and Indian personnel. When she entered the Australian service in 1964 she had been refitted to carry 1,870 single class passengers in some comfort. In 1973 she made Sitmar's last line voyage to Australia and since then she has been entirely engaged in cruising from that country. In this she has been enormously successful, outlasting most of her competitors from P&O and the Russian lines, and at the time of writing (1991) she continues in service despite some recent mechanical problems.

Arosa Line

One more emigrant line might be classed as cosmopolitan. For a concern which was active for a mere seven years, the Arosa Line has attracted a great deal of attention from shipping writers. Like Home Lines, Sitmar and also the Greek Line, it was very much the creation of one man – in this case, Nicolo Rizzi, who was Swiss-domiciled but is said to have been a Yugoslav national (although his name sounds very Italian). The title Arosa was derived from the

The *Fairstar* at 101 Berth, Southampton. A 21,000 ton ex-Bibby Line trooper, she sailed for a while in Sitmar's service to Australia and has since had enormous success as a cruise ship in the Australian market. *K. & D. Lane*

The *Arosa Kulm* was almost the archetypal emigrant steamer. An 8,000 tonner, much converted over the years, she accommodated most of her passengers in dormitories.

Word Ship Society

Swiss mountain of that name, and indeed, the line was run from Geneva. Until the last two years of its life Arosa was purely its trade name and from 1952 to 1957 the operating company, registered in Panama, was called the Compañia Internacional Transportadora. Then the official name Arosa Line Inc. was adopted.

Most of the Arosa Line's sailings were on the emigrant run between Bremerhaven and the Canadian ports. There were, though, voyages on other routes including some bringing West Indian migrants to Britain and – particularly after the line had acquired a rather superior vessel – between Bremerhaven and New York. The line also found employment for its ships with student charters and in the cruise market – although here they suffered several unfortunate mishaps. At the end of 1958 Arosa collapsed under the weight of its debts, its three remaining ships being arrested and sold.

The line's first ship was the *Arosa Kulm* (1920/8,929 gross tons). She was one of those very ordinary vessels which go on to lead remarkable lives. She had started as a US Army transport. She then passed to the American Merchant Line and eventually to United States Lines. At this stage she was known as the *American Banker*, one of a group of ships which maintained a service between New York and London carrying mainly cargo but with accommodation for a limited number of passengers. In 1940 United States Lines transferred her to a Belgian affiliate in order to overcome the trading restrictions imposed by American neutrality. She was now called the *Ville d'Anvers* and was the only one of her group to survive the War. In 1946 she reverted to the United States Lines, surprisingly flying the Honduran flag, but they had little use for her and

quickly sold her. A further change of ownership brought her, still registered in Honduras, into the possession of the Sociedad de Navegación Trasatlántica. Under the banner of Stevenson Line she was placed in a service linking Istanbul and other Mediterranean ports with New York. She now bore the name *City of Athens* but was not profitable and was auctioned off, fetching $400,000. The buyers were Panamanian Lines and with them, and their successors Mediterranean Lines, she had perhaps the most successful period of her life. Named *Protea* and now able to accommodate 965 mainly dormitory passengers she became one of the most consistent vessels under charter to the I.R.O. As already recorded, she was sold for about $1 million during the course of her I.R.O. charter. Her new owners were another Panamanian company, Compañia de Operaciones Maritimas who possessed a small fleet of cargo vessels. Finally, in 1951, she was bought by Nicolo Rizzi's company and received the name *Arosa Kulm* some months later. At first she was used in the charter market but early in 1952 she inaugurated the new Arosa Line service from Bremerhaven to Canada.

At the time there were many people requiring transport from Northern Europe to Canada and the *Arosa Kulm* was sufficiently successful for her owners to acquire another passenger-carrier after a couple of years. (For some time they had also owned a small cargo ship.) The choice was an American vessel, the *Puerto Rico*, which had spent most of her life on the New York–San Juan route, latterly as a first class-only cruising vessel belonging to the Bull Line. Arosa spent quite heavily on modernising her appearance and on increasing her passenger capacity from 200 to 806, almost entirely in tourist class but housed in cabins rather than dormitories. She was now called *Arosa Star* (1931/9,070 gross tons). After the collapse of the Arosa Line she was bought cheaply by an operator on the Miami–Nassau run and enjoyed nine years of great popularity as their *Bahama Star* – so much so that when she was finally replaced her successor was called the *New Bahama Star*.

In 1955 the Arosa Line continued its rapid expansion by buying another, and very much larger, vessel. Now called the *Arosa Sun* (1930/20,126 gross tons), the new ship had been the *Felix Roussel* of Messageries Maritimes (named after a former president of the line). She was one of three modernistic motor liners which Messageries called their Nautonaphtes. As built, she had two funnels of square section, each with a prominent lip round the top – reflecting, one supposes, a desire in the late 'twenties to move away from the traditional forms and adopt designs more in keeping with the new, exciting age. (The interior of the *Ile de France* was an earlier manifestation of this view.) In her post-War refit she lost these unusual funnels and received instead one of oval section and of typical motorship design. What she did not lose was her sumptuously decorated interior (at any rate in the first class), much of which was in a style adapted from Kmer art – she ran on the company's Far Eastern route, particularly to the French possessions in Indo-China. Political developments in that area caused her withdrawal and sale. Arosa converted her into a predominantly tourist class ship accommodating 922 passengers of whom only 60 were first class. Quite a lot of the lavish decoration of her public rooms was retained, however, making her surely one of the most sumptuous of the emigrant ships. It has been suggested with hindsight that the company could profitably have used her considerable size to provide capacity for rather more passengers. After the demise of the Arosa Line she was converted into an accommodation ship for workers at a Dutch steel plant, where she remained for thirteen years.

Within two years Arosa had bought another, and in some ways even finer, Messageries liner. As she was largely used for cruising and her transatlantic voyages were made to New York rather than the St Lawrence, she can hardly be classed as an emigrant ship. In any case Arosa found her uneconomic and sold her only sixteen months after she had entered their service. By now the Canadian migrant trade which was the company's mainstay was in decline and the Hamburg Atlantik Line had entered the lists with a service to New York using a very well-appointed vessel. By December, 1958 Arosa's debts were so pressing that the creditors triggered the company's collapse.

One final footnote: Arosa was briefly represented in New York by the well-known Danish shipping concern, the East Asiatic Company during the period 1955-56.

FLEET LIST

Argentina

11,015 gross tons, twin screw, quadruple expansion with low pressure turbine, 16 knots. Built, 1913, by Cammell Laird as the *Bergensfjord*, the second of a pair of liners for the new Norwegian America Line. 1931: as part of an up-grading of the line's passenger service, the *Bergensfjord* had a low pressure turbine added to her original engines, thus raising her speed. 1940: became a troopship

The first Home Lines vessel was the *Argentina*, a former Norwegian liner. The funnel markings were derived from those of the Swedish American Line which initially had an interest in one of the Home Lines companies. *World Ship Society*

under the management of Furness Withy. 1946: returned to the Norwegian America Line but sold to Panamanian Navigation Co, and refitted as their *Argentina* for the Italy–River Plate emigrant trade. 1947: entered service. 1948: transferred to Panamanian Lines. 1949: transferred to Mediterranean Lines. 1953: transferred to Home Lines Inc., thus recognising the trade name under which she and her fleet mates had always operated. 1952: temporarily transferred from the Central American service in which she had operated since 1949 to the North Atlantic. 1953: sold to Zim Israel Lines and as their *Jerusalem* instituted their transatlantic service. Also used within the Mediterranean. 1957: renamed *Aliya*. 1958: laid up. 1959: scrapped at La Spezia.

Arosa Kulm

8,929 gross tons, single screw, geared turbine, 15 knots. Built, 1920, as a US Army transport, *Cantigny*, by the American International Shipbuilding Corpn., Hog Island, Pennsylvania – one of a class known as 'Hog Island Freighters'. 1924: handed over to the American Merchant Line and renamed *American Banker*, mainly for cargo service. 1926: more extensive passenger accommodation installed. 1929: ownership of the line transferred to P.W. Chapman & Co. 1931: US Shipping Board foreclosed on the Chapman company and transferred both the United States Lines and the American Merchant Line to a new concern, United States Lines Co. of Nevada, controlled by the International Mercantile Marine group. 1940: transferred to a Belgian affiliate, Soc. Maritime Anversoise and renamed *Ville d'Anvers*. 1945: handed back to United States Lines who registered her under the Honduran flag and in 1946 sold her to Isbrandtsen Line. 1946: bought by Cia. de Vapores Mediterránea and later Sociedad de Navegación Trasatlántica. Renamed *City of Athens* and placed in Mediterranean service from New York. 1947: sold by auction to meet her owners' debts, becoming the *Protea* of Panamanian Lines who refitted her as an emigrant-carrier. 1948: chartered to the I.R.O. 1949: sold to Cia. de Operaziones Maritimas. 1951: sold to Cia. Internacional Transportadora. 1951: chartered to Incres Line for two voyages from Le Havre to Canada. 1952: opened the Arosa Line service from Bremen to Canada under the name *Arosa*

Kulm. c.1957: transferred to Arosa Line Inc. 1958: arrested for debt at Plymouth on a voyage from the West Indies. 1959: scrapped at Bruges.

Arosa Star

The *Arosa Star*, a compact former American cruise ship, sailed as an emigrant steamer for the Arosa Line for four years until the company collapsed in 1958.　　*World Ship Society*

9,070 gross tons, single screw, geared turbines, 15 knots. Built, 1931, by Bethlehem Shipbuilding, Quincy, Massachusetts as the *Borinquen* for the New York & Porto Rico Steamship Co. (part of the Agwilines group). 1942: became a US Army transport. 1946: returned to her owners. 1949: sold to the Bull Line and renamed *Puerto Rico*. 1954: bought by Cia. Internacional Transportadora (i.e. the Arosa Line), refitted and renamed *Arosa Star*. c.1957: Arosa Line Inc. 1959: bought for $510,000 by McCormick Shipping Corporation of Panama and operated in the Eastern Steamships cruise service as the *Bahama Star*. 1968: withdrawn as the result of more stringent American maritime safety regulation. 1969: sold to Western Steamship Co. (Panama) and taken to California to serve as *La Jenelle*, a floating hotel but wrecked in 1970 at Port Hueneme during a hurricane.

Arosa Sun

20,126 gross tons, twin screw, diesel, 17 knots. Built, 1930, by Ateliers et Chantiers de la Loire, St Nazaire as the *Felix Roussel* for the Messageries Maritimes Far Eastern service. 1935: rebuilt with an extended bow and new engines. 1940: managed as a British troopship by the Bibby Line. 1942: survived a heavy air attack at Singapore. 1946: returned to Messageries Maritimes service. 1948-50: refitted. 1955: sold to Cia. Internacional Transportadora and refitted. Placed in their Canadian service as the *Arosa Sun*. c.1957: Arosa Line Inc. 1958: arrested at Bremen. 1960: sold to the Royal Dutch Steelworks, Ijmuiden as an accommodation vessel. 1974: broken up at Bilbao.

Atlantic

20,553 gross tons, twin screw, geared turbine, 21 knots. Built, 1927, by William Cramp, Philadelphia as *Malolo* for the Matson Line's service to Honolulu. 1927: involved in a serious collision with the *Jacob Christensen* and saved with difficulty. 1937: renamed *Matsonia*. 1942: taken up as a US Navy transport. 1946: returned to Matson Lines who quickly restored her to service. 1948: bought by Panamanian Lines, then transferred to Mediterranean Lines. Renamed *Atlantic* and refitted. Placed in a new Home Lines service from Genoa to New York. 1953: Home Lines Inc. 1954: after three years in an express service between Southampton and Canada, transferred to the Greek register and renamed *Vasilissa Freideriki* (or *Queen Frederica*) for Home Lines' new subsidiary National Hellenic American Line. 1965: National Hellenic American and its ship were sold to the Chandris group who retained the *Queen Frederica* on her Piraeus to New York service until 1967 when stricter US maritime safety rules forced her transfer to the Chandris group's Australian service. 1968: chartered to Sovereign Cruises. 1971: laid up. 1973: reactivated for cruises on Chandris's own account for one season. 1973: laid up again. 1977: scrapping commenced at Elefsis. 1978: the remains of the ship were gutted by fire.

Home Lines refitted their second-hand liners to a very high standard. The *Atlantic* was already an extremely well-found ship when they purchased her from the Matson company.
World Ship Society

Brasil

11,055 gross tons, triple screw, geared turbine, 17 knots. Built, 1905, by Alexander Stephen, Glasgow as *Virginian*, one of two pioneer turbine steamers for the Allan Line service from Liverpool to Canada. 1914: taken up as a troop transport and later as an auxiliary cruiser. 1915: the purchase of the Allan Line by Canadian Pacific (which had actually occurred in 1909) was finally announced. 1920: the *Virginian* was released from naval service and sold to the Swedish American Line who renamed her *Drottningholm*. 1923: fitted with new turbines, geared rather than direct as originally. 1940: began a long series of voyages for the International Red Cross repatriating prisoners of war. 1946: sold to South Atlantic Lines for delivery in 1948. 1948: placed by her new owners in the Home Lines South American service as the *Brasil*. c.1951: transferred to Mediterranean Lines. 1951: after some months on the Italy–New York route inaugurated a new Hamburg–New York service under the new name *Homeland*. 1952: in a general reorganisation of Home Lines services was transferred back to the Genoa–New York route. 1953: owners became Home Lines Inc. 1955: scrapped at Trieste.

Castel Bianco

7,604 gross tons, single screw, geared turbine, 15

knots. Built, 1945, by Bethlehem-Fairfield, Baltimore as the 'Victory' ship *Vassar Victory* for the US Maritime Commission. 1947: bought by Sitmar (Italian flag) and renamed *Castelbianco*. Chartered to the I.R.O. 1952: rebuilt as a full passenger carrier and name amended to *Castel Bianco*, now 10,139 gross tons. Mainly used in the Central American service. 1957: sold to the Spanish Line (Cia. Trasatlántica Española) and renamed *Begoña*. 1974: scrapped at Castellon after breaking down in mid-Atlantic.

Castel Felice

The *Castel Felice*, an ex-British India liner, was a hard working member of the Sitmar fleet. She is seen here after a 1955 refit in which her promenade deck was partially enclosed.
Steffen Weirauch collection

12,150 gross tons, twin screw, geared turbine, 16 knots. Built, 1930, by Alexander Stephen, Glasgow as the British India Line's *Kenya*. 1940: taken up as a troopship and later as a Landing Ship (Infantry). 1941: renamed *Hydra*, then *Keren*. 1946: bought by the Ministry of Transport. 1948: laid up. 1949: ran aground after breaking adrift in a gale. Bought by Alva Steamship Co. (Vlasov group). Renamed successively *Kenya, Keren, Kenya, Fairstone, Kenya* and *Keren*; and transferred first to the Panamanian flag and then the Italian (Sitmar). 1951: rebuilding commenced. 1952: entered the line's Genoa–Australia and Genoa–South America services under the name *Castel Felice*. 1954: started occasional North Atlantic voyages, also began running between northern Europe and Australia. 1968: transferred to the Panamanian flag. 1970: scrapped at Kaohsiung.

Castelverde

7,607 gross tons, single screw, geared turbine, 15 knots. Built, 1945, by California Shipbuilding Corporation, Los Angeles as *Wooster Victory* for the US Maritime Commission. 1947: bought by the Vlasov group and initially registered under the Argentinian flag, later the Panamanian, without change of name. Chartered to the I.R.O. 1950: renamed *Castelverde* and shortly afterwards transferred to the Sitmar company (Italian flag). 1953: rebuilt (9,008 gross tons). Now *Castel Verde*, in the Central American service. 1957: bought by the Spanish Line and called *Montserrat*. 1970: serious boiler and mechanical problems left the ship adrift, but she was repaired and returned to service. 1973: scrapped at Castellon.

Fairsea

Sitmar's *Fairsea*, here photographed at Sydney, was another conversion from a C3 escort carrier. In 1955 she caused alarm to British shipowners by being the first foreign vessel to be awarded a long-term contract to carry migrants for the Australian government. *Steffen Weirauch collection*

11,678 gross tons, single screw, diesel, 16 knots. Built, 1942, by Sun Shipbuilding, Chester, Pennsylvania. Launched as a C3-type cargo vessel, *Rio de La Plata*, for Moore-McCormack Lines but completed as an auxiliary aircraft carrier. 1942: handed over to the Royal Navy as HMS *Charger*, later returning to the US Navy. 1949: bought by the Vlasov group and registered as *Fairsea* by Alvion Steamship Corpn., Panama. Rebuilt as a passenger ship and chartered to the I.R.O., later running in the Sitmar service to Australia and on the North Atlantic. 1955: inaugurated the line's new Southampton–Australia service. 1958: refitted, 13,432 gross tons, and transferred to the Italian flag. 1968: switched back to the Panamanian flag. 1969: caught fire during a crossing of the Pacific which led to her being sold for scrapping at La Spezia.

Fairsky

12,464 gross tons, single screw, geared turbine, 17½ knots. Built, 1942, by Western Pipe & Steel, San Francisco. Laid down as a C3-type, *Steel Artisan* for Isthmian Lines but completed as an auxiliary aircraft-carrier, USS *Barnes*, for the US Navy. Handed over to the Royal Navy as HMS *Attacker*. 1946: returned to the US Navy and laid up. 1948: sold to American-flag owners and later to the Vlasov group who had plans to convert her into a cargo vessel. Renamed *Castelforte*, later *Castel Forte*, remaining unconverted until 1957 when she was rebuilt as the passenger ship, *Fairsky*

TV. FAIR SKY

CROSSING EQUATORIAL LINE

To-day's Events

4.30 P.M. - *King Neptune and His Court will board the Ship.*

4.30 P.M. - *Strike up the Band! The Regal Parade will take charge of the Festivities and BAPTISM OF PASSENGERS.*

(Liberian register). 1972: laid up. 1973: reactivated, mainly as a cruise ship. 1977: struck a wreck off Djakarta and beached. Sold for scrapping but later reprieved for conversion into a floating hotel and casino at Manila. 1979: by now called the *Philippine Tourist*, she was badly damaged by fire and sold for scrapping at Hong Kong.

Fairstar

21,619 gross tons, twin screw, geared turbine, 17 knots. Built, 1957, by Fairfield, Glasgow as the *Oxfordshire*, a troopship for Bibby Line under contract to the British government. 1962: the Ministry of Defence cancelled its permanent trooping contracts. 1963: the vessel was chartered to Fairline Shipping Corporation of Liberia (part of the Vlasov group) for use in the Sitmar service to Australia. 1964: bought outright by Vlasov in the name of Fairstar Shipping Corporation and named *Fairstar*. Entered service on completion of her refit. 1973: closed Sitmar's regular liner service and became a fulltime cruise ship based in Australia.

Italia

21,554 gross tons, twin screw, diesel, 17½ knots. Built, 1928, by Blohm & Voss, Hamburg as the *Kungsholm* for the Swedish American Line's Gothenburg–New York service. 1939: based in New York for cruising after the outbreak of the War. 1942: sold to the American government which was threatening to commandeer her, it has since been claimed. Renamed *John Ericsson* and used as a troopship under United States Lines management. 1947: extensively damaged by fire at New York. Sold back to Swedish American who assigned her to South Atlantic Lines. Repaired and refitted and placed in the Home Lines South American service in 1948. 1948: transferred to the North Atlantic routes. 1952: transferred to Mediterranean Lines. 1953: transferred to Home Lines Inc. 1954: ran down the tug *Fairplay I* at Cuxhaven. 1961: started the line's new cruising service from New York to Nassau. 1964: withdrawn and sold to Freeport Bahama Enterprises for use as the floating hotel, *Imperial Bahama*, but the venture was unsuccessful and she was sold for scrapping at Bilbao the following year.

Protea

(see *Arosa Kulm*).

Vasilissa Freideriki

(see *Atlantic*).

Wooster Victory

(see *Castel Verde*).

The *Italia*, formerly the Swedish American *Kungsholm*, was a notable motor liner despite having tall steamship-like funnels. She is here seen arriving at New York.

Steffen Weirauch collection

Chapter Six

The Spaniards, The French, and The Dutch

Spanish Vessels

Spain was not involved in the Second World War but her liner companies were nonetheless at a fairly low ebb in the mid 'forties. They were still recovering from the effects of their country's Civil War (1936-39) in which most of their best ships had been destroyed (or, at the end of hostilities, seized while in Russian ports to which they had been sent by the Republican government to collect war materials).

The Compañía Trasatlántica Española (known as the Spanish Line to the rest of the World) had historically been a large carrier of migrants not only from Spain but also from Italy. In the nineteenth and early twentieth centuries its services had stretched out to the Spanish colonies and former colonies in South America, the Caribbean basin, the west coast of Africa and the Philippines. After the Second World War it had two main services. One was from northern Spanish ports and Portugal to Cuba and Mexico, often via New York. (From 1963 Puerto Rico was substituted for Cuba.) The second route was from Genoa and Barcelona to Venezuela and several islands in the southern Caribbean.

The company's vessels were of medium size, usually combination carriers with a passenger capacity of two or three hundred, divided between first class and tourist. This situation changed in 1957, however, when the Spanish Line bought two converted 'Victory' ships from Sitmar. (See Chapter Five.) The *Begoña* (ex-*Castel Bianco*, 1945/10,139 gross tons) and *Montserrat* (ex-*Castel Verde*, 1945/9,008 gross tons) had accommodation for about 950 and 820 passengers respectively in tourist and, rather superior, special tourist classes. The accommodation was upgraded in 1962, notably by the fitting of full air-conditioning. In their first year with the Spanish Line they ran from Genoa to the Caribbean and the *Begoña* also made two voyages from Italian ports to Australia. In 1958, however, they were switched to a new route from Southampton via Spain and Portugal to Central America and several of the islands of the British West Indies. Like the similar service of the Siosa Line (see Chapter Four), this route took Spanish and Portuguese migrants outwards and then brought West Indians over to settle in Britain on the return leg. The pair remained in service rather later than most emigrant ships, despite bouts of engine trouble. It was one of these which left the *Begoña* stranded in mid-Atlantic in 1974 and brought about the end of the service.

The smaller *Satrustegui* (1949/6,518 gross tons) and *Virginia de Churruca* (1948/6,518 gross tons) were other

The utilitarian 'Victory' ship *Wooster Victory* eventually became the Spanish Line's *Montserrat*. Spanish Line vessels usually had plain black funnels but here the *Montserrat* sports a yellow one decorated with the line's house-flag. *Steffen Weirauch collection*

Spanish Line vessels which might be classed as emigrant carriers, although their passenger capacity was not enormous – after modernisation in the early 'sixties they could carry 44 in first class and 192 in tourist. Initially they were chartered from the Spanish government shipping company under different names, but were bought outright by the Spanish Line in 1952. They were employed on the Genoa–Barcelona–Caribbean route.

Another old Spanish concern had operated passenger ships with extensive accommodation for emigrants before the War. This was the Ybarra company whose squat, modern motorships had run between Genoa, Barcelona and the River Plate ports. The company had the misfortune to lose all but one of its passenger vessels during the Civil War and then suffer the destruction by fire of that single survivor a few months later. In 1939-40 the possibilities for finding replacements were distinctly limited. Eventually, however, the Ybarra company managed to acquire, through intermediaries, a pair of passenger steamers of one of the standard types which the Americans had built in some quantity immediately after the First World War. As the *Cabo de Buena Esperanza* (1922/12,594 gross tons) and *Cabo de Hornos* (1921/12,597 gross tons)[1] they maintained Ybarra's South American passenger service for nearly two decades until 1958 and 1959 respectively. They had an old-fashioned passenger configuration for some years – 850 in first, third and steerage. In the late 'fifties they were replaced by a very superior pair of 14,000 ton liners, the style of whose accommodation aroused much highly favourable comment.

Ybarra y Cia., based in Seville, was a family-controlled business. Another private company which carried migrants from Spain to South America after the War was the Aznar Line of Bilbao. Like Ybarra they had a fair-sized fleet of smallish cargo vessels in addition to their passenger ships. They are best remembered in Britain, though, for the services they ran between the Canary Islands and London and Liverpool in the 'fifties and 'sixties, carrying fruit and holiday-making passengers. All their ships had names beginning with 'Monte' in recent times.

Two of the vessels which Aznar used to carry migrants had originated as members of a new class of cargo ships, named after Spanish monasteries, which were being built for the state-owned shipping company. However, the government sanctioned their sale to Aznar and they were completed as the *Monte Urbasa* (1948/7,723 gross tons) and *Monte Udala* (1948/10,170 gross tons). Despite the discrepancy in their tonnage they were of identical size. It is thought that originally they carried all their passengers in dormitories but in later years some at least of the accommodation was upgraded. The *Monte Urbasa* ran on a rather wandering route to the Caribbean ending up at New Orleans, but the *Monte Udala* maintained the company's main service to Rio de Janeiro and the River Plate ports.[2] Like most northern Spanish liners she called at Vigo to pick up Portuguese traffic. In 1959 she was joined in the South

American service by the *Monte Umbe* (1959/9,961 gross tons), a development of the 'Monasterio' class which had curvaceous modern lines. Her emigrant passengers travelled in small cabins and, as with her two running mates latterly, there was a limited amount of air-conditioned accommodation for first and tourist class customers. The South American service survived until the late 'seventies.

SPANISH FLEET LIST

The Spanish Line's *Begoña* during her early years on the West Indies to Southampton run. Also in the picture is the Southampton tug-tender *Paladin*.　　*World Ship Society*

Begoña

10,139 gross tons, single screw, geared turbine, 15 knots. Built, 1945, by Bethlehem–Fairfield, Baltimore as the 'Victory' ship *Vassar Victory* for the U.S. Maritime Commission. 1947: bought by Società Italiana Trasporti Marittimi (the Sitmar Line) and renamed *Castelbianco*. Chartered to the I.R.O. 1952: rebuilt and renamed *Castel Bianco*. Gross tonnage increased to the above figure from 7,604. 1957: bought by the Spanish Line and renamed *Begoña*. Initially ran from the Mediterranean to the Caribbean and to Australia, but quickly transferred to a Southampton–Caribbean service via Spain and Portugal. 1974: broke down in mid-Atlantic. Scrapped at Castellon.

Cabo de Buena Esperanza

12,594 gross tons, twin screw, geared turbine, 17 knots. Built, 1922, by New York Shipbuilding Corporation, Camden, New Jersey for the United States Shipping Board as the *Hoosier State*, but quickly renamed *President Lincoln*. She was allotted to the Pacific Mail Line who placed her in their Far Eastern service from San Francisco. 1925: absorbed by the Dollar Line. Continued to run to the Far East but later used on the San Francisco–New York route. 1938: on the collapse of the Dollar Line its ships and services were transferred to the American President Line which was set up with encouragement from the U.S. government. 1940: sold to Berge y Cia. and renamed *Maria*

1　i.e. Cape of Good Hope and Cape Horn. All Ybarra liners had 'cape' names.

2　Aznar voyages varied considerably, many starting from ports outside Spain. Some of the South American voyages continued beyond Buenos Aires, round the toe of the continent and up the west coast to Valparaiso and Antofagasta.

For nearly two decades the *Cabo de Buena Esperanza* and her sister maintained Ybarra's South American passenger service from Barcelona. Members of one of the standard classes the Americans built after the First World War, they had four goal-post masts.   *A. Scrimali*

del Carmen. Almost immediately re-sold to Ybarra y Cia and renamed *Cabo de Buena Esperanza*, being placed in service between Barcelona and the River Plate. 1958: scrapped at Barcelona.

Cabo de Hornos

12,597 gross tons, twin screw, geared turbine, 17 knots. Built, 1921, by New York Shipbuilding Corporation, Camden, New Jersey as *Empire State* for the United States Shipping Board and allotted to the Pacific Mail Steamship Co. for their Far Eastern route. 1922: renamed *President Wilson*. 1925: absorbed by the Dollar Line and subsequently used on other Dollar services. 1938: transferred to the American President Line. 1940: sold to Berge y Cia. and renamed *Maria Pipa*, but re-sold to Ybarra and placed on the South American route as the *Cabo de Hornos*. 1959: scrapped at Aviles.

Monte Udala

10,170 gross tons, single screw, diesel, 16 knots. Launched in 1946 by Cia. Euskalduna, Bilbao as a cargo vessel for the Empresa Nacional Elcano but completed, 1948, as the passenger–cargo ship *Monte Udala* for Naviera Aznar. Placed on the South American run. 1971: foundered in mid-Atlantic.

Monte Umbe

9,961 gross tons, single screw, diesel, 17 knots. Built, 1959, by Cia. Euskalduna, Bilbao for Naviera Aznar and employed in their South American service (subsequently in the Canary Islands to UK trade). 1975: sold to Dem Line of Beirut and renamed *Liban*. 1979: scrapped at Gadani Beach.

Monte Urbasa

7,723 gross tons, single screw, diesel, 16 knots. Launched, 1945, by Soc. Española de Construccion Naval, Bilbao as the 'Monasterio'-class freighter *Escorial* for the Empresa Nacional Elcano. 1947: bought by the Aznar Line while still under construction. 1948: completed as the *Monte Urbasa* and used on the Central American run. 1969: sold to Ybarra y Cia who renamed her *Cabo Santa Paula* and converted to a cargo-only vessel. 1977: sold to Cypriot owners and renamed *Esperos I*, then *Eurostar*. 1978: scrapped at Beirut.

Montserrat

9,008 gross tons, single screw, geared turbine, 15 knots. Built, 1945, by the California Shipbuilding Corporation, Los Angeles as the 'Victory' ship *Wooster Victory* for the US Maritime Commission. 1947: bought by the Vlasov group and initially registered under the Argentinian flag and later the Panamanian flag, both without change of name. Chartered to the I.R.O. 1950: renamed *Castelverde* and subsequently transferred to the Società Italiana Trasporti Marittimi (Sitmar Line). 1953: rebuilt (now, 9,008 gross tons, rather than the original 7,607). Renamed *Castel Verde* and placed in the Central American service. 1957: bought by the Spanish Line and renamed *Montserrat*. 1970: adrift in the Atlantic with boiler and mechanical disorders, but later repaired. 1973: scrapped at Castellon.

Satrustegui

6,518 gross tons, twin screw, diesel, 16 knots. Built, 1948, by Union Navale de Levante, Valencia as *Explorador Iradier* for Empresa Nacional Elcano and chartered to Cia. Trasatlnática (i.e. the Spanish Line). 1952: bought by the Spanish Line and renamed *Satrustegui*. 1973: sold to Cia. Trasmediterranea who intended to rename her *Isla de Cabrera*, but she was damaged by fire while in dock and was scrapped at Castellon in 1974.

The *Monte Umbe* ran for the Aznar Line from Spain to South America, although perhaps better known for her service on the company's route between the Canary Islands and Britain.
Steffen Weirauch collection

The Spanish Line's *Satrustegui* (under her original name of *Explorador Iradier*) was a compact post-War motor liner.
Laurence Dunn collection

Virginia de Churruca

6,518 gross tons, twin screw, diesel, 16 knots. Built, 1949, as *Conde de Argelejo* for Empresa Nacional Elcano by Union Navale de Levante, Valencia. Chartered to the Spanish Line who, in 1952, bought her and renamed her *Virginia de Churruca*. 1973: sold to Cia Trasmediterranea and renamed *Isla de Formentera*. 1979: scrapped at Barcelona.

S.G.T.M.

The French probably carried fewer migrants than most major shipping powers after the War, although the trans-Mediterranean ferries catered for the Algerian labour which was drawn to France in the same way that West Indians flocked to Britain.

There were three French lines running passenger ships to South America: the Société Générale de Transports Maritimes whose vessels were based at Marseilles but often also called at Genoa; and Chargeurs Réunis and their associated company Cie. de Navigation Sud Atlantique who together operated from Bordeaux and Le Havre but whose voyages frequently originated at Hamburg. The South American services of the latter two concerns were taken over by Messageries Maritimes in 1962. Of the three, it was Transports Maritimes (SGTM) who competed for the emigrant traffic from Italy and Spain to South America. In 1951 and 1952 they introduced two liners which made very adequate provision for this trade. The *Provence* (1951/15,719 gross tons) could carry 736 in a fourth (dormitory) class as against 148 first, 167 tourist and 436 third class. The *Bretagne* (1952/16,355 gross tons) carried rather more third and rather fewer fourth class passengers. The pair were smart-looking ships but not, it would seem, very profitable and in the early 'sixties the *Bretagne* was chartered and later sold to Chandris for their new Australian service. She did not last long, being irreparably damaged by fire in 1963. In 1961 the *Provence* started to run in joint harness with the Costa Line ships on the South American route. Finally, in 1965 she was sold outright to Costa. Refitted with a rather different passenger configuration she became their *Enrico C* and as this is written is still running for them as a cruise ship.

A number of French ships on the colonial routes to Indo-China and West Africa carried third, and sometimes fourth, class passengers in dormitories or very basic cabins. It does not seem likely, however, that many emigrants were carried on these routes. As often as not, this accommodation was occupied by troops or police – like the Portuguese, the French made use of the regular liner services to transport their troops. Nor would it seem that the Messageries Maritimes services to Australia were great carriers of migrants. There were two of these – one, via Suez, was maintained for some years by two ex-British war-time standard cargo ships with accommodation for 36 passengers only; the other route, via Panama, was primarily a link with the French possessions in the South Seas rather than a through route to the Antipodes. Finally, although the great French Line's service to the West Indies called at several British islands there and returned via Plymouth, virtually no provision was made for the booming migrant trade on the route in the 'fifties and 'sixties.

FRENCH FLEET LIST

Bretagne

16,335 gross tons, twin screw, geared turbine, 18 knots. Built, 1952, by Chantiers et Ateliers de St. Nazaire, Penhoet for SGTM's South American service. 1960: chartered to the Chandris group for their recently established Australian service. 1961: bought by Chandris. 1962: renamed *Brittany*. 1963: severely damaged by fire while undergoing repairs at Piraeus. 1964: the remains were scrapped at La Spezia.

Provence

15,719 gross tons, twin screw, geared turbine, 18 knots. Built, 1951, by Swan Hunter & Wigham Richardson, Newcastle-upon-Tyne for SGTM. 1954: very badly damaged in a collision with the tanker *Saxonsea*. 1961: commenced running jointly with the Costa Line service on the South American route. 1965: sold to Costa who renamed her *Enrico C*. 1990: refitted and given new diesel engines. By now called *Enrico Costa*.

The Dutch Government

For a while in 1949-50 emigration was a two-way traffic for the Dutch. On the one hand the Dutch settlers

The old-established SGTM service from Marseilles and Genoa to the River Plate was maintained in the 'fifties by two smart new sisters. The *Provence*, which eventually became the Costa Line's *Enrico C*, carried no fewer than four separate classes of passengers.

A. Duncan

who had either survived the Japanese occupation of the East Indies or had returned there after the War were now having to be evacuated speedily, along with the troops who had been stationed there. On the other hand, some of the inhabitants of their Netherlands homeland were leaving for new lives abroad. The evacuation from the East Indies took place partly, of course, in the ships which had been regularly employed in the big Dutch companies' services to the area. Also, however, a number of the vessels which carried European migrants to Australia were diverted to Batavia on their empty homeward voyages to assist in the process. The *Cameronia* made several such calls and the *Empire Brent* and the Bibby liners were also involved in the operation. Ships under charter to the I.R.O. were also diverted on their way back from Australia, including the *Dundalk Bay*, the Swedish *Anna Salén*, the Norwegian *Goya* and *Skaugum*, the Panamanian *Nelly* and *Fairsea*, the Hong Kong–Greek *Hellenic Prince* and a number of American troopships.

For some time the Dutch government had been encouraging people to leave their small, crowded country. They chartered several well-known passenger ships to transport emigrants to Canada, the USA, Australia and, in view of the strong historical and cultural ties between the two countries, South Africa. Eventually they set up their own shipping company to perform this function. The political struggle in the Dutch East Indies which eventually led to the formation of the independent state of Indonesia restricted the post-War recovery of the traditional Nederland Line and Royal Rotterdam Lloyd services to that country. Like the Bibby Line who faced similar problems in their trade to Burma, the two Dutch companies found that, despite war losses, they had more passenger liners than they now needed. Naturally, therefore, these concerns were pleased to provide the Dutch government with a pair of emigrant ships. Royal Rotterdam Lloyd's *Kota Inten* (1927/7,191 gross tons) and Nederland's *Tabinta* (1930/8,156 gross tons) made a number of voyages to Canada in 1948-49. They were followed by two larger vessels.

Thus, between 1950 and 1958 the Nederland Line's *Johan Van Oldenbarnevelt* (1930/19,787 gross tons) operated under charter to the government carrying migrants to Australia, with some summer voyages to Canada. In her day a notable motor liner – both companies were enthusiasts for this form of propulsion – she was named after a historical national hero. Understandably her rather cumbersome title was frequently abbreviated to *JVO*. After a major refit in 1952 she could accommodate 1,414 passengers, mainly in 4-, 5- and 6-berth cabins but with several dormitories also. During the same period Royal Rotterdam Lloyd contributed their *Sibajak* (1928/12,226 gross tons) to the emigrant service.

The government also chartered the Holland–America Line's turbine steamer *Volendam* (1922/15,434 gross tons).

After war-time trooping service (and a narrow escape from sinking following a torpedo attack in 1940[1]) she was not considered a worthwhile candidate for restoration as a fully-fledged passenger liner. Initially she was used for further trooping, to the East Indies now, but she also made several emigrant voyages to Australia. Then between 1948 and 1951, still under charter to the government, she often carried migrants from Holland to Canada, and sometimes to the USA. She had been given a very limited refit after her war-time trooping and she therefore accommodated her passengers in fairly spartan quarters.[2] (She was one of a series of similar intermediate liners which had been built in the 'twenties by Harland & Wolff, mainly for constituents of the International Mercantile Marine group. By then Holland–America had severed their financial links with the combine but they continued to order their passenger ships from Harland & Wolff which was the I.M.M.'s shipbuilding arm.)

The *Volendam*'s retirement in 1951 coincided with the introduction into emigrant service of three other ships which had served as Dutch troopers. Unlike their fleet mates they were actually owned by the government. They were 'Victory' ships which the Americans had sold to the Dutch in 1947. Although they were placed under the auspices of the Directoraat-Generaal van Scheepvart, management was in the hands of Royal Rotterdam Lloyd (two ships) and the Nederland Line (one). In 1951-52 they were converted into emigrant-carriers but, unlike the Sitmar 'Victories' which underwent a similar operation, they remained ugly, functional-looking ships. They could carry approximately 900 passengers each in multi-berth cabins and dormitories. Changes took place in the management some time later: the *Zuiderkruis* (1944/9,126 gross tons) which had been operated by Royal Rotterdam Lloyd now became the responsibility of Nederland; *Groote Beer* (1944/9,140 gross tons) was transferred from Nederland to Holland–America management; *Waterman* (1945/9,124 gross tons) remained in the charge of Royal Rotterdam Lloyd. In the mid-'fifties the trio were making as many as twenty or more transatlantic voyages a year from Rotterdam – usually, but not invariably, to Canada. They also made perhaps half a dozen trips to South Africa every year. But the Dutch ships were not confined to their country's emigration programme – space on some of the *Volendam*'s transatlantic voyages was let out to the I.R.O. and some of the vessels carried large contingents of students at times, in addition to making a few further trooping voyages. Often when returning from Canada, Australia or South Africa they would carry ordinary passengers, charging very low fares since their accommodation was far from luxurious. In 1962 the *Groote Beer* served as a hotel ship at Fremantle during the Commonwealth Games.

By then the ownership of the three ex-'Victory' ships had changed. In 1961 they were transferred to Trans-Oceaan, a concern formed by the government in

---

1   It is said that when she was dry-docked for repairs after having been badly holed by one torpedo, it was discovered that a second, unexploded, was still lodged in her hull.
2   Some indication of the nature of *Volendam*'s accommodation after the war can be gained from the fact that she carried 1,682 passengers in a single class whereas her sister *Veendam* carried 586.

conjunction with the shipping companies. Operation remained in the hands of their existing managers. At about the same time improvements were made in the accommodation and facilities which they offered their passengers, but they did not remain in service for long. In 1963 the *Zuiderkruis* became a naval depot and accommodation ship and the other two were sold to John S. Latsis. Like the former *Stratheden* and *Strathmore* they were used by him as seasonal pilgrim ships, but with a more varied sailing pattern than the ex-P&O ships. Despite the change of ownership, the *Groote Beer* also reappeared on the Atlantic for two more brief seasons of student voyages and made one trip to Australia.

Circumstances forced some of the Dutch lines to be innovative. Nederland placed the *Johan Van Oldenbarnevelt* in a round-the-world service when her charter to the government expired. In this she partnered the bigger *Oranje* which had become available with the final closure of the Indonesian passenger service. The new service did not last for long and in 1963 the *JVO* was sold to the Greek Line to become their cruise liner *Lakonia*. Later that year she was destroyed by fire, 132 people losing their lives. Royal Rotterdam Lloyd ran their big *Willem Roys* on a round-the-world route in informal partnership with the Nederland Line vessels after she too had been withdrawn from the Indonesian trade. Again, this proved to be a short-lived venture.

Europe–Canada Line

Holland–America also experimented with a few round-the-world voyages in the 'sixties using the almost single-class intermediate liners *Ryndam* and *Maasdam*; and these vessels were also employed in Bremen to New York and Rotterdam to Canada services which lasted for some years. The line's real involvement in the emigrant trade of the time was through the Europe–Canada Line, however. Holland–America bought this venture jointly with Royal Rotterdam Lloyd in 1955, becoming sole owners in 1963. Europe–Canada (also known variously as Europa–Kanada, Europa–Canada and ECL Shipping) was based in Bremen in order to participate in the boom in emigration to Canada from Germany. Its ships flew the German flag and were manned by German crews who, as explained in Chapter Three, were less costly than those of many other nationalities. It was nevertheless a Dutch enterprise. For some years it had a measure of success.

Operations started in 1955 using the chartered *Seven Seas* (1941/12,575 gross tons), Panamanian-registered but Scandinavian-controlled. Her earlier career is outlined in Chapter Seven. Suffice it to say here that she was another of the former war-time escort carriers which had been laid down as C3-type merchant ships. For some years she had been running as an emigrant-carrier belonging to the Caribbean Land & Shipping Corporation. After a season on the Bremen–Montreal route Europe–Canada bought her outright. She was a typical emigrant ship of the time carrying 987 'tourist' class passengers mainly in dormitories and a token 20 first class passengers. As was often the case with ships on the Canadian route, she was diverted to Halifax and New York in the winter months when the St. Lawrence became impassable. As the Canadian emigrant boom subsided, New York became her usual year-round

terminus. There may have been three reasons why the Europe–Canada Line survived for nearly a decade longer than the rival Arosa Line. With such parents, it was obviously more securely financed; it was successful in building up student trade when the flow of emigrants began to wane; and it did not indulge in over-optimistic expansion.

In fact, Royal Rotterdam Lloyd did lend the company their *Willem Ruys* (1947/21,119 gross tons) for a couple of round voyages in 1958 when they were looking for employment for her, but she was perhaps too big for this trade. The *Seven Seas* was disabled by an engine room fire in 1965 but returned in 1966. After a few months, however, she was sold as a floating hostel. She was briefly replaced by the Holland–America company's *Ryndam* but by now trade had declined seriously and the company was closed down.

DUTCH FLEET LIST

The *Groote Beer* and *Waterman* laid up at Rotterdam in October, 1963. Former 'Victory' ships, the Dutch government employed them as troopers, emigrant ships and in student voyages. *Steffen Weirauch collection*

Groote Beer

9,140 gross tons, single screw, geared turbine, 15 knots. Built, 1944, by Permanente Metals Corpn., Richmond, California as *Costa Rica Victory*, a standard 'Victory' ship. 1947: sold to the Netherlands government for use as a troopship under Nederland Line management. Renamed *Groote Beer*. 1952: converted into an emigrant steamer, later being transferred to Holland–America Line management. 1961: transferred to Trans-Oceaan, a semi-government concern which retained the ship in emigrant service. 1963: sold to John S. Latsis and renamed *Marianna IV*, being mainly employed in the pilgrim trade, but also making transatlantic student voyages for the Dutch under her old name of *Groote Beer*. 1966: laid up. 1971: scrapped at Eleusis.

Johan Van Oldenbarnevelt

19,787 gross tons, twin screw, diesel, 17 knots. Built, 1930, by Nederlandsche Scheepsbouw, Amsterdam for the Nederland Line's service from Amsterdam to the East Indies. 1939: briefly chartered to the Holland–America Line to help with the rush of passengers returning to America before the outbreak of war. 1940: with the invasion of

Holland, her registration was transferred to Batavia. 1941: taken up as an allied troopship under Orient Line management. Now registered in the Netherlands Antilles. 1946: returned to her owners' service. 1950: chartered to the Dutch government for emigrant service, mainly to Australia but also making a few transatlantic voyages. 1951: substantially refitted. 1959: entered the Nederland company's new round-the-world service from Amsterdam and Southampton. 1963: acquired by the Greek Line for use as the cruising liner *Lakonia*. 1963: destroyed by fire near Madeira in a notorious incident which cost 132 lives.

Kota Inten

7,191 gross tons, twin screw, diesel, 14 knots. Built, 1927, by Fijenoord, Rotterdam for Rotterdam Lloyd, later Royal Rotterdam Lloyd. 1948: chartered to the Dutch government for a number of emigrant sailings to Canada, returning to Royal Rotterdam Lloyd's own service after one season. 1957: scrapped at Hong Kong.

The Panamanian-flag *Seven Seas*, converted from a C3 escort carrier, was chartered by the Europe-Canada Line in 1955 and bought by them the following year.   *K. & D. Lane*

Seven Seas

12,575 gross tons, single screw, diesel, 16½ knots. Launched, 1940, as *Mormacmail*, a C3-type cargo liner for Moore–McCormack Lines by Sun Shipbuilding, Chester, Pennsylvania; but completed, 1941, as an auxiliary aircraft-carrier USS *Long Island*. 1946: laid up. 1947: sold, then re-sold the following year. 1948: bought by the Caribbean Land & Shipping Corporation and converted into the emigrant-carrier *Nelly* (Panamanian flag). Also used for student voyages. 1953: refitted and renamed *Seven Seas*. 1955: by now under the control of the Salén group, she was chartered to the Europe–Canada Line for their new Bremen–Canada service. 1956: bought by Europe–Canada. 1965: caught fire in mid-Atlantic, being out of service for nearly a year. 1966: sold for use as a hostel at Rotterdam. 1977: scrapped at Ghent.

Sibajak

12,226 gross tons, twin screw, diesel, 17 knots. Built, 1928, by De Schelde, Vlissingen for the Rotterdam Lloyd's service to the Dutch East Indies. 1940: became a troop transport under P&O management. Temporarily registered in the Netherlands Antilles. 1947: her owners received the title Royal Rotterdam Lloyd. 1951: chartered to the Dutch government for emigrant service, mainly to Australia but also across the Atlantic, with occasional trooping voyages

and stints on her owners' Indonesian service. 1959: scrapped at Hong Kong.

Tabinta

8,156 gross tons, single screw, diesel, 15 knots. Built, 1930, by Nederlandsche Scheepsbouw, Amsterdam for the Nederland Line. 1948: chartered by the Dutch government for North Atlantic migrant sailings. 1949: returned to the Nederland Line. 1961: scrapped at Hong Kong.

Volendam

15,434 gross tons, twin screw, geared turbine, 15 knots. Built, 1922, by Harland & Wolff, Govan for the Holland–America Line. 1940: came under British control, managed by Cunard–White Star Line. 1940: torpedoed in mid-Atlantic but towed to safety. 1941: returned to service, now as a troopship. 1945: handed back to Holland–America but remained in service as a trooper with the British under charter. 1946: chartered to the Netherlands government, initially as a troopship but after about a year as an emigrant-carrier. 1952: scrapped at Hendrick Ido Ambacht.

Waterman

9,124 gross tons, single screw, geared turbine, 15 knots. Built, 1945, by Oregon Shipbuilding Corporation, Portland as *La Grande Victory*, a 'Victory' ship. 1947: sold to the Dutch government who renamed her *Waterman* and placed her under Royal Rotterdam Lloyd management as a troopship. 1952: converted into a migrant ship. 1961: transferred to Trans-Oceaan. 1963: bought by John S. Latsis and used mainly as a pilgrim ship, under the name *Margarita*. 1968: chartered to Pacific University for student cruising. 1970: scrapped at Hiroshima.

Willem Ruys

21,119 gross tons, twin screw, diesel, 22 knots. Laid down in 1939 by De Schelde, Vlissingen for the Rotterdam Lloyd. Construction greatly slowed during the war. Completed, 1947, as the *Willem Ruys* and entered Royal Rotterdam Lloyd's Rotterdam to the East Indies service. 1958: after being withdrawn from the Indonesian service she made several North Atlantic voyages including two from Bremen to Montreal under charter to the Europe–Canada Line. 1959: following a major refit was transferred to a new round-the-world service. 1964: sold to Achille Lauro and much rebuilt. 1966: entered Lauro's Australian services under the name *Achille Lauro*. 1972: transferred to fulltime cruising. 1982: seized for debt and did not resume service until 1984 by which time the Flotta Lauro's financial crisis had been partly resolved. 1985: hijacked by terrorists. 1987: ownership transferred to Starlauro.

Zuiderkruis

9,126 gross tons, single screw, geared turbine, 15 knots. Built, 1944, by Oregon Shipbuilding Corporation, Portland as the American 'Victory' ship *Cranston Victory*. 1947: released for purchase by the Dutch government who placed her in service as the troopship *Zuiderkruis*, managed by Royal Rotterdam Lloyd. 1951: converted to an emigrant ship. Now managed by Nederland. 1961: transferred to Trans-Oceaan. 1963: transferred to the Dutch Navy. 1969: scrapped at Bilbao.

A popular Holland-America Line intermediate liner before the War, the *Volendam* made emigrant voyages for the Dutch government after the conflict. She is here seen as a troopship.   *A. Duncan*

Chapter Seven
Some Scandinavians and a Pole

Pride of place among the Scandinavian owners who involved themselves in the emigrant trades must go to the Salén group of Stockholm. This family-controlled concern is perhaps best remembered for having been for many years one of the biggest operators of reefers (i.e. refrigerated cargo ships). As briefly mentioned in Chapter One, however, the group was also involved in the process of setting up the I.R.O.'s emigrant shipping operation. In March 1949, a Swedish shipping journal reported that Salén had not only chartered their own *Anna Salén* to the I.R.O. but had also organised the charter of 13 other vessels of up to 12,000 tons. These, it was claimed, included Norwegians, Americans, Panamanians and Greeks.

The *Anna Salén* (1940/11,672 gross tons) was another of the C3 cargo vessels which had been taken in hand for conversion into aircraft carriers during construction and had been released after the War for sale for commercial use. Like her near-sisters, she was rebuilt for her new owners as a passenger carrier. Photographs show her to have had a typical emigrant ship appearance with double banks of life-boats, necessary in a ship of that size carrying up to 1,500 passengers. She also had a stylised riband painted round her bow, as did several of the I.R.O. vessels. Salén kept her until 1955 when they sold her to the Hellenic Mediterranean Lines for their Australian service.

Salén would also seem to have had a connection with the *Seven Seas* in the period before she was bought by Europe–Canada Line in 1955 (see the previous chapter). She was also a former C3 ship and was acquired by the Caribbean Land & Shipping Corporation in 1948. They too converted their new purchase into an emigrant-carrier. They registered her in Panama and called her *Nelly* (1941/11,086 gross tons). Mainly she sailed between Europe and Australia. Her owners, who also had a couple of smaller ships, originally had connections with the American–Norwegian firm of T. Gotaas but within a few years Lloyd's Register was listing them c/o Salén Rederei. In 1953 she was renamed *Seven Seas* and was refitted, now carrying about 1,000 passengers as against her previous 1,300 – mostly still accommodated in dormitories, however.

One of the ships which Salén recruited for the I.R.O. was the *Goya* (1938/6,996 gross tons) belonging to the Norwegian owner Johann Ludwig Mowinckels. She was one of the several former German vessels which, having been seized by the Allies during or after the War, subsequently appeared in the emigrant trades. She had been the *Kamerun*, built for the South and East African service run jointly by the Woermann and Deutsche Ost Afrika lines. Mowinckels had been using her as a cargo vessel but had her converted into a passenger ship at Hamburg early

The Norwegian owners I.M. Skaugen ordered the *Skaubryn* as a cargo vessel but had her completed as an emigrant carrier. She was one of the best-equipped of the early post-War migrant ships.
World Ship Society

in 1949 for the I.R.O. charter. She lasted in this form for a mere two years before reverting to a cargo-only role. Her conversion in 1949 may indeed have been planned with that possibility in mind since very little in the way of extra superstructure was built up – although, of course, the usual rows of lifeboats were added. She carried up to 900 passengers.

The *Goya* was used by the I.R.O. on the Australian run, as was her sister the former *Togo*[1], which had become the Norwegian Navy's *Svalbard* (1938/6,789 gross tons). Whereas ships on commercial voyages would normally call at several Australian ports, those on charter to the I.R.O. often delivered their passengers to just one. The *Svalbard* had undergone a very similar conversion to her sister and was used as a naval transport except during her interlude with the I.R.O. in 1948-49. She remained in naval service until 1955 when she was sold to commercial owners. Thereafter she had a varied career, latterly with a Colombian line, which ended with her stranding off the Mexican coast in 1985. That event caused a small flurry of comment in the shipping journals since as the *Togo* she had served the German navy in several capacities during the War and towards the end of her life had apparently become something of a mascot for the German communities in various South American ports.

Another former German ship was chartered to the I.R.O. by I.M. Skaugen.[2] She was the *Skaugum* (1949/11,626 gross tons) which had been launched early in 1940 as a diesel-electric cargo ship for the Hamburg–America Line but had lain uncompleted until the British government, whose property she had become after the War, sold her to Skaugen in 1948. They had her finished as an emigrant ship capable of carrying no less than 1,700 passengers. Again the layout was typical of these conversions from cargo vessels – little superstructure but the hull packed with simple passenger accommodation; tall ventilators, no doubt very necessary during passages through the Red Sea; and the inevitable rows of lifeboats. Mention has already been made (in Chapter One) of the facilities which were provided on this ship. It was also commented at the time that she had a very large Provision Room so that food could be bought wherever it was cheapest along the route. It was claimed that she would be capable of over 20 knots but that her schedules would be based on an average of between 17 and 18 knots. It is doubtful whether in the event this was the case but, even so, she was almost certainly somewhat faster than most of the older vessels which the I.R.O. employed.

The *Skaugum* worked mainly between the Mediterranean and Australia and was presumably successful since in 1951 she was joined by the *Skaubryn* (1951/9,786 gross tons) running to Australia out of Bremen. One of the few completely new ships introduced into this type of trade, she had been laid down as a cargo vessel but at an early stage in her construction Skaugen had decided that she could be profitably employed as an emigrant-carrier and had some rather superior accommodation built into her. Like Sitmar, Skaugen continued to operate on the Australian route after the I.R.O. charters expired. Other employment was also found for the two ships. The *Skaubryn* made trooping voyages for the French and British and was chartered for transatlantic voyages by the Greek Line and the Dutch government passenger service. The *Skaugum* was chartered to the Pakistanis for pilgrim work. Unfortunately the *Skaubryn* was destroyed by fire in March 1958 while crossing the Indian Ocean, happily without direct loss of life. At about the same time the *Skaugum* was withdrawn from passenger service and converted into a cargo vessel.

Some years ago a correspondent wrote to the magazine 'Sea Breezes' suggesting that the Norwegian freighters *Dicto* (belonging to A.B. Aaby) and *Vivita* (of the Ugland group), and also the British *Harpathian* owned by J. & C. Harrison, may have been used as temporary emigrant ships. It is true that all three did visit Australian ports in 1950-51. They may have carried passengers but a study of their movements leaves the impression that they were primarily, if not solely, carrying cargo.[3]

One of the ships in regular liner service in which the I.R.O. announced its intention of making block bookings in the year to the end of June, 1950 was the Polish *Sobieski* (1939/11,030 gross tons). She was a modern motor ship which had been built for the state-owned Gdynia–America Line's pre-war passenger service to South America. After the invasion of Poland she had become a troopship under British control, one of a small fleet of Polish liners which was placed under the management of Lamport & Holt. When she was handed back to Gdynia–America they placed her in a new service which they started early in 1947 from Genoa to Halifax and New York. This lasted until early 1950 when the company withdrew from the route – owing perhaps to increased competition and also possibly to the international political climate which made Westerners less willing to travel in Polish ships. Having now no obvious employment for the vessel, the Poles sold her to the Russians.

FLEET LIST

Anna Salén

11,672 gross tons, single screw, diesel, 17 knots. Built, 1940, by Sun Shipbuilding & Drydock, Chester, Pennsylvania. Intended as a C3-type cargo ship, *Mormacland* for the Moore–McCormack Lines, but taken over by the US Navy and completed as an auxiliary aircraft carrier. 1941: transferred to the Royal Navy and commissioned as HMS *Archer*. 1945: refitted as a cargo vessel, *Empire Lagan* by the Ministry of War Transport and placed under the man-

---

1 The *Kamerun* and the *Togo* were named after African territories served by their original owners.
2 Skaugen remains one of the major Norwegian shipping concerns and was for some years one of the owners of the Royal Caribbean Cruise Line.
3 The Dutch shipping writer Arie Lagendijk has ascertained that all three of these vessels were under charter to the Dutch at one time, but his enquiries confirm that they were not used in the evacuation from the East Indies.

Another converted C3 escort carrier, the Swedish *Anna Salén* had the usual rows of lifeboats and many tall ventilators to keep her 1,500 passengers as cool as could be managed in hot latitudes.   *World Ship Society*

agement of the Blue Funnel Line (Alfred Holt, managers). 1946: returned to the US Maritime Commission and eventually released for sale to the Salén group. 1949: entered service as the emigrant ship *Anna Salén*. 1955: bought by Cia. Naviera Tasmania (Hellenic Mediterranean Lines) and renamed *Tasmania* for their regular Mediterranean–Australia service. 1961: sold to China Union Lines of Taiwan and renamed *Union Reliance*, but soon after the sale she was involved in a collision and fire and in 1962 she was scrapped at New Orleans.

Goya

6,996 gross tons, single screw, diesel. Built, 1938, by Bremer Vulkan, Vegesack as *Kamerun* for the joint Woermann and Deutsche Ost Afrika service to Africa. 1946: in sole Woermann ownership. 1946: passed to the Norwegian government and allocated to Johann Ludwig Mowinckels who named her *Goya* (5,042 gross tons). 1949: converted for emigrant transport. 1950: reverted to a cargo carrier (5,239 gross tons). 1960: sold to T.J. Skogland and renamed *Reina*. 1962: sold to Trygve Matland Jr. and renamed *Svanholm*. 1963: sold to Christen K. Gran and renamed *Hilde*. 1964: sold to Meldaf Shipping Co. (Greek) and renamed *Melina*. 1969: scrapped in Taiwan.

Nelly

11,086 gross tons, single screw, diesel, 16½ knots. Launched, 1940, as *Mormacmail*, a C3 cargo liner for Moore–McCormack, by Sun Shipbuilding, Chester, Pennsylvania; but completed, 1941, as an auxiliary aircraft carrier USS *Long Island*. 1947: laid up and sold. 1948: bought by the Caribbean Land & Shipping Corporation who converted her into an emigrant-carrier and renamed her *Nelly* (Panamanian flag). 1953: refitted and renamed

The *Goya*, belonging to J.L. Mowinckels, became a temporary passenger ship in 1949 when she was chartered to the I.R.O. She was a war prize, having been seized from the Germans.   *J. Ludwig Mowinckels Rederi*

The Polish *Sobieski* was built on the Tyne shortly before the War. This photograph was taken when she was on her trials.

Laurence Dunn collection

Seven Seas. 1955: chartered to the Europe–Canada Line for their new transatlantic service from Bremen. 1956: bought by Europe–Canada Line. 1963: previously jointly owned by Royal Rotterdam Lloyd and Holland–America, the Europe–Canada Line now became a wholly-owned subsidiary of the latter company. 1965: caught fire in mid-Atlantic and out of service for nearly a year. 1966: sold as a hostel in Rotterdam. 1977: scrapped at Ghent.

Seven Seas
(See *Nelly*).

Skaubryn
9,786 gross tons, single screw, diesel, 16 knot. Built, 1951, as a cargo vessel for I.M. Skaugen by Oresundsvarvet, Landskrona but completed as an emigrant-carrier. Mainly used on the Bremen to Australia route but also spent considerable time out on charter. 1958: destroyed by fire in mid-Indian Ocean during an Australian voyage.

Skaugum
11,626 gross tons, twin screw, diesel-electric, 15 knots. Launched, 1940, as the Hamburg America Line cargo ship *Ostmark* by Germaniawerft, Kiel but not completed. 1945: seized by the British but still not completed. 1948: sold to I.M. Skaugen and converted to the emigrant ship *Skaugum*. 1949: completed and placed in service, initially on charter to the I.R.O. 1957: rebuilt as a cargo vessel with normal diesel propulsion. 1964: bought by Ocean Shipping & Enterprises of Liberia and renamed *Ocean Builder*. 1972: scrapped at Kaohsiung.

Sobieski
11,030 gross tons, twin screw, diesel, 16 knots. Built, 1939, by Swan Hunter & Wigham Richardson, Newcastle for the Gdynia–America Line. 1939: control assumed by the British government who passed management to Lamport & Holt. 1946: returned to her owners who, in 1947, placed her in a new service from Genoa to New York. 1950: sold to USSR and renamed *Gruziya*. 1975: scrapped at La Spezia.

Svalbard
6,789 gross tons, single screw, diesel. Built, 1939, by Bremer Vulkan, Vegesack as *Togo* for the joint Woermann and Deutsche Ost Afrika service to South and East Africa. 1939: became a German government troop transport. 1940: mined but stayed afloat. 1940: converted to a mine-layer. 1943: converted to an armed raider but on entering service she grounded near Dunkirk and was attacked, but survived. 1943: converted into a fighter direction ship, later a troop transport and finally used as a refugee carrier during the evacuation of the eastern territories. 1945: taken over by the British, later passing to the Americans and eventually being handed over to the Norwegian Navy who used her as a transport, *Svalbard*. 1948: chartered to the I.R.O. as an emigrant ship. 1949: reverted to her naval duties. 1954: sold to Norwegian commercial owners and converted into the cargo vessel *Tilthorn*. 1956: *Stella*. 1960: bought by Deutsche Afrika Line and once again became the *Togo*. 1968: bought by Panamanian-flag owners and renamed *Lacasielle*. 1975: became the *Topeka* of the Lineas Agromar of Colombia (still Panamanian flag). 1985: stranded off the Mexican coast and declared a total loss.

Chapter Eight
The Greek Fleet

Although the Greeks are one of the most enterprising of the maritime races, it was not until after the Second World War that they became heavily involved in deep sea passenger shipping; and it was not until the late 'sixties that they became one of the leaders in the field.

Greek Line

Nevertheless, they had a transatlantic passenger line – known as the Greek Line and starting operations in 1939. Its first ship was a redundant Anchor liner, previously called the *Tuscania*, which was bought by the General Steam Navigation Company of Greece. This concern was set up by members of the Goulandris family, a well-known London–Greek shipping clan. They named their new purchase the *Nea Hellas* (1922/16,991 gross tons). In appearance she was very like the Cunard intermediate liners of the period, which was not surprising since at the time she was built the Anchor Line was a Cunard subsidiary. In 1941, with Greece now involved in the War, she became a British troopship, once again under the management of the Anchor Line. Her new passengers, in the cavalier fashion in which British soldiers have always treated foreign names, transliterated *Nea Hellas* into 'Nellie Wallace', the name of a well-known music hall comedienne of the day.

After the War the *Nea Hellas* was returned initially to Goulandris Brothers Ltd., the family's London company; but by 1947 she was back in the hands of the General Steam Navigation Company of Greece and registered at Piraeus. She re-entered the line's service in 1947 and, although she made one voyage to Australia in 1949, she was mainly employed on the Piraeus to New York route, often via Valetta, Naples, Lisbon and Halifax. She was one of the ships on whose regular line voyages the I.R.O. made block bookings in the 1949-50 period. In 1955 she was switched to the Bremerhaven–New York service and assumed the name *New York*, now having accommodation for just 80 first class passengers and 1,300 tourist.

Like Home Lines and Arosa, the Greek Line had for some time been filling the gap created by the absence of the big German liner companies from the passenger business. In 1951 they had started two services from Bremerhaven: one to New York; and one to Quebec and Montreal. The latter was something of a 'natural' for them as Goulandris Brothers were already involved in the Canadian cargo trades. At first the two ships they used on the Canadian run were elderly former Australian coastal liners which they had bought in the immediate post-war period. It is almost certain that in better times they would both have been scrapped by 1946-47 but such was the shortage

Lifeboat drill on board the Greek Line's *Columbia*.

Steffen Weirauch collection

In less straitened times the Australian coastal liner *Canberra*, would have been scrapped. But in 1947 she was a valuable property and was bought by the Greek Line.

World Ship Society

of viable passenger ships then that they were snapped up by the Goulandris interests. A few weeks earlier the *Canberra* (1913/7,710 gross tons) had been bought by Singapore Chinese, but by the time she reached Singapore they had already sold her on to the Greeks. Goulandris did not change her name and employed her on various emigrant routes before allotting her to the Canadian run, at first from the Mediterranean but eventually from Bremerhaven. In 1954, at the age of forty-one, she was sold – surprisingly, for further service. Her new owners were the government of the Dominican Republic who renamed her *España* and used her to bring emigrants from Spain. It is said that on the return voyages she carried cargoes of sugar. She lasted for another five years.

The other ex-Australian was the *Katoomba* (1913/8,473 gross tons), which after a few years with the Greek Line was renamed *Columbia*. Between 1947 and 1949 they chartered her to the French Line for the West Indies service but thereafter they mainly used her on their own Canadian routes. In 1949 both the *Canberra* and the *Katoomba*, which had hitherto still been coal-burners, were converted to oil-firing. The *Canberra* now accommodated 64 first and 646 tourist class passengers; the equivalent figures for the *Katoomba* were 52 and 754. Many of the tourist class passengers slept in dormitories. The fares for these two ships were among the lowest on the Atlantic. As in most similar vessels operating out of North German ports, the 'hotel' staff was German. Both ships were registered in Panama, in the name of the Compañía Maritima

del Este which was increasingly becoming the vehicle for the Goulandris shipowning activities – by 1949 its fleet consisted of eight vessels of which three were passenger ships.

The third passenger vessel bought for the Cia. Maritima del Este, and the one which initiated the Bremerhaven–New York service, was the *Neptunia* (1920/10,519 gross tons). She had been the *Johan de Witt* of the Nederland Line. When bought by Goulandris late in 1948 she was sent for a refit during which her mainmast and her second funnel were removed. The result was that she acquired a rather front-heavy appearance, but not a displeasing one. Her new owners were reported to have paid about £250,000 for her. Just over a year later the rather larger P&O/New Zealand Shipping Co. liner *Rimutaka* was sold for between £90,000 and £100,000. Lloyd's List quoted the two sales as a measure of the extent to which the scramble for passenger tonnage had abated by early 1950. The *Neptunia* would seem to have had slightly superior accommodation to that on the two older ships but she was still very predominantly a tourist class carrier (39 first class and 748 tourist). After the sale of the *Canberra* she was switched to the Bremerhaven–Canada route. Her career was ended, however, by a brush with a rock near Cobh in 1957.

By the early 'fifties the Greek Line was in a position to order a new-building, rather than resort to the second-hand market again. Despite early turbine disorders, the new ship, the *Olympia*, proved to be a fine acquisition which –

GREEK LINE

1958

EDITION 4/58

SAILING SCHEDULE

NORTH ATLANTIC SERVICE from

SOUTHAMPTON
LIVERPOOL
LONDON
GREENOCK
COBH

also BREMERHAVEN - LE HAVRE CHERBOURG

to CANADA and U.S.A.

See your authorised Travel Agent

He can help you

GREEK LINE
PASSENGER SERVICE
29 PICCADILLY, LONDON, W.1.
TEL. REGENT 4141

GREEK LINE

1958

MINIMUM STERLING FARES

To/From NEW YORK and CANADA

Effective for all Sailings WESTBOUND to 31st May, 1958 EASTBOUND to 31st March, 1958	Effective Feb. 10th 1958 for all Sailings WESTBOUND from 1st Nov. 1958 EASTBOUND from 1st Sept. 1958		Effective for Sailings WESTBOUND June 1 to Oct. 31 1958 (incl.) EASTBOUND April 1 to Aug. 31 1958 (incl.)
		T.S.S. New York	
80 10 0	84 0 0	First Class	98 0 0
58 0 0	59 10 0	Tourist Class	65 0 0
57 0 0	58 10 0	Tourist Class (B Deck Forward)	64 10 0
55 10 0	57 0 0	Dormitory	62 10 0
		S.S. Arkadia	
87 10 0	90 10 0	First Class	96 10 0
59 0 0	60 10 0	Tourist Class	64 10 0
58 0 0	59 10 0	Tourist Class (D. Deck)	63 10 0

HALIFAX, N.S.   The above Tourist Class rates will be reduced by £5 per adult for Westbound sailings to Halifax, N.S. during the period 1st December, 1958 to 31st March, 1959 when the St. Lawrence is closed.

FARES FOR CHILDREN

Over 12 years		Full Fare
1-12 years		Half Fare
Under 1 year - First Class		£7 . 0 . 0
Under 1 year - Tourist Class		£3 . 10 . 0

EMBARKATION FRANCE, GERMANY or BELGIUM

Please refer General Fares and Information Booklet for Tariff.

Courtesy Southampton Museums

S.S. ARKADIA 20256 BRT.

WESTBOUND
EUROPE - CANADA - NEW YORK

STEAMER	Bremerhaven	London	Le Havre	Southampton	Cherbourg	Cobh	Liverpool	Greenock	Halifax	Quebec	Montreal	New York
NEW YORK	April 4	—	April 5	April 6	—	April 7	—	—	—	April 14	—	—
NEW YORK	—	—	—	—	—	—	April 26	April 27	—	May 5	—	May 9
ARKADIA	May 22	—	—	May 24	May 23	—	May 25	May 26	—	June 2	June 3	—
NEW YORK	May 24	—	May 25	May 26	—	May 28	May 27	—	June 3	—	—	June 5
ARKADIA	June 17	—	—	June 18	June 19	June 19	—	—	—	June 25	June 26	—
NEW YORK	June 22	June 23	—	—	June 24	June 25	—	—	—	July 2	—	July 7
ARKADIA	July 9	—	—	July 10	July 11	July 11	—	—	—	July 17	July 18	—
NEW YORK	July 24	—	July 25	July 26	—	July 27	—	—	—	—	—	Aug. 4
ARKADIA	July 31	—	—	Aug. 1	Aug. 2	Aug. 2	—	—	—	Aug. 8	Aug. 9	—
NEW YORK	Aug. 18	—	Aug. 19	Aug. 20	—	Aug. 21	—	—	—	—	—	Aug. 29
ARKADIA	Aug. 24	—	—	Aug. 25	Aug. 26	Aug. 26	—	—	—	Sept. 1	Sept. 2	—
NEW YORK	Sept. 14	—	Sept. 15	Sept. 16	—	Sept. 17	—	—	—	—	—	Sept. 25
ARKADIA	Sept. 15	—	—	Sept. 16	Sept. 17	Sept. 17	—	—	—	Sept. 23	Sept. 24	—
ARKADIA	Oct. 7	—	—	Oct. 8	Oct. 9	Oct. 9	—	—	—	Oct. 15	Oct. 16	—
NEW YORK	Oct. 9	—	Oct. 10	Oct. 11	—	Oct. 12	—	—	—	—	—	Oct. 20
ARKADIA	Nov. 1	—	—	Nov. 2	Nov. 2	—	Nov. 3	Nov. 4	—	Nov. 10	—	—
NEW YORK	Nov. 3	—	Nov. 4	Nov. 5	—	Nov. 6	—	—	—	—	—	Nov. 14
ARKADIA	Nov. 19	Nov. 20	—	—	—	Nov. 22	—	—	—	—	—	Nov. 28
NEW YORK	Nov. 28	—	Nov. 29	Nov. 30	—	Dec. 1	—	—	—	Dec. 8	—	—
ARKADIA	Dec. 12	—	—	Dec. 13	Dec. 14	Dec. 14	—	—	Dec. 20	—	—	Dec. 22

(Left margin label: SUMMER SEASON — spanning the June 17 through Oct. 20 rows)

Courtesy Southampton Museums

in the much-modified form – now sails as the Commodore Cruise Line's *Caribe 1*. She was one of the earliest Atlantic liners to be built specifically to cater mainly for tourist class passengers. Rather arbitrarily, however, I do not rate her as an emigrant ship. Her line voyages were in the New York services which, despite calls at Halifax en route, were by 1954 probably not mainly patronised by migrants.

The *Arkadia* (1931/20,259 gross tons), on the other hand, was definitely an emigrant ship. Her transatlantic service for the Greek Line was on the Bremerhaven–Quebec–Montreal route and she also made a few winter sailings to Australia, thus returning to the country which she had previously served as the *New Australia* (see Chapter Two). For much of her Greek Line career she could carry 50 passengers in first class and 1,337 in tourist. It is said that she was prone to emit large clouds of black smoke; and I am told that the dockers at Tilbury, where she called en route to Canada, named her the 'Arkadia' – with the emphasis on the penultimate syllable in order to distinguish her from the P&O *Arcadia* which they regarded much more fondly. However, she served the Greek Line for eight years, being sold for scrap in 1966. Unlike most of her fleet mates, she flew the Greek flag.

Like many other passenger shipping companies, the Greek Line eventually switched almost entirely to cruising. It collapsed, however, in 1975. Perhaps rather unfairly, it is remembered as much for the notorious loss by fire of the cruise ship *Lakonia* (the former *Johan Van Oldenbarnevelt*) as for its three decades of Atlantic service.

Livanos and Yannoulatos

Another London–Greek concern, John Livanos & Sons, was also involved in the emigrant business in the years following the war. Whereas Goulandris bought secondhand passenger liners, Livanos were less ambitious in their purchases and may, perhaps be compared with some of the opportunist Italian entrants.

The first Livanos passenger ship was the tiny *Cairo* (1907/1,344 gross tons) which was placed under the flag of Palestine (as it then was) in 1945. In her youth she had been well-known around the Scottish coasts, at first as MacBrayne's clipper-bowed *Chieftain* and later in the employment of the 'North company' on the routes to the Orkneys and Shetlands. There followed twenty years of service on the west coast of Canada before Livanos bought her and registered her in the name of the Oriental Navigation Co. of Tel Aviv. By then she had long since lost her clipper bow. She would seem to have proved a willing little workhorse. Until early 1947 she ran regularly between Marseilles and Alexandria via Haifa and it is probable that she participated in the migrant traffic to Haifa from Marseilles and the various Italian ports at which she often called. Her passenger capacity was 194. In 1947 she was switched to a new route from Marseilles to Mombasa and Beira and at about the same time ownership was transferred to another Livanos company, the Zarati Steamship Co. of Panama. If the East African service was an unlikely one in which to employ a small elderly steamer built for short haul

The Greek Line *Arkadia*. Compare with her photograph as the *New Australia* in Chapter Two.   *Laurence Dunn collection*

coastal runs, an even greater improbability occurred in 1948 – she became a transatlantic liner, with a series of voyages between Marseilles and the southern Caribbean (Trinidad, La Guaira and Fort de France). It is not clear whether she carried passengers on her East African and Caribbean journeyings but she remained in service until 1950.

Another Livanos passenger ship proved considerably less dependable than the *Cairo*. The *Derna* (1915/5,751 gross tons) was a cargo ship which they bought in 1948 from the French Line. She had been built for the Deutsche Ost Afrika Line but had passed to the French when the spoils of the First World War were divided up. Livanos installed emigrant accommodation and sent her off on a voyage to Australia from Marseilles. She took 67 days to reach Melbourne which would seem to imply that the trip was not trouble-free. It was some months before she returned to service, by which time she had received a new name, *Assimina*, and had been transferred from the Zarati company to another Panamanian-registered Livanos concern, Cia. de Navegación Dos Oceanos. She now mainly sailed from Mediterranean ports to South America but was scrapped in 1952.

The largest of the three Livanos ships was the *Jenny* (1918/7,914 gross tons). She was converted from a First World War standard British cargo vessel which had belonged to the White Star Line. On the demise of that company the Clan Line had bought her. After two years in the Livanos fleet she was converted to an emigrant-carrier and also placed on the South American run. Like the *Assimina* she was registered in Panama in the name of the Dos Oceanos company. Shortly before being sold in 1952 she was taken up for a brief spell of trooping by the British government.

Yannoulatos was another well-known name in the dynastic world of Greek shipping. Then, as now, their offices were in the Electric Railway Station Building in Piraeus and they operated under the title Hellenic Mediterranean Lines. In the post-war years, though, they also had an off-shoot in Hong Kong, the China Hellenic Lines. It was through this company that they bought a very odd vessel indeed, which they rebuilt as the emigrant ship *Hellenic Prince* (1928/6,522 gross tons). Originally she had been the *Albatross*, a Royal Australian Navy seaplane-carrier which later served as a repair ship with the British Navy. After the War, plans to convert her into a floating hotel moored permanently off the coast of Devon proved abortive. At the time of her conversion into the *Hellenic Prince* her former chief engineer was quoted as saying that she had 'the bows of a battleship, the waist of a destroyer and the stern of a cruiser.' She was chartered to the I.R.O. for two years and then did a little trooping for the British but she was probably never intended to be more than a temporary passenger ship.

This was not the case with the *Cyrenia* (1911/7,527 gross tons) which Hellenic Mediterranean Lines operated

The extraordinary *Hellenic Prince* was one of the improvised emigrant-carriers of the post-War years. She had been a seaplane-carrier in the Royal Australian Navy. She is seen here shortly after being converted in South Wales. *Laurence Dunn collection*

in their own name, although ownership was vested in an associated Panamanian-flag company. She had been built for the Union Steamship Company of New Zealand who had used her on their trans-Tasman and trans-Pacific routes. She served as a troopship during the First World War and as a hospital ship in the Second, one of her final official duties being to bring the New Zealand contingent to the Victory celebrations in London. On regaining possession, her owners thought her too old and worn to be worth reconditioning. (It was reported that she had steamed a total of 2,184,081 miles.) Hellenic Mediterranean did not share this view and bought her, giving her a name ending in '-ia', as was their custom. For them she sailed from Piraeus and Genoa to Fremantle and Melbourne. She lasted until 1957.

Hellenic Mediterranean maintained their Australian service fairly regularly until the early 'sixties, latterly with the *Tasmania* (1940/11,672 gross tons), the former *Anna Salén* which they bought in 1955 (see Chapter Seven). It will be remembered that she had been one of the C3 ships which became auxiliary aircraft carriers and then, after the War, were converted into passenger ships. After they abandoned the Australian service, the group concentrated on their shorter routes within the Mediterranean.

In 1959 John S. Latsis announced that he would operate a service between the Mediterranean ports and Australia. For this purpose he bought two motor liners which had been built in the 'twenties for the Nelson Line (and later Royal Mail Lines) route from Britain to the River Plate ports. In the event, however, Mr Latsis's plan was stillborn. Within six months one of the pair was sold to a Czech organisation, but it would seem that they were merely nominees for the Chinese People's Republic since after a very few days she was on her way to the East and a new career under Chinese ownership. The remaining vessel was refitted and emerged with one modern funnel instead of the previous two stumpy ones, typical of pre-war motor ships. Named the *Marianna*, she was placed in pilgrim service in which she was later joined by four subsequent Latsis purchases – the former *Stratheden* and *Strathmore* and two of the Dutch government's ex-Victory ships. (See Chapters Two and Six.)

Chandris

Latsis was not the only Greek owner eyeing the Australian trade in 1959. Hitherto the involvement of the Chandris family in passenger shipping had been through the Charlton Steam Shipping Co. as recorded in Chapter Three. Latterly they had been concentrating on the dry cargo and tanker trades. Now, however, they bought the Union-Castle liner *Bloemfontein Castle* which had been built for an emigrant trade from Britain to Southern Africa which had quickly withered (see Chapter Two). She was only nine years old when Chandris bought her and called her *Patris* (1950/16,259 gross tons). Her registered owners became the National Greek–Australian Line but it should be noted that although the group's passenger ships were registered in a variety of names they soon became known as the Chandris Line. Chandris, or their naval architects, were adept at fitting as many cabins as possible into their ships and in the case of the *Patris* the previous passenger complement of 721 was increased to 1,036 (36 in first class

and the balance tourist class). She was placed in service between Piraeus, Fremantle, Melbourne and Sydney via Suez. She remained on this run until 1972 when she was switched to cruising, and then in 1975 she underwent a conversion unusual for a deep sea liner of this size – she was turned into a passenger and car ferry with roll on-roll off facilities through side doors. She sailed from Patras to Venice and to Ancona for Chandris until they quit the ferry business in 1979 and sold her to Karageorgis.

The early months of *Patris*'s Australian service were sufficiently successful for Chandris to secure a running mate for her. Accordingly, they chartered – with an option to purchase – the S.G.T.M. liner *Bretagne*. Within a year the option was exercised and she became the *Brittany* (1952/16,644 gross tons) registered in Greece in the name of the Europe–Australia Line. Eventually she began a new Chandris service between Southampton and Australia via Suez. She did not serve her new owners long, being destroyed by fire while under repair at Skaramanga in 1963. Her S.G.T.M. sister ship, the *Provence*, has survived much longer as the Costa Line's *Enrico C*.

Later in 1963 Chandris found a replacement for the lost *Brittany*. She was the *Lurline*, one of the four notable luxury liners which Matson had placed on their routes to Hawaii and Australia in the inter-war years. Chandris sent her for repair of the turbine damage which had precipitated her withdrawal from Matson service; and for a refit from which she emerged not only with a passenger capacity enlarged from 761 to 1,668 but with a modernised appearance. She now had a raked bow, a single streamlined mast and tapered funnels. With her white hull and her blue funnels, each bearing the large white Chandris X, she presented a striking appearance. Now named the *Ellinis* (1932/18,564 gross tons), she took over the Southampton to Australia service. Sometimes she returned via Panama and called additionally at Rotterdam. She was the first of a number of American-built ships which the Chandris group bought during the next few years of hectic expansion of their liner and cruise ship fleets. She remained active until 1980, latterly in cruising service – ample justification of the acquisition of a vessel which was already 31 years old when Chandris bought her. In fact, her life was extended in 1974 by the transplant of a turbine from one of her sister ships which was being scrapped after lengthy service as Home Lines' *Homeric*.

Chandris's predilection for American ships was again evident when, not much more than a year after buying the *Ellinis*, they made their most important purchase. She was the *America* which, until the arrival of the great *United States*, had been the biggest and one of the most prestigious ships in the US merchant fleet. Although not intended as a record breaker, she was a major competitor in the Atlantic passenger market and was in some ways a preliminary run for the design of the *United States*. There were great similarities in appearance and some of the safety features of the latter ship's design had been incorporated in the *America*. Her attraction for Chandris, who were reported to have bought her for $4.25 million, may partly have been that within her massive-looking hull and superstructure there was ample scope for another exercise in mass transportation. Without much in the way of structural alteration it proved possible to increase her passenger capacity from

1,046 in two classes to no less than 2,300 in one.

It should be emphasised that, although Chandris vessels carried large numbers of passengers, they were air-conditioned and provided cabin accommodation and public facilities which would have been thought the height of luxury by the emigrants of a decade earlier. The *America* was now called the *Australis* (1940/26,486 gross tons[1]). She was placed in a similar service to that of the *Ellinis*. By now Sitmar must have been very conscious of Chandris breathing down their necks.

Late in 1965, only a year after buying the *Australis*, Chandris purchased the National Hellenic American Line from Home Lines and with it the *Vasilissa Freideriki*, or as she was usually known *Queen Frederica* (1927/16,435 gross tons). Another former American liner, she had been the first and the smallest of the famous Matson quartet. Chandris kept her on the Mediterranean–New York run for a while, still under the National Hellenic American name, but she also made some trips to Australia. A considerable tightening of American safety regulations prompted her withdrawal from the Atlantic service in late 1967. After one final Australian sailing she was chartered out in 1968 for the new low-priced Mediterranean fly-cruising programme which Sovereign Cruises were marketing aggressively in Britain. When, after three seasons, Sovereign ill-advisedly moved into ship-owning themselves, the *Queen Frederica* found herself unemployed. She did some Mediterranean cruising on Chandris's own account but mainly she remained in lay-up. In 1977, by now fifty years old, she was sold for scrap. Before the process could be completed she was destroyed by fire.

By the mid-'sixties there were in effect two Chandris passenger shipping lines. There were the big ships on the Australian and Atlantic runs which were the responsibility of Mr Anthony Chandris and there was a fleet of much smaller vessels, mainly converted ferries, which ran cheap cruises in the Mediterranean. These were usually owned by International Cruises S.A., a company operated by Mr Demetrios Chandris, but they traded under the name Chandris Cruises and wore the customary Chandris livery. By 1967 the two fleets had not far short of 100,000 gross tons of passenger shipping in operation. The brothers' interest in the tourist trade also took them into hotel ownership.

Another aspect of the Chandris operation is worthy of comment. In 1967, having bought the Union-Castle *Kenya Castle* (renamed *Amerikanis*) in order to replace the *Queen Frederica* in the National Hellenic American service, they refitted her at their own repair facility at Perama. Here, without the expensive infrastructure of a normal shipyard and with a versatile and flexible workforce, it proved possible to increase her passenger capacity at a fraction of what the work would normally have cost. (When, some time later, the *President Roosevelt* was drastically converted into the cruise ship *Atlantis*, it was reported – with what accuracy is not known – that rebuilding which would have cost $24 million in a British shipyard and would have been utterly prohibitive if done in America, was accomplished

for no more than $8½ million.) In 1971 Chandris were said to be having talks with Cunard about refitting the *Carmania* and *Franconia*, and possibly also operating them. To revert to the *Amerikanis*, she does not really qualify as an emigrant ship. She maintained the Mediterranean–New York service for two final years before becoming a very successful fulltime cruise ship.

By now, the name of Chandris was being linked with almost any sizeable passenger ship which might remotely be suspected of being for sale. Two more big vessels did pass into Chandris hands. The Norddeutscher Lloyd *Bremen* (ex-*Pasteur*) became the cruise ship *Regina Magna* and the Matson Line's *Lurline* (ex-*Matsonia*, ex-*Monterey*) was bought in 1970 and became the *Britanis* (1932/18,254 gross tons). With her passenger capacity increased to 1,655 she was placed in the Australian service. Although a sister ship of the *Ellinis*, she had been much less used, having lain idle for ten years during the post-war period until being brought back into Matson service in 1957. This may partly explain her extraordinary longevity – as this is written in 1991, she is, at the age of 59, still active as a very popular cruise ship in the American market. Despite successive rebuildings by both Matson and Chandris she retains a 'period' appearance. The task of keeping her in service has been eased by the availability of parts from the *Ellinis* which was retired in 1980.

With the introduction of the *Britanis*, Chandris had four large vessels on the Australian run. When the emigrant contract came up for re-negotiation in 1969, Chandris succeeded in wresting it from Sitmar, thus effectively spelling the end of that company's liner service. As a result, from 1970 onwards Chandris enjoyed a guaranteed flow of migrant passengers on the outward voyages from Southampton to the Australian ports. They retained this traffic until it was finally switched completely to the air, leaving the regular liner service no longer a viable proposition.

At the end of 1977 the big *Australis* made the last voyage of what is generally thought to have been an extremely profitable service. Whereas her running mates went on to have successful careers as cruise ships, the *Australis* endured a long and sad period of idleness punctuated by two brief spells of cruising. The first of these followed her sale to an American concern called Venture Cruise Lines. After only two short cruises the company collapsed under the weight of passenger complaints, adverse publicity, the strictures of the health authorities and financial problems exacerbated by fines said to total $½ million. Chandris bought their ship back and used her for just one season of Mediterranean cruising. After that she was the subject of several sales, rumoured and actual, including one to owners who proposed to use her as a hotel ship on the West African coast. There was also a plan for her to become a floating hotel on the River Hudson. Throughout the whole sad saga the once notable liner has remained laid up at Perama.

Before leaving the Chandris operations in the emigrant trade, it should be mentioned that with the closure of the Suez Canal in 1967 it became necessary for their ships, and those of other lines still operating on the Australian

---

1   As the *America* she had rated 33,961 gross tons, but ship measurement is a very inexact science.

route, to make the long trek round the Cape of Good Hope when sailing in the eastbound direction.

Other Greeks

Another Greek owner who ran an emigrant service – very briefly – was Constantine S. Efthymiadis. He was mainly known as an operator of cruise ships in the Mediterranean and of ferries around the Greek coast. It was the loss by fire of one of his ferries, a converted tanker which was found to have been grossly overloaded, which set in train a long battle through the courts and eventually helped to bring about the collapse of the company. Before that however, in 1970, Efthymiadis operated his *Delphi* (1952/10,882 gross tons) in a service which, inter alia, carried Jewish migrants to Haifa. He had signed an agreement with the Jewish Agency and Israel's Absorption Ministry to bring 450 migrants per month from Marseilles, Naples and Palermo over a period of six months with an option for a further six months. The *Delphi* was one of several former French intermediate liners which he bought mainly for use as cruise ships. She had been Messageries Maritimes' *Ferdinand de Lesseps* and, after many refits, she still survives as *La Palma* of the Intercruise company.

One more Greek – or rather, Egyptian-Greek – ship must be mentioned. Of all the varied vessels which were placed in the emigrant trades, the *Rena* (1906/1,619 gross tons) was perhaps the most improbable. Long ago she had been built for the run between Scotland and Ireland as G. & J. Burns's *Woodcock*. Now she was owned by the Panamanian-flag Cia. de Naviera Rena, managed from Alexandria by Panos Protopapas, and mainly used in the Mediterranean and the Red Sea. However, in 1948 – by which time she was already 42 years old – she made a migrant voyage from Piraeus to Buenos Aires followed by another from Genoa to Melbourne. On her return from Australia she called at Shanghai and Hong Kong with the object, one might speculate, of participating in the evacuation of refugees from the Communist advance through China. Of course, she was no smaller than many of the vessels which made such long voyages in the nineteenth century; and her accommodation for 360 passengers can have been no more cramped than would once have been considered normal. But it was surely a sign of the shortage of passenger tonnage that such a ship was pressed into such service in the middle of the twentieth century. She typified the improvisation which shipowners found necessary in the immediate post-War era, and also the opportunities which many of them tried to seize.

The massive-looking *Australis* at Fremantle in 1977 on the last voyage of the Chandris service to Australia.

Chris Gee (Steffen Weirauch collection)

GREEK FLEET LIST

Arkadia

20,259 gross tons, quadruple screw, turbo-electric, 19 knots. Built, 1931, by Vickers-Armstrongs, Newcastle-upon-Tyne for the Furness Bermuda Line and named *Monarch of Bermuda*. 1939: taken up as a troop transport. 1947: during refurbishment was partly destroyed by fire, after which she was bought by the Ministry of Transport and rebuilt as the emigrant carrier *New Australia*. 1950: entered service on the Australian route under Shaw, Savill & Albion management. 1958: bought by the Greek Line, modernised and renamed *Arkadia*, registered under the Greek flag (Arcadia Steamship Corporation). 1966: scrapped at Valencia.

Assimina

5,751 gross tons, single screw, quadruple expansion. Built, 1915, as the cargo ship *Kagera* for the Deutsche Ost Afrika Line by Bremer Vulkan, Vegesack. 1920: became the *Indiana* of the Cie. Générale Transatlantique. 1948: bought by the Zarati Steamship Co., Panama (J. Livanos) and renamed *Derna*; refitted as a temporary emigrant carrier and made one voyage to Australia. 1949: transferred to Cia. de Navegación Dos Oceanos (also of Panama and also a J. Livanos company), renamed *Assimina* and used mainly on the Mediterranean–River Plate route. 1952: scrapped at Blyth.

Australis

26,486 gross tons, twin screw, geared turbine, 22 knots. Built, 1940, by Newport News Shipbuilding & Drydock as the *America* for United States Lines' New York to Southampton and Le Havre service, but owing to the war she was initially used for cruising. 1941: taken over by the US Navy for use as a troopship and renamed *West Point* the following year. 1946: handed back to her owners, once again becoming the *America* and at last entering the Atlantic service for which she had been intended. 1964: sold to the Chandris company, Okeania S.A. and, after a refit, placed in the Chandris round-the-world service from Southampton to Australia. 1969: gross tonnage re-measured, now becoming 34,449. 1970: damaged by fire off Suva. 1977: laid up after her final sailing to Australia and New Zealand (she had in all carried more than a quarter of a million passengers for Chandris.) 1978: sold to the American Cruise Line which was rapidly renamed Venture Cruise Lines. Once again assuming the name *America*, she made two spectacularly unsuccessful cruises before Venture Cruise Lines collapsed and she was sold at auction to her former owners who now called her *Italis* and refitted her with a single funnel. 1979: undertook a brief season of Mediterranean cruising, but remained in lay-up for the rest of her life. 1980: sold to the Intercommerce Corporation (Panama) and renamed *Noga*. Later passed without change of name to Imro Maritime (Liberian company, managed by Gulf Oceanic Shipmanagement). 1984: renamed *Alferdoss* and bought by Silver Moon Ferries.

The *Assimina* was a freighter which Livanos employed in emigrant work for a few years after the War. *World Ship Society*

Britanis

18,254 gross tons, twin screw, geared turbine, 20 knots. Built, 1932, by the Bethlehem Shipbuilding Corpn., Quincy, Mass. as the *Monterey* for the Matson-Oceanic service from San Francisco to Sydney. 1941: taken up for trooping by the US Government. 1946: returned to her owners who at first intended to return her to service but by 1947 rising costs led to the suspension of the refitting work and she lay idle until being sold to the US Government in 1952. 1956: bought back by the Matson Line and refitted. 1957: placed in the San Francisco–Honolulu service under the name *Matsonia*. 1963: following the sale to Chandris of her sister *Lurline*, she assumed her name. 1970: bought by Ajax Navigation Corporation, a Greek-flag Chandris company, renamed *Britanis* and refitted for the Australian service. 1975: devoted entirely to cruising, latterly under the Chandris–Fantasy trade name in the American market.

The remarkable *Britanis*, built in 1932, is still operating as a very successful cruise ship.   *Steffen Weirauch collection*

Brittany

16,644 gross tons, twin screw, geared turbine, 18 knots. Built, 1952, by Chantiers et Ateliers de St. Nazaire, Penhoet as the *Bretagne* for the South American service of the Société Générale de Transports Maritimes. 1960: chartered to the Chandris group for the Australian service. 1961: bought by Chandris and registered as the *Brittany* in the name of Europe–Australia Line (Greek flag). 1963: swept by fire while repairing at Skaramanga. 1964: the remains scrapped at La Spezia.

Cairo

1,334 gross tons, single screw, triple expansion, 14 knots. Built, 1907, by Ailsa Shipbuilding, Troon as *Chieftain* for David MacBrayne, operating on the west coast of Scotland. 1919: sold to the North of Scotland & Orkney and Shetland Steam Navigation Co. and renamed *St. Margaret*. 1925: bought by Canadian National Steamship Co. and refitted as *Prince Charles*, losing her clipper bow in the process. Used on the coast of British Columbia. 1932: laid up. 1934: reactivated. 1940: sold to Union Steamships Ltd when that company took over the route on which she operated. Renamed *Camsoun*. 1945: bought by J. Livanos and registered under the Palestine flag in the name of Oriental Navigation Co. Renamed *Cairo* and

placed in a service from Marseilles to Haifa and Alexandria. 1947: transferred to Zarati Steamship Co. (still within the Livanos group, registered in Panama.) 1950: laid up. 1952: scrapped at La Spezia.

Canberra

7,710 gross tons, twin screw, quadruple expansion, 15 knots. Built, 1913, by Alexander Stephen, Glasgow for Australian Steamships Pty. Ltd. (Howard Smith). Service along the east coast of Australia. 1917: requisitioned as a troopship. 1919: handed back to her owners, re-entering service the following year. 1921: briefly laid up due to an outbreak of plague along the coast. 1925: seriously damaged by fire. It was never established whether this was due to sabotage. 1926: re-entered service. 1941: requisitioned, but remained in her regular service. 1947: the last Howard Smith passenger liner, she was sold to Singapore Chinese interests but rapidly re-sold to the Goulandris group who retained her name but registered her in the ownership of Cia. Maritima del Este (Panama). 1949: substantially refitted. 1954: sold to the Navy of the Dominican Republic and renamed *España*. 1959: scrapped.

Columbia

(see *Katoomba*).

Cyrenia

7,527 gross tons, twin screw, quadruple expansion, 17 knots. Built, 1911, by Fairfield, Glasgow as *Maunganui* for the Union Steamship Co. of New Zealand for their trans-Tasman and trans-Pacific routes. 1914: requisitioned by the New Zealand government as a troopship. 1919: handed back to her owners but not ready to return to service until 1922. 1941: taken up as a hospital ship. 1946: carried the New Zealand contingent to the Victory Celebrations in London. 1946: handed back to the Union company but sold the following year to Cia. Naviera del Atlántica (Panama) and placed in a Hellenic Mediterranean Lines service from Genoa and Piraeus to Melbourne under the name *Cyrenia*. 1952: briefly laid up. 1957: scrapped at Savona.

The *Cyrenia* ran between the Mediterranean and Australia for Hellenic Mediterranean Lines.   *World Ship Society*

Chandris liked to buy big, well-built American liners into which they could construct accommodation for large numbers of passengers. This is the *Ellinis* (ex-*Lurline*). *K. & D. Lane*

Delphi

10,822 gross tons, twin screw, diesel, 17 knots. Built, 1952, by Chantiers de la Gironde as the *Ferdinand de Lesseps* for the Mauritius service of Messageries Maritimes. 1968: bought by Constantine S. Efthymiadis and renamed *Delphi*. Refitted several times and used in Mediterranean services. 1974: thought to have been sold for scrapping in Spain but survived and emerged in 1977 as *La Perla* of Perla Cruises of Cyprus. 1980: arrested for debt at Liverpool after several troubled cruises under charter to a British company. Sold by auction to Intercruise, also of Cyprus, renamed *La Palma* and resumed Mediterranean cruising. Still in service at the time of writing.

Derna

(see *Assimina*).

Ellinis

18,564 gross tons, twin screw, geared turbines, 19½ knots. Built, 1932, as the *Lurline* by Bethlehem Shipbuilding Corporation, Quincy, Massachusetts for the Matson Navigation Co.'s San Francisco to Honolulu service. 1941: became an American troopship. 1946: returned to the Matson Line and refitted, returning to service in 1948. 1963: bought by Chandris and registered under the Greek flag in the name of Marfuerza Cia. Maritima, a Panamanian concern within the group. Now named *Ellinis*, she was placed in the round-the-world service after being extensively refitted and modernised. 1975: devoted entirely to

cruising. 1979: registered ownership transferred to Australia Line S.A., still within the Chandris group. 1980: laid up. 1986: scrapped in Taiwan.

Hellenic Prince

6,522 gross tons, twin screw, geared turbine. Built, 1928, by Cockatoo Docks & Engineering, Sydney as HMAS *Albatross*, a seaplane carrier with the Royal Australian Navy and later a repair ship with the Royal Navy. 1946: sold to the South Western Steam Navigation Co. and renamed *Pride of Torquay*. There were plans to convert her into a liner or a floating hotel but in the event she was merely used as a storage hulk. 1947: bought by China Hellenic Lines and rebuilt as an emigrant ship, *Hellenic Prince*. 1949: chartered for two years to the I.R.O. 1952: trooping for the British Ministry of Transport. 1953: laid up. 1954: scrapped at Hong Kong.

Jenny

7,914 gross tons, single screw, triple expansion. Built, 1918, by Workman Clark, Belfast as *War Argus*, a standard G-type cargo ship for the Shipping Controller (White Star Line, managers). 1919: bought by the Oceanic Steam Navigation Co. (i.e. the White Star Line) and renamed *Gallic*. 1933: bought by the Clan Line and renamed *Clan Colquhoun*. 1947: bought by Zarati Steamship Co. (J. Livanos) and renamed *Ioannis Livanos*. 1949: transferred to Dos Oceanos Cia. de Nav., another Livanos company, and renamed *Jenny* for the emigrant service. 1952: trooping for the British Ministry of Transport. 1951: sold to Djakarta Lloyd and renamed *Iman Bondjel*. 1952: further renamed *Djatinegara*. 1956: scrapped at Osaka after having to be beached while under tow.

The *Nea Hellas*, formerly of the Anchor Line, was the Greek Line's first ship. *World Ship Society*

With the German lines out of action, several companies moved in to provide cheap transatlantic passages from German ports. The *Columbia* was one of the Greek Line ships in this trade.
World Ship Society

Katoomba

8,473 gross tons, triple screw, triple expansion and low pressure turbine, 15 knots. Built, 1913, by Harland & Wolff as the *Katoomba* for McIlwraith McEacharn for the Australian coastal passenger trade. 1918: briefly taken up as a troopship. 1919: returned to her owners, entering service the following year. 1941: again requisitioned and used as a troopship by the Australian government. 1941: a short interlude of commercial service was followed by a return to trooping. 1942: commercial service again, but soon reverted to trooping. 1946: released, but quickly sold to Goulandris and registered under the Panamanian flag in the ownership of Cia. Maritima del Este. Refitted. No change of name. After one voyage for her new owners, she was chartered to the French Line for their West Indies service. 1949: returned to her owners, refitted again and, under the name, *Columbia*, placed in the Greek Line Canadian service, initially from the Mediterranean but

eventually from Bremerhaven. 1954: transferred within the Goulandris group to the Neptunia Shipping Co., still under the Panamanian flag. 1957: laid up. 1959: scrapped at Nagasaki.

Nea Hellas

16,991 gross tons, twin screw, geared turbine, 16½ knots. Built, 1922, by Fairfield, Glasgow as *Tuscania* for the Anchor Line who intended her for their North Atlantic services. In the event, Anchor found themselves with a surplus of tonnage and *Tuscania* was chartered in 1926 to the line's parent company, Cunard, for their London–New York service. 1930: laid up. 1931: reactivated and thereafter often used for trooping, cruising and seasonal voyages on the Indian route. 1939: sold to General Steam Navigation Co. of Greece, renamed *Nea Hellas* and placed in the Greek Line service from Piraeus to New York. 1941: requisitioned as a troopship by the British Ministry of War Transport and placed under the management of her former owners, Anchor Line. 1947: returned to the Greek Line. 1955: renamed *New York* and switched to the Bremerhaven–New York route. 1959: laid up. 1961: scrapped at Onomichi.

Neptunia

10,519 gross tons, twin screw, triple expansion, 15 knots. Built, 1920, by Nederlandsche Scheepsbouw,

The *Neptunia* of the Greek Line had been one of a number of Dutch vessels made redundant by political developments in the East Indies. This photograph must have been taken after 1954 as she carries a trident motif on her funnel.
World Ship Society

Amsterdam as the *Johan de Witt* for the Nederland Line's service from Amsterdam to the Dutch East Indies. 1930: laid up. 1932: reactivated. 1933: rebuilt with a new bow. 1940: taken up as a troopship under British management (Orient Line). 1945: returned to the Nederland Line. 1948: sold to the Cia Maritima del Este and renamed *Neptunia*, having been substantially rebuilt, now with only one funnel instead of two. 1949: entered Greek Line service, at first on the Piraeus–New York route, but after 1951 on the routes from Bremerhaven to Canada and to New York. 1957: struck a rock at Cobh and declared a total loss, being scrapped at Hendrik Ido Ambacht in 1958.

New York
(see *Nea Hellas*).

Patris
16,259 gross tons, twin screw, diesel, 18½ knots. Built, 1950, by Harland & Wolff, Belfast as the *Bloemfontein Castle*, a one-class vessel for the Union-Castle Line, plying between London and South and East Africa. 1959: bought by the Greek–Australian Line S.A. (Chandris group, Greek flag) and after a refit placed in a new service from the Mediterranean to Australia. Now named *Patris*. By the early 1970s mainly employed in cruising from Australian ports. 1975: used as a temporary accommodation ship after the devastation of the city of Darwin by a storm. 1976: converted into a side-loading passenger and car ferry and placed on routes between Greece and Italy. 1979: on the withdrawal of Chandris from the ferry market, sold to Michael Karageorgis and renamed *Mediterranean Island*, continuing in service between Venice and Patras. 1981: renamed *Mediterranean Star*. 1986: chartered to the Star Navigation Co. for a service from Piraeus to Alexandria which ceased after a few months. 1987: scrapped at Gadani Beach.

Patris started the Chandris brothers' regular Australian service. Comparison with the photograph in Chapter Two of her as the Union-Castle *Bloemfontein Castle* reveals little exterior change except the addition of extra lifeboats.

Queen Frederica
(see *Vasilissa Freideriki*).

Rena
1,619 gross tons, single screw, triple expansion. Built, 1906, by John Brown, Clydebank as *Woodcock* for G. & J. Burns. 1915: renamed *Woodnut*. 1920: reverted to *Woodcock*. 1923: transferred to Burns & Laird Lines, still on the services between Scotland and Ireland. 1930: renamed *Lairdswood*. 1930: bought by the Aberdeen Steam Navigation Co. and renamed *Lochnagar*. 1946: bought by Rena Cia de Naviera (Panamanian flag, managed by Panos Protopapas) and renamed *Rena*. 1948: made one voyage to South America and one to Australia. 1952: renamed *Blue Star*. 1952: scrapped at La Spezia.

Tasmania
11,672 gross tons, single screw, diesel, 17 knots. Built, 1940, by Sun Shipbuilding & Drydock, Chester, Pennsylvania. Intended as a C3 cargo ship for the Moore-McCormack Lines, to be named *Mormacland*, but taken over by the US Navy and completed as an auxiliary aircraft carrier. 1941: transferred to the Royal Navy and commissioned as HMS *Archer*. 1945: refitted as a cargo vessel, *Empire Lagan* by the Ministry of War Transport and managed by the Blue Funnel Line. 1946: returned to the US Maritime Commission, later being sold to the Salén group. 1949: entered service as the emigrant ship *Anna Salén*. 1955: sold to the Yannoulatos group for their Hellenic Mediterranean Lines service to Australia and named *Tasmania* (Cia. Naviera Tasmania). 1961: sold to China Union Lines and renamed *Union Reliance*. 1961: collided with a tanker and caught fire. 1962: scrapped at New Orleans.

Vasilissa Freideriki
16,435 gross tons, twin screw, geared turbine, 21 knots. Built, 1927, by William Cramp, Philadelphia as *Malolo* for the Matson Navigation Co.'s service from San Francisco to Honolulu. 1927: involved in a collision with a Norwegian ship after which she was very nearly lost. 1937: modernised and renamed *Matsonia*. 1942: became a US Navy transport. 1946: returned to the Matson Line and restored to the Honolulu service. 1948: bought by Panamanian Lines and later transferred to Mediterranean Lines; and as the *Atlantic* placed in the Home Lines service between Genoa and New York. 1953: transferred to Home Lines Inc., continuing in her Southampton–Canada service. 1954: transferred to the Greek register and renamed *Vasilissa Freideriki* (alternatively known as *Queen Frederica*). Now owned by a new Home Lines subsidiary, National Hellenic American Line and placed in service between Piraeus and other Mediterranean ports and New York. 1965: National Hellenic American Line and its ship sold to the Chandris group who kept the *Vasilissa Freideriki* on the New York run until 1967, although she also made some Australian voyages. Her gross tonnage was now 16,435 as against 21,329 previously. 1968: chartered to Sovereign Cruises for Mediterranean fly-cruises. 1971: laid up. 1973: reactivated for cruises on Chandris's own account. Laid up again at the end of the summer season. Mechanical problems prevented her undertaking a further programme the following year. 1977: scrapping commenced at Elefsis. 1978: the remains of the ship were gutted by fire.

Chapter Nine
The American Contingent

In all fairness, this book should really have started with the American ships. Overwhelmingly, the Americans were making the largest contribution to repairing the ravages of the War and to setting up the organisations which, it was hoped, would provide the world with a better social, economic and political climate. The Marshall Plan and the American contributions to the United Nations were examples of their generous involvement. The International Refugee Organisation was another body which relied heavily on American finance and participation. The United States provided over half its operating funds. America also took in a good proportion of the people the I.R.O. was trying to place. In his book on the refugee problems of twentieth century Europe,[1] Michael R. Marrus reminds his readers that of the 1,039,150 people resettled by the I.R.O. between 1947 and 1951 329,000 were accepted into the United States. (Other figures were Australia: 182,000; Israel: 132,000; Canada: 123,000; Western Europe: 70,000, over half of whom came to Great Britain.)

America was also the main provider of the fleet of ships which carried those members of this vast group of migrants whom the I.R.O. was settling outside Europe. Some indication of the extent to which American troopships were employed in this work has already been given in Chapter One. However, a little more detail should perhaps be provided. In July 1947, the I.R.O. took over from the Inter-Governmental Committee on Refugees the charter of three US Army troopships which, it was stated, were the only passenger vessels then available. By early 1949, the I.R.O. fleet had grown to thirty three. Just how great was the American government's contribution by then can be seen from the following lists of the ships which the I.R.O. had arranged to employ in the year to July 1950:-

US Transports

General C.H. Muir	General W.M. Black
General C.C. Ballou	General S.D. Sturgis
General Harry Taylor	General Stuart Heintzelman
General Le Roy Eltinge	General M.B. Stewart
General R.L. Howze	General W.G. Langfitt
General J.H. McRae	General M.L. Hersey
General W.G. Haan	General Omar Bundy
General A.W. Greely	General R.M. Blatchford
Willard A. Holbrook	Mercy (hospital ship)
Marine Jumper	Marine Marlin

Commercial Charters

Svalbard (Norwegian Government)
Charlton Sovereign (Charlton Steam Shipping Co.)
Castelbianco (Sitmar)
Wooster Victory (Sitmar)
Mozaffari (Mogul Line)
Protea (Cia. de Operaziones Maritimas)

Block Space taken in
Nea Hellas (Greek Line)
Sobieski (Gdynia-America Line)
Samaria (Cunard-White Star Line)
Scythia (Cunard-White Star Line)
Volendam (Holland-America Line)
Olimpia (Flotta Lauro)
Istanbul (Turkish Maritime Lines)

In the event, other commercial vessels were also employed during this period and it is believed that at its peak, in late 1949, the total fleet amounted to 39 ships. In March 1950, however, it was reported that the number was being reduced to 29 as a result of a reduction in the admissions into the United States and Australia. There were two main routes. One was from Bremerhaven to New York (although the American troopships made some voyages to Boston or New Orleans and vessels frequently called at Halifax en route). The second was from Naples to Australia. On this route voyages took anything between 24 and 28 days. At least seven of the American ships returned via Batavia during the Dutch evacuation from the East Indies. There were also some sailings from Naples to South America.

American Troopships

With the exception of the Mercy and the Willard A. Holbrook, all the American vessels were members of the C4 class. This was one of the standard types which the authorities had ordered in large numbers in the period immediately before and during America's involvement in the Second World War. There were several variants of the C4 design, including cargo vessels, troop transports and hospital ships. Their configuration was almost tanker-like, the engines being situated aft. The troopships could in some cases carry between 3,000 and 3,500 men, mainly within the hulls. This was an astonishing capacity for ships which were rated at about 12,600 gross tons. Naturally, their long decks were lined with large numbers of life-boats and rafts. The majority of the C4 class was built in the West Coast yards which had been specially set up by Henry J. Kaiser, a civil engineering magnate, to assemble standard ships, literally by the hundred.

Those vessels named after various Generals – and it is astonishing how many there apparently were in the American forces at the time – belonged to the US Army, although they had originally been built for the Navy. Those with names beginning with Marine .... belonged to the War Shipping Administration, and later the US Maritime Commission.

The other two Americans named in the I.R.O. list were also products of US Government standard ship programmes, although one was of an earlier generation. The Willard A. Holbrook (1921/12,562 gross tons) was a 535-type which had spent the pre-war years in trans-Pacific

1   Unwanted: European Refugees in the Twentieth Century by Michael R. Marrus (Oxford University Press, 1985).

service as the passenger vessel *President Taft*, mainly for the Dollar Line. She was a near-sister to the Ybarra Line's *Cabo de Hornos* and *Cabo de Buena Esperanza* (see Chapter Six). The *Mercy* (1943/6,750 gross tons) was a hospital ship variant of the C1 class, smaller than the C4s and with her machinery in a conventional mid-ships position.

Other troopships may have made I.R.O. voyages, including the *General Alex M. Patch* and the *General Maurice Rose*. Certainly both those vessels were shuttling between Bremerhaven and New York in late 1949 but they may, of course, have been carrying military personnel only. They were P2-type turbo-electric vessels of about 17,100 gross tons. Each had accommodation for no less than 4,680 troops. It has been stated that on 250 voyages between 1949 and 1952 US transports carried 271,717 passengers to New York and Boston. There were also many voyages to other parts of the world.

The American authorities also made some of their troopships available to commercial liner companies for use as stop-gaps until more conventional passenger ships became available. The American President, Matson and New York & Porto Rico lines placed these vessels in services which could hardly be described as emigrant-carriers but three other companies used them on routes where many of the passengers must have fallen into that category. In these services the passenger capacity of the C4 vessels was usually limited to about 900, but still mainly in dormitories. American Scantic Line (an off-shoot of Moore McCormack) ran the *Marine Perch*, *Marine Jumper* and *Ernie Pyle* from New York to Scandinavia and the Baltic between 1946 and 1948. Many of their voyages called at Bremen and were run on joint account with United States Lines; some extended as far east as Gdynia. These three ships also made voyages for United States Lines alone on the routes from New York to Bremen and to Southampton and Le Havre, as did the *Marine Flasher*, *Marine Marlin*, *Marine Falcon*, *Marine Tiger*, *Marine Shark* and *Marine Swallow*. They had all finished their United States Lines service by 1949. Although the pre-war American Export Lines service from New York to the Mediterranean had almost exclusively carried first-class travellers, this concern operated a number of troopships in a very basic passenger service between 1946 and 1949. The vessels involved at various times were the *Marine Shark*, *Marine Carp*, *Marine Flasher*, *Marine Perch* and *Marine Jumper*. In addition, the *Vulcania* made several austerity voyages for American Export Lines before being handed back to the Italians in 1946.

Once the C4 ships had been returned to the US Maritime Commission, the established American lines did not specifically participate in the emigrant trades from Europe to any great extent. One vessel should, however, be included in this survey. The *Washington* (1933/23,626 gross tons) was one of a pair of large liners which had been built for United States Lines in the early 'thirties. In view of the economic and social climate of the times they had been fitted out as cabin-class ships and they did not purport to be fast luxury liners. They were nevertheless very popular on the Atlantic, particularly with American travellers. After the war, only one of the duo returned to civilian service. At least one of the *Washington*'s early post-war voyages was specifically dedicated to carrying war brides and their children, as with similar voyages by the *Queen Mary* and *Aquitania* (see Chapter Two). In her later post-war form the *Washington* could accommodate 1,106 one-class passengers, of whom many slept in communal cabins for up to twelve people. From 1949 onwards her route was extended eastwards from the Channel ports to Hamburg. In late 1951 United States Lines returned her to the US Maritime Commission, from whom they had been chartering her, and for the next fourteen years she languished as part of her country's Reserve Fleet.

Arnold Bernstein

Although he was responsible for only six voyages which fall within the scope of this book, Arnold Bernstein deserves mention – if only for his remarkable persistence. It is worth digressing to outline the history of his various ventures. Of German-Jewish origin, he emerged as a shipowner in Hamburg after the First World War. He amassed a fleet of small cargo ships and was also connected with a company called the Deutsche-Russische Transithandelsgesellschaft which presumably operated within the Baltic. Already he may have been involved in carrying motor vehicles – two of his ships were called *Tractor* and *Fordtransport IV*. By the late 'twenties he had several larger, though elderly, vessels which were operating a transatlantic cargo service, particularly carrying American cars to the European market. Passenger accommodation was added to three of these ships a few years later and they maintained a regular service between Antwerp and New York.

In 1935 he made his most ambitious move, buying the historic but failing Red Star Line from the International Mercantile Marine group. In this he had the financial backing of the Chemical Bank of New York. Now German-registered, the two remaining Red Star liners continued on the Antwerp–New York route. The venture may not have been successful – certainly, during the legal wrangles in which Bernstein was involved after the War, Chemical Bank claimed that by 1937 the Red Star Line was bankrupt. In that year Bernstein was imprisoned by the Nazis for alleged currency offences, his shipping assets being seized and eventually sold off.

Fortunately he was released before the War started and was able to reach New York. He became an American citizen and formed the Arnold Bernstein Shipping Company. It is not easy to disentangle his subsequent operations. In particular, it is unclear in some cases whether Bernstein was merely acting as general agent for some passenger shipping ventures or whether he had at least a partial financial stake in them. He was also involved with various cargo vessels, at least one of which, the *Orbis*, he owned.

Possibly the first venture with which he was connected after he had settled in America was a short-lived Panamanian concern, Cia. Trasatlántica Centro-Americana. In 1940 this company had two ships, one of which was an elderly passenger vessel called *Panamanian*. She was a sister of the much-travelled *Santa Cruz* which later ran for Italia on the South American run (see Chapter Four). *Panamanian* sank in Baltimore harbour shortly before she was due to make her first Atlantic crossing for the new company. She was salvaged and sold to Far Eastern owners but not before she had been arrested for debt. Thereafter Trasatlántica Centro-Americana disappears from the lists of shipowners.

The resilient Bernstein bounced back. After the War he fought long battles on two fronts. He went through the courts trying to obtain compensation for his lost German assets. Among the concerns he attempted to sue in America were the Holland–America Line and a firm of Belgian shipbreakers both of whom had bought former Bernstein vessels from the Nazi authorities. (He claimed $11 million from Holland–America but after nine years settled for a fraction of this sum.) While he was engaged in this struggle, he was also seeking a government subsidy for an American-flag passenger-cargo service on his old New York–Antwerp route. Perhaps to prove his point – his application was being heard at the time – the Arnold Bernstein Shipping Company chartered a ship for four voyages on the route in 1948. The *Continental* (1902/10,005 gross tons) was another superannuated ex-American. She had one claim to fame – as the Panama Railroad Company's *Ancon* she had officially opened the Panama Canal in 1914. Now owned by a San Francisco company, but flying the Panamanian flag, she could carry 350 passengers in a single class and her voyages for Bernstein may well qualify her for inclusion in the ranks of emigrant-carriers. Her other post-War activities are documented in Chapter Ten.

While still battling for his subsidised service, Bernstein was also involved in an attempt to establish a Panamanian-flag transatlantic line in 1950-51. This was maintained for two seasons (again between Antwerp and New York, with a call at Plymouth) by the *Europa*. She was a former P&O and New Zealand Shipping Co. vessel belonging to the Incres Line, which also owned some cargo ships. Some sources suggest that Bernstein was the founder of the company; others maintain that his connection was purely as general agent through the Arnold Bernstein Shipping Company. Lloyd's List announced the new service as the Bernstein Line but it seems to have been generally known by the Incres name[1]. In any case, it was not successful. On one voyage the *Europa* is said to have carried just a single passenger. After two seasons the service was abandoned, the connection with Bernstein ceased and Incres converted the *Europa* into a very successful cruise liner, the *Nassau*.

Perhaps the most significant of the Incres transatlantic sailings were two made to Canada in 1951 by a vessel called the *Protea* (1920/8,929 gross tons) which they had chartered. These voyages may be regarded as the forerunners of the Arosa Line service – within a few months the *Protea* had become the *Arosa Kulm* and was sailing under the Arosa Line name between Bremerhaven and the Canadian ports. (This apparently insignificant vessel figured quite prominently as a migrant transport in the post-war period and her career is detailed in the sections on the Home Lines and the Arosa Line in Chapter Five.) With her dormitory accommodation she was very much an emigrant ship.

It had originally been intended that the Incres/Bernstein service to New York from Antwerp and Plymouth should be maintained by two ships, with the *Europa* being joined by a curious vessel based on a converted British tank landing ship. Belonging to a Swiss owner but soon transferred to a Panamanian company, she did not in the event run in the Atlantic service (for which she was almost certainly ill-suited.) Instead she became the *Silverstar* and, painted in a silver livery, was used for some years on cruises from American ports with Bernstein's company as general agents.

At last, in 1958, Bernstein's plan for a subsidised service from New York to the Low Countries came to fruition when the *Atlantic*, an extensively converted Mariner-class freighter, made the first sailing of the new American Banner Line from New York to Zeebrugge and Amsterdam, competing head-on with the Holland–America Line. Bernstein thus abandoned his long connection with Antwerp which, truth to tell, had not been a greatly successful transatlantic port in the past half-century. In one respect Bernstein remained faithful to the methods of his early days. Although the *Atlantic*'s space was almost entirely devoted to good accommodation for tourist class passengers, she could also carry a limited number of automobiles. Sad to say, the new line was not successful and after two seasons it was closed. By now Bernstein was about seventy and he finally retired after a career marked by an extraordinary capacity to rally after adversity.

FLEET LIST

Continental

10,005 gross tons, twin screw, triple expansion, 13 knots. Built, 1902, by the Maryland Steel Co., Sparrow's Point, Maryland as *Shawmut* for the Boston Steamship Co. 1909: bought by the Panama Railroad Co. and renamed *Ancon*, still American-registered. Refitted with passenger accommodation. 1940: bought by the Permanente Steamship Co., a concern connected with Henry J. Kaiser, and renamed *Permanente*. 1941: taken over as a transport by the US Army. 1946: bought by the Tidewater Commercial Co. Inc. of San Francisco, but registered in Panama under the name *Tidewater*. 1948: chartered to the Arnold Bernstein Shipping Co. Inc. for Atlantic service under the name *Continental*. 1948: returned to her owners but retained the name *Continental*. 1950: scrapped at Genoa.

Ernie Pyle

12,420 gross tons, single screw, geared turbine, 17 knots. Built, 1945, by Kaiser Company, Vancouver, Washington as a C4-S-A3-type troop transport for the War Shipping Administration. 1946: chartered to the United States Lines for Atlantic passenger service. 1947: made some joint United States Lines – American Scantic sailings. 1949: charter to United States Lines ended and the vessel was placed in the US Maritime Commission Reserve Fleet and laid up. 1965: sold to Central Gulf Steamship Co. and rebuilt as the cargo ship *Green Lake*. 1978: broken up at Kaohsiung.

General A.W. Greely

12,665 gross tons, single screw, geared turbine, 17 knots. Built, 1945, by Kaiser Company, Richmond, Cali-

---

1   Said to be an anagram of Scerni, an Italian shipping agency.

fornia as a C4-S-A1 transport for the US Navy. 1946: passed to the US Army and refitted to their specifications. Later chartered to the I.R.O. 1950: transferred back to the US Navy. 1959: transferred to Marad (the Maritime Administration) and laid up. 1969: sold to Pacific Far East Line and converted into the container ship *Hawaii Bear*. 1975: bought by Farrell Lines and renamed *Austral Glade*. 1979: renamed *Pacific Enterprise*. 1982: bought by Vanessa Trading Co. and renamed *Caribe Enterprise*. 1983: scrapped.

General C.C. Ballou

12,666 gross tons, single screw, geared turbine, 17 knots. Built, 1945, by Kaiser Company, Richmond, California as a C4-S-A1 transport for the US Navy. 1946: transferred to the US Army and refitted. Used for I.R.O. service. 1950: returned to the US Navy. 1954: laid up. 1960: transferred to Marad, still laid up. 1968: sold to Sea-Land Service and converted into a container vessel, *Brooklyn*. 1975: sold to the Puerto Rico Maritime Shipping Authority and became their *Humacao*. 1981: sold to Eastern Star Maritime and renamed *Eastern Light*. 1981: scrapped at Kaohsiung.

General C.H. Muir

13,000 gross tons, single screw, geared turbine, 17 knots. Built, 1945, by Kaiser Company, Richmond, California as a C4-S-A1 transport for the US Navy. 1946: handed over to the US Army and refitted. Chartered for a period to the I.R.O. 1960: transferred to the Marad Reserve and laid up. 1968: sold to Sea-Land Services and renamed *Chicago* after conversion to a container ship. 1975: sold to Puerto Rico and renamed *San Juan*.

General Harry Taylor

12,544 gross tons, single screw, geared turbine, 17 knots. Built, 1944, by Kaiser Company, Richmond, California as a US Navy transport (type C4-S-A1). 1946: transferred to the US Army and modified. Later allotted to I.R.O. service. 1950: handed back to the Navy. 1958: laid up in the Marad Reserve Fleet. 1963: converted to the missile-tracking vessel *General Hoyt S. Vandenberg*.

The *General Harry Taylor* was one of the type-C4 transports which the US Army made available to the I.R.O. Her troop-decks could accommodate as many as 3,000 people.

General Le Roy Eltinge

13,100 gross tons, single screw, geared turbine, 17 knots. Built, 1945, by Kaiser Company, Richmond, California for the US Navy (C4-S-A1 class). 1946: converted into an Army troopship. Used by the I.R.O. 1950: taken over by the US Navy. 1968: placed in the Marad Reserve. 1969: sold to the Waterman group and converted into the container ship *Robert E. Lee*. 1973: renamed *Robert Toombs*. 1980: scrapped at Kaohsiung.

General J.H. McRae

12,496 gross tons, single screw, geared turbine, 17 knots. Built, 1944, by Kaiser Company, Richmond, California as a US Navy transport (C4-S-A1). 1946: converted to a US Army troopship. Later chartered to the I.R.O. 1950: transferred back to the US Navy. 1960: laid up in the Marad Reserve Fleet. 1968: sold to Hudson Waterways and rebuilt as a container ship, *Transhawaii*. 1975: sold to the Puerto Rico Maritime Shipping Authority and renamed *Aguadilla*. 1982: sold to the Merchant Terminal Corporation and renamed *Amoco Voyager*.

General M.B. Stewart

12,521 gross tons, single screw, geared turbine, 17 knots. Built, 1945, for the US Navy as a transport by Kaiser Company, Richmond, California (C4-S-A1 type). 1946: handed over to the US Army and refitted as a troopship. Later used for an I.R.O. charter. 1950: returned to the Navy. 1958: laid up in the Maritime Administration reserve fleet. 1967: bought by Albany River Transport and rebuilt as the cargo vessel *Albany*. 1974: converted to the drilling ship *Mission Viking* for Mission Drilling & Exploration. 1981: sold to Manufacturers Hanover Leasing.

General M.L. Hersey

12,326 gross tons, single screw, geared turbine, 17 knots. Built, 1944, by Kaiser Company, Richmond, California as the US Navy transport *General Mark L. Hersey* of the C4-S-A1 class. 1946: transferred to the US Army, renamed as above and refitted for service as a troopship. Later made I.R.O. voyages. 1950: returned to the US Navy. 1951: collided with the Argentinian passenger liner *Maipu* which sank. 1954: laid up. 1959: transferred to the Marad Reserve Fleet. 1968: sold to Sea Land Service, lengthened and rebuilt as a container ship initially called *Pittsburgh* but in 1969 further renamed *St. Louis*. 1988: scrapped, Kaohsiung.

General Omar Bundy

12,544 gross tons, single screw, geared turbine, 17 knots. Built, 1944, by Kaiser Company, Richmond, California as a C4-S-A1 transport for the US Navy. 1946: transferred to the US Army and refitted as a troopship. Made some voyages for the I.R.O. 1949: laid up. 1964: sold to Bethlehem Steel and rebuilt as the cargo vessel *Portmar* for their subsidiary Calmar Steamship Co. 1976: sold to Adbury Steamship Co. and renamed *Port*. 1979: sold to Hawaiian Eugenia Corpn. and renamed *Poet*. 1980: lost without trace.

General R.L. Howze

12,544 gross tons, single screw, geared turbine, 17 knots. Built, 1944, by Kaiser Company, Richmond,

The *General C.C. Ballou*, one of the type-C4 transports built in Henry Kaiser's mass-production shipyards on the West Coast.

California as the US Navy transport *General Robert L. Howze* of the C4-S-A1 type. 1946: renamed *General R.L. Howze* on transfer to the US Army and refitted as a troopship. Subsequently used on charter to the I.R.O. 1950: transferred back to the Navy. 1958: laid up in the Marad Reserve Fleet. 1968: bought by Pacific Far East line and rebuilt as the container ship *Guam Bear*. 1975: renamed *New Zealand Bear*. 1976: bought by Farrell Lines after the collapse of Pacific Far East and renamed *Austral Glade*. 1979: renamed *Pacific Endeavor*. 1981: broken up at Gadani Beach.

General R.M. Blatchford

13,100 gross tons, single screw, geared turbine, 17 knots. Built, 1944, by Kaiser Company, Richmond, California as a transport for the US Navy (C4-S-A1 class). 1946: converted to a troopship for the US Army. Later chartered to the I.R.O. 1950: returned to the Navy. 1968: laid up in the Maritime Administration Reserve Fleet. 1969: sold to Waterman Carriers and rebuilt as a container ship, *Stonewall Jackson*. 1974: renamed *Alex Stephens*. 1980: scrapped at Kaohsiung.

General S.D. Sturgis

12,349 gross tons, single screw, geared turbine, 17 knots. Built, 1944, by Kaiser Company, Richmond, California as the C4-S-A1 type transport *General Samuel D. Sturgis* for the US Navy. 1946: taken over by the US Army, refitted as a troopship and renamed as above. Later chartered to the I.R.O. 1950: returned to the US Navy. 1958: laid up in the Marad Reserve Fleet. 1967: sold to Central Gulf Steamship, rebuilt as a cargo ship and renamed *Green Port*. 1980: scrapped at Kaohsiung.

General Stuart Heintzelman

12,666 gross tons, single screw, geared turbine, 17 knots. Built 1945, the last of the C4-S-A1 transports for the US Navy, by Kaiser Company, Richmond, California. 1946: transferred to the US Army and converted into a troopship. For some time used on charter by the I.R.O. 1950: reverted to the US Navy. 1954: laid up. 1959: transferred to the Marad Reserve Fleet, still laid up. 1968: converted to the container ship *Mobile* of Sea Land Services. 1984: scrapped at Inchion.

General W.G. Haan

12,511 gross tons, single screw, geared turbine, 17 knots. Built, 1945, as a C4-S-A1 transport for the US Navy by Kaiser Company, Richmond, California. 1946: transferred to the US Army and refitted for trooping. Used by the I.R.O. for a period. 1950: returned to the US Navy. 1958: laid up in the Marad Reserve Fleet. 1968: sold to Hudson Waterways, lengthened and converted into the container ship *Transoregon*. 1975: sold to the Puerto Rico Maritime Shipping Authority and renamed *Mayaguez*. 1982: sold to Merchant Terminal and renamed *Amoco Trader*. 1985: laid up.

General W.G. Langfitt

12,544 gross tons, single screw, geared turbine, 17 knots. Built, 1944, by Kaiser Company, Richmond, California for the US Navy as a C4-S-A1 class transport. 1946: passed to the US Army and refitted as a troopship. Chartered to the I.R.O. for some time. 1950: returned to the Navy. 1958: laid up as part of the Marad Reserve Fleet. 1968: sold to Hudson Waterways and converted to a container ship, the process involving lengthening her. Renamed *Transindiana*. 1978: laid up. 1983: scrapped at Brownsville.

General W.M. Black

12,551 gross tons, single screw, geared turbine, 17 knots. Built, 1944, by Kaiser Company, Richmond, California as the C4-S-A1 transport *General William M. Black* for the US Navy. 1946: transferred to the US Army and refitted as the troopship *General W.M. Black*. Chartered later to the I.R.O. 1950: returned to the US Navy. 1956: laid up in the Marad Reserve Fleet. 1967: sold to Central Gulf Steamship who converted her into a cargo vessel and named her *Green Forest*. 1980: scrapped at Kaohsiung.

Marine Carp

12,420 gross tons, single screw, geared turbine, 17knots. Built, 1945, by Kaiser Company, Vancouver, Washington as a C4-S-A3 transport for the War Shipping Administration. 1946: chartered to American Export Lines for service between New York and the Mediterranean. 1949: handed over to the US Maritime Commission and laid up. 1952: passed to the US Navy for use as a transport. 1958: joined the Marad fleet of laid up vessels. 1967: sold to Central Gulf Steamship and converted into the cargo vessel *Green Springs*. 1979: scrapped at Kaohsiung.

Marine Falcon

12,420 gross tons, single screw, geared turbine, 17 knots. Built, 1945, by Kaiser Company, Vancouver, Washington as a War Shipping Administration C4-S-A3 transport. 1947: chartered to United States Lines. 1949: returned to the Government (US Maritime Commission) and laid up. 1966: sold to Litton Industries who had her lengthened and converted into the container ship *Trenton*. 1975: sold to Puerto Rico Maritime Shipping Authority and renamed *Borinquen*.

Marine Flasher

12,420 gross tons, single screw, geared turbine, 17 knots. Built, 1945, by Kaiser Company, Vancouver, Washington as a C4-S-A3 troop transport for the War Shipping Administration. 1946: chartered to United States Lines and later, briefly, to American Export Lines. 1949: handed back to the US Maritime Commission and laid up. 1966: sold to Litton Industries and lengthened during conversion into the container vessel *Long Beach*. 1975: sold to Reynolds Leasing. 1988: grounded at San Juan, becoming a Constructive Total Loss.

Marine Jumper

12,420 gross tons, single screw, geared turbine, 17 knots. Built, 1945, by Kaiser Company, Vancouver, Washington as a W.S.A. transport (C4-S-A3 class). 1947: chartered to United States, American Scantic and American Export Lines severally until 1949 when she was chartered to the I.R.O. 1949: laid up by the US Maritime Commission. 1966: sold to Litton Industries, lengthened and converted into the container ship *Panama*. 1975: sold to Reynolds Leasing.

Marine Marlin

12,420 gross tons, single screw, geared turbine, 17 knots. Built, 1945, by Kaiser Company, Vancouver, Washington as a C4-S-A3 type transport for the W.S.A.

1946: chartered to United States Lines for their New York to Bremen service. 1949: charter ended and she was then briefly used for I.R.O. voyages before being laid up. 1965: sold to Central Gulf Steamship Corporation, converted into a cargo vessel and renamed *Green Bay*. 1971: sank after an underwater explosion attributed to the Vietcong while in a Vietnamese port. Salvaged but sold for scrapping at Hong Kong.

Marine Perch

12,410 gross tons, single screw, geared turbine, 17 knots. Built, 1945, by Kaiser Company, Richmond, California as a C4-S-A3 transport for the War Shipping Administration. 1946: chartered to American Scantic, later to American Scantic and United States Lines jointly and then to American Export. 1948: laid up by the US Maritime Commission. 1965: sold to Rio Grande Transport and converted to the bulk-carrier *Yellowstone*. 1978: sunk in a collision.

Marine Shark

12,420 gross tons, single screw, geared turbine, 17 knots. Built, 1945, by Kaiser Company, Vancouver, Washington for the W.S.A. (C4-S-A3 transport). 1946: chartered to American Export Lines and later to United States Lines. 1949: handed back to the US Maritime Commission and laid up. 1967: sold to Litton Industries and rebuilt as the container vessel *Charleston*.

Marine Swallow

12,410 gross tons, single screw, geared turbine, 17 knots. Built, 1945, by Kaiser Company, Richmond, California as a War Shipping Administration troop transport of the C4-S-A3 class. 1946: laid up. 1948: briefly chartered to United States Lines for their New York to Bremen service, then laid up again. 1965: sold to Meadowbrook Transport and converted into the bulker *Missouri*. 1974: became the Panamanian-registered *Ogden Missouri*. 1977: became the *Linnet*, still Panamanian-flagged. 1978: scrapped at Kaohsiung.

Marine Tiger

12,420 gross tons, single screw, geared turbine, 17 knots. Built, 1945, by Kaiser Company, Vancouver, Washington for the War Shipping Administration as a C4-S-A3 transport. 1947: chartered to United States Lines. 1949: handed over to the US Maritime Commission and laid up. 1966: sold to Litton Industries, lengthened and converted into the container ship *Oakland*. 1988: sold for breaking up but wrecked off Vietnam.

Mercy

6,750 gross tons, single screw, geared turbine, 14 knots. Laid down by Consolidated Steel, Wilmington, California and completed, 1943, by the Los Angeles Shipbuilding & Dry Dock Co. as a US Navy hospital ship (Class C1-B). 1946: transferred to the US Army. 1949: transferred to the US Maritime Commission. 1956: became the *Empire State III* (State University of New York Maritime College). 1960: transferred to Marad and laid up. 1971: scrapped at Valencia.

Protea

8,929 gross tons, single screw, geared turbine, 15 knots. Built, 1920, as the US Army transport *Cantigny* by American International Shipbuilding Corporation, Hog Island, Pennsylvania. 1924: allotted to the American Merchant Line and renamed *American Banker*. At this stage in her career she was largely a cargo vessel but over the years her passenger accommodation was extended several times. 1929: ownership of the American Merchant Line and of United States Lines transferred to P.W. Chapman & Co. 1931: US Shipping Board foreclosed on the Chapman company and the two lines were transferred to a new concern, United States Lines Co. of Nevada, controlled by the International Mercantile Marine group. 1940: switched to a Belgian affiliate, Société Maritime Anversoise and renamed *Ville D'Anvers*. 1945: reverted to United States Lines but in 1946 sold to Isbrandtsen Line. 1946: bought by Cia. de Vapores Mediterránea and later Sociedad de Navegación Trasatlántica. Renamed *City of Athens* and placed in a service between the Mediterranean and New York. 1947: auctioned to meet her owners' debts, becoming the *Protea* of Panamanian Lines, one of the constituent firms of Home Lines, who refitted her as an emigrant-carrier. 1948: chartered to the I.R.O. 1949: sold to Cia. de Operaziones Maritimas, still on her I.R.O. charter. 1951: sold to Cia Internacional Transportadora. 1951: chartered to Incres Line for two voyages from Le Havre to Canada. 1952: opened the Arosa Line service from Bremer haven to Canada under the name *Arosa Kulm*. c.1957: transferred to Arosa Line Inc. 1958: arrested for debt. 1959: scrapped at Bruges.

Washington

23,626 gross tons, twin screw, geared turbine, 20 knots. Built, 1933, for United States Lines' New York–Hamburg service by New York Shipbuilding, Camden, New Jersey. 1940: owing to the provisions of America's Neutrality Act, she was no longer able to run to combatant countries and was accordingly switched to a New York–Genoa service and subsequently to the New York–San Francisco route. 1941: taken up as the troop transport *Mount Vernon*. 1942: sold to the US Maritime Commission, continuing as a trooper. 1945: resumed her old name of *Washington*. 1946: returned to United States Lines under charter and used initially on austerity voyages from New York to Southampton. 1948: refitted and, from 1949, resumed sailings on the New York–Hamburg route. 1951: laid up at the end of the charter. 1965: scrapped at Kearny, New Jersey.

Willard A. Holbrook

12,562 gross tons, twin screw, geared turbine, 17 knots. Built, 1921, by Bethlehem Shipbuilding Corpn., Sparrow's Point, Maryland for the US Shipping Board as the *Buckeye State*. Allotted to the Pacific Mail Line for their service from San Francisco to the Far East. 1922: renamed *President Taft*. 1925: bought by the Dollar Line and retained on the Far East run. 1938: on the failure of the Dollar Line, was taken over by the American President Line. 1941: taken over as a US Army transport, *Willard A. Holbrook*. 1943: refit as a hospital ship commenced but not completed. 1947: transferred to the US Maritime Commission. 1952: scrapped.

The P2-type turbo-electric troopship *General Maurice Rose* may have carried refugees from Bremerhaven to New York in 1949.
Steffen Weirauch collection

Chapter Ten
Zionists, Israelis and Others

There were many Jews requiring resettlement after the war. Not only were there the battered survivors of the Holocaust but there were also many refugees from the countries of what was becoming the Eastern bloc. In Poland, for instance, there was a brutally anti-Semitic climate and many Jews found it advisable to leave – and indeed were encouraged to do so. Some were eventually settled by the I.R.O. and other agencies, often being carried by the ships described in earlier chapters. Large numbers were sent to the new state of Israel after its formation in 1948.

Before the foundation of Israel, however, the Zionist movement was already organising a clandestine migration to what was then Palestine. Thousands of Jews were secretly helped to make their way to camps near the French and Italian coasts. From there they were to embark for the Jewish Homeland. The ships into which they were crammed were a tatterdemalion lot – old, tiny, vastly overcrowded and quite lacking in facilities for such large numbers of passengers. As a result they were often utterly filthy and insanitary by the time they reached their destination. They belonged to shadowy owners, often acting as fronts for the Haganah (the Palestinian Jewish military organisation) and its offshoot the Mossad Le'Aliya Bet. The crews often contained many American Zionist sympathisers or exiled Spanish Republicans. In order to reach Palestine the ships had to run the naval blockade by which Britain, as the Mandatory Power, sought to prevent illegal immigration. For the British sailors involved in the patrol, it was a hazardous and extremely unpleasant duty. There were many dramatic skirmishes which usually ended with the arrest of the Zionist ships. Some of them lay at Haifa for many months, abandoned and rusting. After 1946 the passengers of the arrested vessels were deported, usually to Cyprus where they remained discontentedly in camps, awaiting their turn in the very limited quota of legal immigration. It was reported that up to March 1947 the Royal Navy had intercepted 78 ships carrying some 70,000 illegal immigrants. A further 21 vessels were known to have eluded the blockade. In the next twelve months 40 ships

An atmospheric shot of the *Kedmah*. This small British-owned liner flew the Palestine flag and then, after 1948, the Israeli during her years on charter to Zim Israel.
Zim Israel Navigation

An incredible view of illegal migrants in the hold of a Zionist ship.   *Author's collection*

The *Exodus* sustained damage during her capture by the Royal Navy. Here some of her passengers demonstrate while under armed guard..   *Author's collection*

were intercepted and it was thought that only four had got through.

The Haganah operation was extremely complex and expensive. It is thought to have been largely financed by overseas supporters, largely in America. Their ships were usually given Hebrew names, although still officially registered in other names under flags of convenience. They usually displayed the legend 'Haganah Ship' prominently once they were intercepted. Initially most of the vessels on this illegal run were very small – often no more than fishing boats or caiques. Others were aged steamers bought for one last voyage. Later, rather larger vessels were sometimes used. Some were lost owing to their decrepit and over-crowded condition. One is thought to have been sunk by a Russian submarine.

The Panamanian-flag *Anal* (1877/253 gross tons) mader her one dash for the Palestinian coast in May 1947 under the pseudonym *Yehuda Halevy*. She was a tiny but notable vessel. As the *Earl of Zetland* she had served the Shetlands for nearly seventy years. Then in 1946 she was bought by a Mr. 'Fatty' Pandelis and was next heard of as an illegal Jewish immigrant ship. Her old hull was constructed of iron, a fact which may have stood her in good stead in the clashes which some sources suggest took place at the end of that final voyage. (Other sources claim that she surrendered without resistance.) After her arrest she was left to rot at Haifa – a sad end to a stout little ship.

Without doubt, though, the most famous of the Zionist ships was the *Exodus 1947*, sometimes known simply as *Exodus* and officially registered as the *President Warfield* (1928/1,814 gross tons).[1] She was a former overnight liner on the American coast. After war service (which involved, among other exploits, a hazardous crossing of the Atlantic for which she and her similar companions were utterly unsuited) she was sold for scrap. She re-emerged, however, as a Zionist blockade runner, sailing from Sète in 1947 with an incredible 4,500 passengers. Her interception and arrest took place in a glare of worldwide publicity, which was one of the Haganah's objects in despatching her. A British attempt to return her passengers to France backfired when they refused to leave the ships which took them there. In the end they were taken on to Hamburg and forcibly removed amid much further publicity. The affair became a cause célèbre, the source of much sympathetic attention for the Zionist movement. Some years later there was a scheme to turn the *Exodus 1947* into a floating museum but she was gutted by fire and had to be scrapped.

The biggest of the would-be blockade runners were the *Pan Crescent* (1901/4,605 gross tons) and the *Pan York* (1901/4,507 gross tons). They left the Bulgarian port of Burgas in December, 1947 with no fewer than 15,236 migrants. A few of these were Bulgarians but about 14,800 were Rumanians. The Rumanian authorities connived at this exodus in order to rid themselves of part of a trouble-some minority but also to exacerbate the unstable situation in the Middle East which the Communist powers were hoping to exploit. Both ships had enjoyed long careers with American owners, latterly as banana boats with United Fruit from whom the Haganah bought them for about $200,000 apiece. Further large sums were spent on fitting them out for their new task and although their 'passengers' still lived in incredibly cramped quarters in the holds the facilities included quite sophisticated hospitals. Some of the work on the *Pan Crescent* was done at Venice but, after an unsuccessful attempt by British agents to sink her, she and her sister were taken to Constantza to be refitted. Both ships were registered in Panama in the name of F&B Shipping of Miami. (This was a Haganah front-company whose initials, it was later claimed, represented a sentiment which was both extremely vulgar and very anti-British.) The *Pan Crescent* and the *Pan York*, having provoked a very complicated political situation, agreed in the end to be escorted by the Royal Navy to Cyprus. Once there, their passengers joined the many already waiting to get to Palestine. A few months later, after the formation of the new state of Israel, they finally reached their destination. The two ships passed into the ownership of Ships & Vessels Ltd., a Haifa-based concern associated with the Zim Israel Navigation Company. As the *Atzmaut* and the *Komiyut* they carried many migrants to the new country and were scrapped in 1950 and 1952 respectively.

Zim Lines became the national shipping company of Israel but it had begun operating before the emergence of the state. It is ironic that a British firm, Harris & Dixon, was much involved in the management for some years. One of Zim's first ships was the *Kedmah* (1927/3,504 gross tons), chartered from Harris & Dixon who in due course transferred her to the Palestine, and later Israeli, flag. She was a smart little steamer which had been the pride of the Straits Steamship Co. of Singapore before the War. The change of ownership entailed little alteration in her name – she had previously been the *Kedah*. Towards the end of her charter to Zim she was returned to the British flag and renamed *Golden Isles*. She remained in Zim service until 1955.

In 1948 Zim placed three other small and elderly liners in service. The largest was the *Negbah* (1915/5,544 gross tons). She had been built for a Dutch company for service to the Netherlands Antilles but had been variously employed by several American companies over the years. For a while she was a member of the small fleet of ex-liners used by Libby's, the food group, to transport seasonal labour and stores to their salmon canneries along the Alaskan coast. Immediately before passing to Zim she was the *Luxor* belonging to a Panamanian company. My suspicion that there might have been a connection with the Palestine-registered *Cairo* which J. Livanos was running between Marseilles, Haifa and Alexandria at the time would seem to be unfounded. Her owners were represented by the very Jewish-sounding Blidberg Rothchild Agency of New York. In any case she saw no service as the *Luxor*, being sold instead to Zim.

Another of the Zim ships was the *Galilah* (1913/3,899 gross tons), a former American river liner well-known

---

1   Not a mis-spelling of President Garfield. Mr. Warfield was the president not of the USA but of the Old Bay Line, her original owners. Some accounts give her unofficial name as *Exodus From Europe 1947*.

between the wars as the *De Witt Clinton* of the Hudson River Day Line. Finally, there was the relatively youthful *Artsa* (1930/3,213 gross tons) which had been a fruit-carrier for the Laeisz group of Germany and had later had a spell in Italian ownership.

The main Zim service was from Marseilles to Haifa, calling at other Mediterranean ports en route. Between 1948 and 1951 no fewer than 700,000 migrants were carried to Israel.

In 1953 Zim Israel Lines entered the Atlantic trade. Whereas the emigrant passengers of most Atlantic lines had always travelled westward, the equivalent Zim passengers were going in the opposite direction. The vessel which established this service was the *Jerusalem* (1913/11,105 gross tons), one of the original Norwegian America Line vessels which we met in Chapter Five as Home Lines' *Argentina*.

In 1955-58 Zim Israel's passenger fleet was transformed by the advent of four new liners built by Deutsche Werft of Hamburg as part of the War Reparations programme. These vessels, and a number of freighters received under the same agreement, meant that the company no longer had to make do with small and superannuated tonnage, which was all it had been able to obtain in the 'forties.

For some years Zim Israel was in the habit of chartering medium-sized liners to supplement its own fleet at times of particular demand. Thus, the *Charlton Star* was chartered in 1957 to carry Jewish exiles from Poland (see Chapter Three). Vessels chartered on other occasions included the *Flaminia* and *Surriento* (both covered in Chapter Four).

Anal

253 gross tons, single screw, compound. Built, 1877, by J. Fullerton, Paisley as the *Earl of Zetland* for the Shetland Isles Steam Navigation Co., which was absorbed by the North of Scotland & Orkney & Shetlands Steam Navigation Co. in 1890. 1884: lengthened. 1939: renamed *Earl of Zetland II* on the advent of a new vessel which was to replace her. However, the outbreak of the war resulted in her being reprieved and retained in service. 1946: sold to Anal Compañía Provencial (Panama) and renamed *Anal*. 1947: arrested by the Royal Navy while attempting to run the blockade of Palestine under the unofficial name of *Yehuda Halevy*. 1950: scrapped after lying at Haifa for about three years.

Artsa

3,213 gross tons, single screw, triple expansion. Built, 1930, by Bremer Vulkan, Vegesack as *Panther*, a fruit-carrier, for Afrikanische Frucht (F. Laeisz). c.1939: became the *Lech*; and later passed into the hands of Lloyd Mediterraneo who named her *Mare Liguria*. 1949: bought by the Zim Israel Navigation Co. and renamed *Artsa*. 1963: scrapped.

Atzmaut

4,605 gross tons, single screw, triple expansion. Built, 1901, by the Newport News Shipbuilding & Dry Dock Co. as the *El Valle* for the Southern Pacific Co., later the Southern Pacific Steamship Lines. 1941: became the *Pan Crescent* of the Pan Atlantic Steamship Co. (Waterman Steamship, managers). c.1945: passed to the United Fruit Steamship Corporation. c.1946: bought by F&B Shipping for use as an illegal immigrant carrier. 1947: made one run and was intercepted but remained in the hands of her crew. 1948: passed to Ships & Vessels Ltd. and chartered to Zim as the *Atzmaut*. 1950: scrapped at Haifa.

After 45 years as a respectable American freighter and a brief episode as an illegal Zionist blockade-runner, the *Atzmaut* ended her days with Zim Israel Lines.

Laurence Dunn collection

Exodus

(see *President Warfield*).

Galilah

3,899 gross tons, twin screw, triple expansion. Built, 1913, by Harlan & Hollingsworth, Wilmington, Delaware as the *Manhattan* for the Central Vermont Transportation Co. During the First World War became the *Nopatin* of the US Government (Navy Department) and afterwards the *De Witt Clinton* of the Hudson River Day Line. In the

In its early days the Zim Israel company had to find small passenger ships as best it could. The *Artsa* was a conversion from a former German fruit-carrier.

Zim Israel Navigation

Zim Israel's *Galilah* had once been the American river liner *De Witt Clinton*.
Zim Israel Navigation

Second World War ownership passed to the US War Shipping Administration and, after the War, to the US Maritime Commission. 1948: sold to Samuel Derecktor of New York and renamed initially *Col. Frederick C. Johnson* and then *Derecktor*. Brownsam Corporation of Panama became the registered owners. 1948: bought by the Ness Shipping Co. of Haifa and became the *Galilah* in the Zim Israel fleet. 1953: scrapped in Italy.

Golden Isles
(see *Kedmah*).

Jerusalem
11,105 gross tons, twin screw, quadruple expansion with low pressure turbine, 16 knots. Built, 1913, by Cammell Laird, Birkenhead as the *Bergensfjord* for the Norwegian America Line. 1931: low pressure turbine added to her original engines. 1940: became a troopship under the management of Furness Withy. 1946: returned to the Norwegian America Line but sold to Panamanian Navigation Co. and renamed *Argentina* for the Home Lines service to South America which she entered the following year after a refit. 1948: ownership transferred to Panamanian Lines Inc. and in 1949 to Mediterranean Lines (still

employed in the Home Lines service). 1953: transferred to Home Lines Inc. 1953: sold to Zim Israel, renamed *Jerusalem* and instituted their service to New York; also used in the Mediterranean. 1957: renamed *Aliya*, leaving the name *Jerusalem* available for one of the company's new ships. 1958: laid up. 1959: scrapped at La Spezia.

In 1953 Zim Israel bought Home Lines' veteran *Argentina* and used her to open their new transatlantic service as the *Jerusalem*.
Zim Israel Navigation

Kedmah

3,504 gross tons, twin screw, geared turbine, 16½ knots. Built, 1927, by Vickers, Barrow-in-Furness for the Straits Steamship Co. as the *Kedah* for their express service between Singapore and Penang. 1939: requisitioned by the Royal Navy as an armed auxiliary. 1942: involved in the evacuation operations from Singapore and Malaya. 1946: handed back to her owners but sold to Harris & Dixon who renamed her *Kedmah* under the British flag; but soon registered her under the Palestine, and later Israeli, flag in the name of Kedem Palestine Line Ltd. of Haifa and eventually Kedem Israel Line. Employed in the Zim Line service between Marseilles and Haifa. 1952: became the *Golden Isles* of Harris & Dixon but still on charter to Zim Israel. 1955: laid up and, in 1956, scrapped at Newport.

Komiyut

4,570 gross tons, single screw, triple expansion. Built, 1901, by Newport News Shipbuilding & Dry Dock as the *El Dia* for the Southern Pacific Co., subsequently Southern Pacific Steamship Lines. Briefly called *Roanoke*, then reverted to *El Dia*. 1941: became the *Pan York* of the Pan Atlantic Steamship Co. c.1945: owned by the United Fruit Steamship Corporation. c.1946: bought by F&B Shipping for use as an illegal immigrant carrier. 1948: passed to Ships & Vessels Ltd and renamed *Komiyut*. 1952: scrapped at Briton Ferry.

Negbah

5,544 gross tons, single screw, triple expansion, 14 knots. Built, 1915, by De Schelde, Vlissingen as *Ecuador* for the Dutch Royal West Indian Mail Line, but bought by Pacific Mail Line in 1916. 1925: bought by the Panama Mail Line. 1931: transferred to the Grace Line as *Santa Olivia*. 1937: bought by Libby, McNeil & Libby to serve their Alaskan canneries and named *David W. Branch*. 1941: taken over as a US Army transport. 1947: bought by Cia. Victoria de Vapores of Panama and renamed *Luxor* but did not enter service. 1948: bought by Zim Israel, refitted and renamed *Negbah* (initially managed by Harris & Dixon). 1956: scrapped at Savona.

President Warfield

1,814 gross tons, single screw, triple expansion. Built, 1928, by the Pusey & Jones Company, Wilmington, Delaware for the Baltimore Steam Packet Co. (the Old Bay Line). 1941: taken over by the US War Shipping Administration and used, inter alia, as a cross-Channel troopship. 1947: sold to Potomac Shipwrecking Co. of Washington, D.C. but re-sold to F&B Shipping and registered in

Zim Israel's *Negbah* had spent several years on the Alaskan coast before the War, serving Libby's salmon canneries.

Zim Israel Navigation

Honduras (although she remained in Potomac's name in Lloyd's Register for some years). Her new owners used her for an attempt to run the British blockade of Palestine, but she was intercepted. 1947 onwards: she lay at Haifa for some years. Plans were made to convert her into a floating museum. 1952: badly damaged by fire and subsequently scrapped at Haifa.

Yehuda Halevy
(see *Anal*).

Rumania

Among the Eastern Bloc countries anxious to export their Jewish population, Rumania announced in 1950 that to assist in the migration of, it was said, 250,000 Jews to Israel, the liner *Transilvania* (1938/6,672 gross tons) would operate a weekly service from Constantza to Haifa. In this service she would carry up to 1,500 passengers per trip. She was one of a notable pair of handsome motor liners built in Denmark for the Rumanians shortly before the war. Her sister passed to the Russians in the mid-'forties but the *Transilvania* remained in the hands of the Rumanian government and in the later 'fifties and early 'sixties she became a well-known cruise ship operating round the eastern Mediterranean and much patronised by German passengers.

Transilvania
6,672 gross tons, twin screw, diesel, 20 knots. Built, 1938, by Burmeister & Wain, Copenhagen for the Rumanian express service from Constantza to Alexandria. Operated by Navrom, the Rumanian Maritime & Fluvial Navigation concern after the War. Fate uncertain; she is reputed to have capsized.

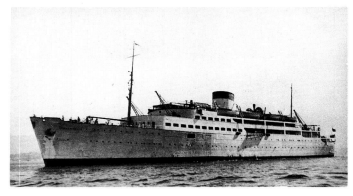

The Rumanian *Transilvania* had been considered the height of modernity when delivered by Danish builders in 1938. This picture is taken from a postcard, probably French.
Laurence Dunn collection

China

Before we leave the subject of post-war Jewish migration, mention must be made of the Chinese liner *Hwa Lien* (1907/3,488 gross tons) and her passengers. One of the most extraordinary aspects of the attempts by European Jews to escape Nazism had been the way in which thousands of them made their way to Shanghai in 1938-39.

Shanghai, already captured by the Japanese in their invasion of China, was still an open house – one of the few places in the world which it was possible to enter without papers. Late in 1946 the *Hwa Lien* set sail for Australia with some of the survivors of this pre-War Shanghai Jewish community. The voyage was not without its troubles and the *Hwa Lien* had to put into Darwin to replenish her food and water. A twin-funnelled former New Zealand liner, she had recently been bought by the United Corporation of China Ltd. of Shanghai. Her subsequent career on the China coast was cut short by the Communist advance in the Chinese Civil War and she was finally used to evacuate Nationalists to Taiwan.

Hwa Lien
3,488 gross tons, triple screw, geared turbine, 19 knots. Built, 1907, as *Maori* by William Denny, Dumbarton for the Union Steamship Company of New Zealand's express service between the North and South Islands. 1944: laid up. 1946: bought by the United Corporation of China and renamed *Hwa Lien*, making one voyage with displaced persons from China to Australia and then entering the Chinese coastal trade. 1949: laid up. 1950: carried Nationalists to Formosa (Taiwan) and laid up again. 1951: sank in a cyclone, was raised and scrapped.

India

Another surprising Eastern involvement in the migrant trades was the charter by the I.R.O. of two Indian liners for voyages from the Mediterranean to Australia. The Mogul Line of Bombay, part of the P&O group at this time, operated passenger ships between the sub-continent and the Red Sea ports – notably Jeddah, to which it carried many Muslim pilgrims on their way to Mecca during the annual Hajj season. Even after Partition it continued to carry pilgrims not only from the new state of India but also from East Pakistan. Unlike some of its competitors the Mogul Line was in the habit of having new ships built especially for it. The *Mohammedi* (1947/7,026 gross tons) and *Mozaffari* (1947/7,024 gross tons) were a sturdy-looking pair, although their single, rather short funnels gave them a slightly under-endowed appearance. In 1950 they each made one immigrant voyage to Australia. For reasons which are not clear their names were temporarily changed to *Ocean Triumph* and *Ocean Victory*, respectively.

Ocean Triumph
7,026 gross tons, single screw, triple expansion with exhaust turbine, 14½ knots. Built, 1947, by Lithgow, Glasgow as the Mogul Line's *Mohammedi*, initially under the British flag. 1950: renamed *Ocean Triumph* for one immigrant voyage for the I.R.O. and then reverted to *Mohammedi*. 1960: the Mogul Line became Indian-owned. 1978: scrapped at Bombay.

Ocean Victory
7,024 gross tons, single screw, triple expansion with exhaust turbine, 14½ knots. Built, 1947, by Lithgow, Glasgow for the Mogul Line as their *Mozaffari*, at first

British-registered. 1950: renamed *Ocean Victory* for a Malta–Australia voyage for the I.R.O., then reverted to *Mozaffari*. 1960: the Mogul Line was acquired by Indian interests. 1977: scrapped at Bombay.

Egypt

The Egyptian lines operated mainly in the Mediterranean and the Red Sea. The Khedivial Mail Line did, however, have a passenger/cargo service to New York for some years after the War. Later the United Arab Maritime Company, into which the major Egyptian lines had been merged, ran a short-lived service between Alexandria and Canadian ports. These operations may well have carried some migrants but they do not seem to have been primarily emigrant-carriers.

On the other hand, there were a few voyages to Australia which undoubtedly came within the ambit of this book. Khedivial Mail's *Gumhuryat Misr* (1938/7,830 gross tons) made one voyage in 1956 and fell foul of the Australian authorities' safety regulations (see Chapter Four). She had been one of a quartet of well-proportioned steamers originally built for the Canadian National company's services between Canada and the British West Indies.

The Société Misr de Navigation Maritime vessels *Al Sudan* (1944/7,372 gross tons) and *Misr* (1943/7,367 gross tons) ran to Australia on a number of occasions between 1947 and 1956. They were American-built war-time ships based on the C3 design, which were members of a class specially constructed as Landing Ships (Infantry) for the British forces.

Al Sudan

7,372 gross tons, twin screw, geared turbine, 14½ knots. Built, 1914, by Consolidated Steel Corporation, Wilmington as a Landing Ship (Infantry). Launched as *Cape St. Vincent* but completed as *Empire Arquebus* and bareboat chartered by the American government (War Shipping Administration) to the British Ministry of War Transport for whom she was managed by Donaldson Bros. & Black. 1945: became HMS *Cicero* but reverted to *Empire Arquebus* the following year. 1947: sold to Société Misr de Navigation Maritime, converted into a passenger ship and renamed *Al Sudan*. 1962: transferred to the United Arab Maritime Company. Idle since 1980.

Gumhuryat Misr

The Khedivial Mail Line's *Gumhuryat Misr* fell foul of Australian safety regulations in 1956. *World Ship Society*

7,830 gross tons, twin screw, geared turbine, 12½ knots. Built, 1928, by Cammell Laird, Birkenhead as *Lady Nelson* for the Canadian National Steamships service between Canada and the British West Indies. 1942: sunk by a German submarine while in harbour at St. Lucia, but was salvaged and restored as a hospital ship for the Royal Canadian Navy. 1947: returned to her owners' service. 1952: laid up. 1953: bought by the Khedivial Mail Line, refitted and renamed *Gumhuryat Misr*. 1960: renamed *Alwadi*. 1961: Khedivial Mail Line nationalised. 1962: the company was merged into United Arab Maritime. 1965: the *Alwadi* sank at her lay-up berth.

Misr

7,367 gross tons, twin screw, geared turbine, 14½ knots. Built, 1943, by Consolidated Steel Corporation, Wilmington, California as a Landing Ship (Infantry). Launched as *Cape St. Roque* but completed as *Empire Mace* and bareboat chartered by the War Shipping Administration to the British Ministry of War Transport (managers: Anchor Line). 1947: briefly became HMS *Galtee More*. 1947: sold to Société Misr de Navigation Maritime and renamed *Misr*. 1962: transferred to United Arab Maritime. 1981: believed scrapped.

The Egyptian *Misr* had been a Landing Ship (Infantry) during the War. *A. Scrimali*

Yugoslavia

In 1947 two former American liners passed into the hands of the newly-formed Yugoslav state enterprise, Jugoslavenska Linijska Plovidba (usually known as Jugolinija). One had been well-known on the West Coast, the other on the East.

The *Radnik* (1908/6,509 gross tons) had been a significant ship – the first major passenger-carrier of the Matson Navigation Company. Like many later Matson ships she had first-class accommodation which in its day was considered rather luxurious. Called the *Lurline*, she was the precursor of a fleet of unusual vessels built for Matson with three masts and with machinery situated aft. They established the company as the dominant force on the run between the West Coast and Hawaii. In the mid-'thirties the *Lurline* was bought by the Alaska Packers Association.

A busy view of Turkish Maritime Lines' *Istanbul* which sailed regularly between Marseilles and the eastern Mediterranean.

A. Scrimali

The former East Coast ship was the *Partizanka* (1927/ 6,267 gross tons) which, as the *Shawnee*, had belonged to the Clyde Line (later Clyde-Mallory), part of the sprawling Agwilines group. She was a neat-looking vessel, typical of the East Coast liners. During the war she served as a US Army transport. Afterwards, with Agwilines running down, she was sold to a short-lived Panamanian-flag company with Portuguese connections. She was soon damaged in a collision, however, and passed into Yugoslav hands.

Jugolinija used the two ships irregularly on voyages either to Australia or to South America from various Mediterranean ports, including Rijeka (their headquarters), Trieste and Valetta. The *Partizanka*'s career was ended by a fire while she was under repair in Split in 1949; but the *Radnik* soldiered on until 1952. It was reported in 1947 that she had sailed from Montreal for Yugoslavia carrying 500 Yugoslavs who were returning home to support the new Tito regime. They took with them half a million pounds' worth of vehicles, tools, farm equipment and other necessary but scarce machinery. It has been stated that normally the *Radnik* could accommodate only 400 passengers. The *Partiznaka* could carry 800. This was considerably more than several other, mainly cargo, vessels which Jugolinija ran to New York and other American ports.

Partizanka

6,267 gross tons, twin screw, geared turbine, 17 knots. Built, 1927, by Newport News Shipbuilding & Dry Dock Co. as the *Shawnee*. Registered in the name of the New York & Miami Steamship Corporation and used in the Clyde Line service. 1928: Clyde amalgamated with another Agwilines company to form the Clyde-Mallory Line. 1939: chartered to United States Lines for a single transatlantic voyage to help with the rush of Americans wishing to return home as war loomed in Europe. 1941: became a US Army troopship. 1946: returned to her owners; by now registered in the name of Agwilines Inc. 1946: sold to Iberian Star Line of Panama and renamed *City of Lisbon*, but damaged in a collision. 1947: became the *Partizanka* of Jugolinija. 1949: badly damaged by fire. 1950: scrapped.

Radnik

6,509 gross tons, single screw, triple expansion, 13 knots. Built, 1908, by Newport News Shipbuilding & Dry Dock Co. as the *Lurline* for the Matson Navigation Co. 1928: sold to Alaska Packers Association and renamed *Chirikof*. 1940: taken up as a US Army transport. 1946: returned to her owners. 1947: became the *Radnik* of Jugolinija. 1952: laid up. 1953: scrapped.

Turkey

Another national shipping company with a predilection for former American passenger vessels was Turkish Maritime Lines. They purchased several in the post-War period. They were registered in the rather ponderous name of the Republic of Turkey, Ministry of Communications, General Direction for the Exploitation of the State Lines. In 1949 the *Istanbul* (1932/5,236 gross tons) was one of the ships on whose regular voyages the I.R.O. announced they had made block bookings for the carriage of emigrants. At the time the *Istanbul* was sailing on a route between Marseilles and Istanbul via either Genoa or Naples and various Eastern Mediterranean ports. She too had been one of the East Coast liners which American companies within the Agwilines group built in some quantity during the late 'twenties and early 'thirties.

Istanbul

5,236 gross tons, single screw, geared turbine, 17 knots. Built, 1932, by Newport News Shipbuilding & Dry Dock Co. as *Colombia* for the Colombian Mail Steamship Co. and operated on the New York–Caribbean route. 1938: Colombian Mail Steamship Co. was absorbed by the New York & Cuba Mail Steamship Co. (the Ward Line) and *Colombia* was renamed *Mexico*. 1942: taken up by the US Government for trooping. 1946: laid up in the US Reserve Fleet. 1947: bought by the Turkish Ministry of Communications and refitted for Turkish Maritime Lines service as the *Istanbul*. 1966: scrapped.

Japan

Before the War there had been a considerable emigrant trade from Japan to the West Coast of America, to Hawaii and to South America. By the end of hostilities the Japanese deep-sea passenger fleet had been almost entirely destroyed. Only two vessels remained. Rebuilding the passenger fleet was not an immediate priority for the defeated nation and, truth to tell, the Japanese never quite recovered their position in the passenger shipping world. This was largely because the Nippon Yusen Kaisha company chose not to add to the single liner which remained to them. The OSK Line (Osaka Shosen Kaisha), on the other hand, did build new passenger ships and in 1951-52 they placed three vessels on a rather extended route from Kobe and Yokohama across to Los Angeles, then down the West Coast and through the Panama Canal to Rio de Janeiro and the River Plate ports. These vessels were the *America Maru* (1950/8,343 gross tons), the *Africa Maru* (1951/8,354 gross tons) and the *Santos Maru* (1952/8,516 gross tons). At first they were freighters with accommodation for just 12 cabin class passengers. Soon, however, they were modified to carry over 500 third class passengers, mainly in dormitories. These were largely emigrants going to settle in South America.

The service was sufficiently successful for two further, superior vessels to be added after a few years. The *Brazil Maru* (1954/10,100 gross tons), with more extensive superstructure than the earlier ships, accommodated 12 first class, 68 tourist and 902 in third class dormitories. She was also rather faster than the others, with a service speed of 16 knots against their 14-14½ knots. Four years later she was followed by the *Argentina Maru* (1958/10,864 gross tons). Although OSK passenger ships had been powered by diesel engines ever since the mid-'twenties, the new vessel was given turbines. She had a more streamlined funnel than the *Brazil Maru* and accommodated 12 first class, 82 tourist and 960 third class passengers. Between 1952 and 1963 OSK carried 43,438 government-sponsored migrants from Japan to South America.

In 1964 OSK formally merged with the Mitsui Line to form Mitsui-OSK, although the passenger fleet had already been registered for some time in the name of an associate, Nihon Ijusen KK (Japanese Emigration Shipping Co.). The new concern soon abandoned the emigrant trade, removing the dormitory accommodation from the three earlier ships which thus became primarily freighters (as originally intended). The *Brazil Maru* and *Argentina Maru* were also rebuilt. They too lost their dormitory spaces and each now carried a small number of first class passengers and about 350 in what was called 'economy class', consisting of cabins sleeping from four to ten persons. Full air-conditioning was installed. The company ceased to operate a full-scale passenger service on the route in 1973.

Africa Maru

8,534 gross tons, single screw, diesel, 14 knots. Built, 1951, by Central Japan Heavy Industries, Kobe, as a freighter for the OSK Line; accommodation added for emigrants. 1964: transferred to the new Mitsui-OSK Lines. 1965: reduced to a 12-passenger freighter again. 1967: sold to Marlene Shipping, Panama-registered and renamed *Vanlene*. 1972: wrecked off Vancouver Island.

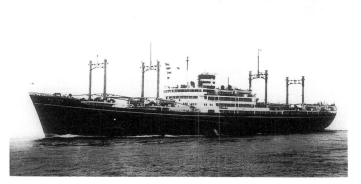

The *Africa Maru* of OSK Line. A freighter-turned-emigrant ship which ran between Japan and South America in the 1950s and 1960s.   *Mitsui-OSK Lines*

America Maru

8,343 gross tons, single screw, diesel, 14 knots. Built, 1950, as a freighter for the OSK Line by Central Japan Heavy Industries, Kobe; accommodation for emigrant passengers added after completion. 1964: on the merger into Mitsui-OSK Lines she was transferred to the new combine's fleet. 1964: converted into a 12-passenger freighter. 1967: sold to the State Shipping Co., Panamanian-registered and renamed *Vankowa*. 1968: renamed *Vanmint*. 1973: scrapped at Kaohsiung.

Argentina Maru

10,864 gross tons, single screw, geared turbine, 16½ knots. Built, 1958, by Mitsubishi Heavy Industries, Kobe for the OSK Line. 1964: OSK merged into Mitsui-OSK Lines. 1965: refitted. 1972: renamed *Nippon Maru* on conversion into a cruise ship. 1976: scrapped at Kaohsiung.

The *Brazil Maru* of OSK Line. A smart motor liner, she initially carried most of her migrant passengers in dormitories but this was changed in a 1965 refit.
Mitsui-OSK Lines

Brazil Maru

10,100 gross tons, single screw, diesel, 16 knots. Built, 1954, for Osaka Shosen Kaisha by Mitsubishi Heavy Industries. Kobe. 1964: OSK merged into Mitsui-OSK Lines. 1965: refitted. 1973: laid up. 1974: converted into a museum ship stationed at Toba.

Santos Maru

Originally intended as a freighter, the *Santos Maru* was converted into an emigrant ship and carried many Japanese to a new life in South America. She belonged to the OSK Line.
Mitsui-OSK Lines

8,516 gross tons, single screw, diesel, 14½ knots. Built, 1952, as a cargo ship for OSK Lines by Mitsubishi Heavy Industries, Kobe; but accommodation installed for emigrant passengers. 1964: became part of the new Mitsui-OSK Lines fleet. 1965: reduced to a 12-passenger freighter. 1972: sold to Liberty Maritime Corporation and renamed *Winona*. 1974: sold to Sincere Navigation Co. of Taiwan and renamed *Hui Hsing*. 1976: scrapped at Kaohsiung.

Argentina

By and large, the countries which received the post-War migrants did not own the ships which carried them. There were, of course, exceptions – Israel was one, as we have already noted in this chapter, and Argentina was another. Between 1949 and 1951 the Compañía Argentina de Navegación Dodero (the Dodero Line) introduced eight passenger vessels into three services between South America and Europe. One service linked Buenos Aires and the River Plate with London and was operated by three newly-built combination liners whose passenger accommodation was limited to roomy and luxurious first-class quarters which attracted very favourable comment when the ships were introduced. Passenger lists on the second service – between Hamburg and Buenos Aires via Amsterdam – were less exclusive and may well have included many migrants. Here too three new ships were built for the route, but they each carried 740 tourist class passengers and only 13 first class. They were Dutch-built motorships with long, low superstructures and were called *Yapeyu* (1951/11,450 gross tons), *Maipu* (1951/11,515 gross tons) and *Alberto Dodero* (1951/11,521 gross tons). The career of the unfortunate *Maipu* ended only five months after she had entered service. She sank after colliding in the Elbe with the US Navy transport *General M.L. Hersey*. No lives were lost.

The third Dodero service was a thorough-going emigrant run from Genoa and Naples to Buenos Aires via Marseilles, Barcelona, Lisbon, Rio de Janeiro and Montevideo. The two main vessels employed on this route had a typically emigrant-ship appearance and history. Like the *Fairsea* and *Fairsky*, *Roma* and *Sydney* et al, they had been laid down in the early 'forties as C3-type cargo liners, part of the American government-sponsored merchant shipbuilding programme. Before they were completed, however, they were taken over and converted into auxiliary aircraft-carriers and allotted to the Royal Navy. When rebuilt as emigrant ships, they had virtually no cargo space and sported an extended superstructure lined with lifeboats. They could each accommodate no less than 1,338 tourist class passengers and a token 4 in first class. They were named *Corrientes* (1942/12,053 gross tons) and *Salta* (1943/12,053 gross tons). Initially, Dodero's service from Genoa was run in conjunction with Italia who had placed the *San Giorgio* on the route. Bringing eight substantial vessels into service within the space of about two years did not constitute the full extent of the Dodero company's commitment to the passenger shipping business. In 1947 they had purchased six of the 'Victory' ships which the American government was making available to foreign owners. All six had been fitted out by the War Shipping Administration as troop transports and in the years before the introduction of the main Dodero liners these ships were used to carry passengers on their troopdecks. Soon after purchase, one of them, the *Buenos Aires*, took Eva Peron back to Argentina after her famous European tour. For this purpose she must have had some rather more glamorous accommodation installed. In the 'fifties the six ships were each refitted with accommodation for about 800 migrant passengers but they lasted in this form for only a few years before becoming freighters. In addition to the *Buenos Aires* (ex-*Smith Victory*, 1945/7,059 gross tons), there were the *Cordoba* (ex-*NYU Victory*, 1945/7,714 gross tons), the *Entre Rios* (ex-*Rock Hill Victory*, 1945/7,604 gross tons), the *Mendoza* (ex-*William and Mary Victory*, 1945/7,722 gross tons), the *Santa Fé* (ex-*Gustavus Victory*, 1945/7,383 gross tons) and the *Tucuman* (ex-*La Crosse Victory*, 1945/7,607 gross tons). In 1961 the *Tucuman* stranded off Bahia Blanca and was declared a Constructive Total Loss, but was salvaged and underwent a most remarkable structural repair at Buenos Aires and saw further service as the *Kismet* and the *Bucephalos*.

By 1955, when the Peron government fell, the Dodero Line was already state-controlled. The change of regime led to the Dodero fleet being transferred to the Flota Argentina de Navegación de Ultramar (literally the Argentinean Overseas Navigation Line, but usually called FANU). Further changes occurred in 1962 when FANU was amalgamated with the Flota Mercante del Estado (the Argentinian State Line) to form the Empresa Lineas Maritimas del Estado (or ELMA).

There followed the gradual run-down of the passenger fleet. In 1964 the *Corrientes* and *Salta* were withdrawn, partly owing to problems with their machinery. Their place on the route to Genoa was taken by the *Yapeyu* and *Alberto Dodero* which remained in this service until it was closed down in 1969. It had been intended that the *Yapeyu* and *Alberto Dodero* should be succeeded on the Hamburg run in 1963-64 by three liners which had maintained a Buenos Aires–New York service for the Argentinian State Line. In fact, one of them was put out of action by fire before she could be converted for her new duties and another also fell victim to fire after a very few voyages. This left just one vessel running to Hamburg, the *Rio Tunuyan*, but although she could accommodate 373 passengers in tourist class only, it would probably be wrong to regard her as an emigrant ship.

The Dodero Line placed three new liners in their Hamburg–Buenos Aires service. The *Alberto Dodero* is seen at Hamburg after the Dodero Line had been taken over by the Fanu company.   *Steffen Weirauch collection*

Alberto Dodero
11,521 gross tons, twin screw, diesel, 18 knots. Built, 1951, by De Schelde, Vlissingen for the Dodero Line's Hamburg route. 1955: passed to FANU. 1962: FANU amalgamated with Flota Mercante del Estado to form ELMA. 1964: transferred to the Genoa route. 1969: sold to Transportes Oceanicos and converted into the livestock-carrier *Cormoran*. 1974: sold to the Cormoran Steamship Co. of Singapore. 1980: sold to Saudi buyers and renamed *Etaiwi I*. 1985: scrapped at Singapore.

Buenos Aires
7,059 gross tons, single screw, geared turbine, 15 knots. Built, 1945, by Bethlehem-Fairfield, Baltimore as the 'Victory' ship *Smith Victory* and operated by the US War Shipping Administration as a troop transport. 1947: sold to the Dodero Line and renamed *Buenos Aires*. 1947: brought Eva Peron back from her European tour. 1955:

refitted as an emigrant steamer in Italy. 1955: transferred to FANU. 1962: transferred to ELMA. 1963: sold to Southwind Shipping Corporation of Liberia and renamed *Fairwind*. 1968: stranded off the Bahamas and scrapped at Bilbao.

Cordoba

7,714 gross tons, single screw, geared turbine, 15 knots. Built, 1945, by Bethlehem-Fairfield, Baltimore as the *NYU Victory* for the War Shipping Administration and used as a transport. 1947: sold to the Dodero Line and renamed *Cordoba*. 1955: transferred to FANU. 1955: refitted at Buenos Aires as an emigrant-carrier. Later became a freighter. 1962: transferred to ELMA. 1972: scrapped at Campana.

Corrientes

12,053 gross tons, single screw, geared turbine, 16½ knots. Built, 1942, by the Seattle Tacoma Shipbuilding Corporation, Tacoma as an auxiliary aircraft carrier, having been laid down as the *Mormacmail*, a cargo liner intended for Moore-McCormack Lines. Handed over to the Royal Navy and named HMS *Tracker*. 1945: Returned to the US Government. 1948: sold to Newport News Shipbuilding & Drydock Co. who re-sold her the following year to the Dodero Line, for whom they converted her into an emigrant ship. Named *Corrientes*. 1955: transferred to FANU. 1962: transferred to ELMA. 1964: engine damage caused her to be taken out of service. Scrapped at Antwerp.

Entre Rios

7,604 gross tons, single screw, geared turbine, 15 knots. Built, 1945, by Bethlehem-Fairfield, Baltimore as the *Rock Hill Victory* for the War Shipping Administration and employed as a troop transport. 1947: sold to the Dodero Line and renamed *Entre Rios*. 1955: transferred to FANU. 1957: converted into an emigrant-carrier in Italy. 1962: transferred to ELMA. By now was being used as a freighter. 1974: laid up. 1977: scrapped at Campana.

Maipu

11,515 gross tons, twin screw, diesel, 18 knots. Built, 1951, by De Schelde, Vlissingen for the Dodero Line's Buenos Aires–Hamburg service. 1951: sank after a collision with the US troop transport *General M.L. Hersey* in the Elbe.

Mendoza

7,722 gross tons, single screw, geared turbine, 15 knots. Built, 1945, by Bethlehem-Fairfield, Baltimore as the *William and Mary Victory*, a troop transport for the War Shipping Administration. 1947: sold to the Dodero Line who renamed her *Mendoza*. 1952: refitted as an emigrant-carrier at Buenos Aires. 1955: transferred to the FANU fleet. 1962: transferred to ELMA. 1972: scrapped at Campana, having been used solely as a freighter for many years.

In 1947 the Dodero Line of the Argentine bought six 'Victory' ships which had been fitted out as troopships. They used them as makeshift passenger vessels. Here is the *Mendoza* later in her career, wearing the colours of the Elma company, one of Dodero's successors.
World Ship Society

Salta

12,053 gross tons, single screw, geared turbine, 16½ knots. Built, 1943, by the Seattle Tacoma Shipbuilding Corporation, Seattle. Intended as a C3-type cargo liner but launched and completed as the auxiliary aircraft carrier *Jamaica* for the US Navy. 1943: transferred to the Royal Navy and renamed HMS *Shah*. 1945: returned to the American government. 1948: sold to the Newport News Shipbuilding & Drydock Co., but re-sold the following year to the Dodero Line. Converted into the emigrant liner *Salta* for their Buenos Aires–Genoa service. 1955: became part of the FANU fleet. 1962: transferred to ELMA. 1964: laid up. 1966: broken up at Buenos Aires.

Santa Fé

7,383 gross tons, single screw, geared turbine, 15 knots. Built, 1945, by Bethlehem-Fairfield, Baltimore as the *Gustavus Victory*, a 'Victory'-type War Shipping Administration troop transport. 1947: sold to the Dodero Line and renamed *Santa Fé*. 1955: transferred to FANU. 1957: converted into an emigrant-carrier in Italy. 1962: transferred to ELMA. 1972: laid up after a long period of use as a cargo vessel. 1974: scrapped at Campana.

Tucuman

7,607 gross tons, single screw, geared turbine, 15 knots. Built, 1945, by Bethlehem-Fairfield, Baltimore as the 'Victory' ship *La Crosse Victory* for the US War Shipping Administration who used her as a troop transport. 1947: sold to the Dodero Line and became their *Tucuman*. 1952: converted into an emigrant ship at Buenos Aires. 1955: transferred to FANU. 1961: ran aground off Bahia Blanca and declared a Constructive Total Loss, but sold to Magellan Strait Development Corporation who had her repaired. 1965: renamed *Kismet* and in 1966: *Bucephalos*. 1969: scrapped at Kaohsiung.

Yapeyu

11,450 gross tons, twin screw, diesel, 18 knots. Built, 1951, by Van de Giessen, Krimpen for the Dodero Line who placed her in their Hamburg service. 1955: transferred to FANU. 1962: following the merger of FANU and Flota Mercante del Estado, ownership passed to ELMA. 1964: transferred to the Genoa service. 1969: sold to Transportes Oceanicos who had her converted into the livestock-carrier *Petrel*. 1973: sold to Transagro. 1974: sold to Cormoran Steamship and renamed *Cremona*. 1976: renamed *Iran Cremona*. 1980: scrapped at Kaohsiung.

Portugal

In August 1948 Fairplay, the shipping magazine, announced that 'a valuable addition to the steamship lines already plying between Genoa and South America will be the monthly service of two 10,000 ton liners *North King* and *Portugal* owned by Sociedade de Navegação Luso-Panamense Ltda. of Lisbon. The two vessels were to be operated by Mr. Arthur Giribaldi (sic) of Genoa and would temporarily fly the Panamanian flag. They would have a capacity of 650 passengers of whom 65 would be in first class. In the event it would seem that the scheme did not come to fruition. The Luso-Panamense company did own a steamer called *North King*, however.

Another Portuguese venture, Tagus Navigation, did get started. Their *Santa Cruz* (1903/15,511 gross tons), a much-travelled former American liner, made a voyage from Lisbon to Buenos Aires in 1947 and another from Genoa to the Caribbean. As already mentioned in Chapter Four, she thereafter ran under charter to Italia who used her on their newly re-established route from Genoa and Naples to Rio de Janeiro, Santos, Montevideo and Buenos Aires. She remained on this route for four years.

Santa Cruz

15,511 gross tons, quadruple expansion, 16 knots. Built, 1903, by the New York Shipbuilding Corporation, Camden, New Jersey. Originally intended as the Atlantic Transport Line's *Minnekahda*, she was transferred to the Pacific Mail Line as their *Manchuria*. 1915: transferred to the Atlantic Transport Line. 1918: taken up as an armed transport by the US Navy. 1919: returned to the International Mercantile Marine group and, this time, allocated to the American Line. 1923: transferred to the New York–San Francisco service of the Panama Pacific Line. 1928: bought by the Dollar Line for their round-the-world service and renamed *President Johnson*. 1932: laid up. 1933: returned to service. 1936: laid up. 1938: Dollar Line collapsed and their fleet was transferred to the new American President Lines who did not, however, reactivate the *President Johnson*. 1941: taken up as a government transport. 1946: laid up. 1947: bought by Tagus Navigation Co. (F. Costa and A. Ribeiro) and renamed *Santa Cruz*. 1947: transferred to the Panamanian flag and chartered to Italia. 1952: scrapped at Savona.

The *Santa Cruz*, a veteran of many years service with various American companies, was chartered by Italia to help re-start their South American service in 1947.

Laurence Dunn collection

Panama

Many of the ships already mentioned in this book flew the flag of the Republic of Panama. It is unlikely, however, that any of them were actually Panamanian-owned. Neither, presumably, were the final two vessels in this record of the emigrant fleets. However, as the true identity of their owners is unclear, the privilege of claiming them shall be accorded to the Panamanians. In one case, it is a very dubious privilege.

In Chapter Nine Arnold Bernstein's token return to the North Atlantic passenger trade with a ship called the *Continental* was described. When he chartered her in 1948 she was known as the *Tidewater* (1902/10,005 gross tons) and belonged to the Tidewater Commercial Co. Inc. of San Francisco. As already noted, she had once been a member of the Panama Railroad Co.'s fleet. Her new owners obtained steady employment for her for several years. In 1947 she sailed from the East Indies to Rotterdam, presumably carrying Dutch passengers returning home because of the political situation in what was to become Indonesia. There followed an emigrant voyage from Genoa and Marseilles to Australia and New Zealand. For the Bernstein charter she received the name *Continental* which she retained henceforth. After her four Bernstein voyages from New York to Plymouth and Antwerp she returned to Genoa via Rotterdam and Gdynia. Finally she made four more trips from Genoa to Australia, being eventually scrapped in 1950.

The *Tidewater/Continental* may have been old and relatively slow but she was respectable. The same cannot be said of the *San Francisco* (1919/8,582 gross tons). In its early days the I.R.O. chartered this vessel from a representative of a concern called the Republic Steamship Corporation. It would seem from a case which came up before a Federal Court Judge in Baltimore in April 1949, that the ship did not actually belong to the Republic corporation at the time. The judge described the affair as 'one of the greatest fiascos ever to come into the court in the form of an Admiralty case'. The I.R.O. had advanced $840,000 to Jose Madeiros, acting for the Republic concern, to convert the ship for use in the refugee programme. It would appear that $450,000 of this money was actually used to buy the vessel, that the corporation was unable to pay for the completion of the work and that the *San Francisco* was not delivered to the I.R.O. at Bremerhaven as agreed. The I.R.O. sued for $1,180,000 and the Maryland Drydock Co. sued for $860,970. It is unlikely that in the event they received anything like these amounts. The *San Francisco* was re-registered in the name of the Maryland Drydock Company and it was about two years before a buyer could be found for her. This was the Djakarta Lloyd and the ageing ship ran for them at first as the *Diponegoro* and later as the *Djakarta Raya*.

Continental

10,005 gross tons, twin screw, triple expansion, 13 knots. Built, 1902, by the Maryland Steel Co., Sparrow's Point, Maryland as the *Shawmut* for the Boston Steamship Co. 1909: bought by the Panama Railroad Co. and renamed *Ancon* still American-registered. Refitted with passenger accommodation. 1940: bought by the Permanente Steamship Co. and renamed *Permanente*. 1941: taken over as a transport by the US Army. 1946: bought by the Tidewater Commercial Co. Inc. and registered under the Panamanian flag as the *Tidewater*. 1948: chartered for the summer to the Arnold Bernstein Shipping Co. Inc. under the name *Continental*. 1948: returned to her owners but retained the name *Continental*. 1950: scrapped at Genoa.

San Francisco

8,582 gross tons, twin screw, geared turbine. Built, 1919, by Sun Shipbuilding, Chester, Pennsylvania as *South Bend*, a US Government transport. 1923: bought by the Luckenbach S.S. Co. and renamed *J.L. Luckenbach*. 1948: chartered to the I.R.O. by the Republic Steamship Corporation who claimed to have bought her. The purchase actually took place subsequently and conversion began into the emigrant ship *San Francisco* but was not completed. 1949: legal proceedings followed the non-delivery of the ship to the I.R.O. She passed into the ownership of the Maryland Drydock Co. 1951: bought by Djakarta Lloyd and renamed *Diponegoro*. 1952: further renamed *Djakarta Raya*. Scrapped.

Tidewater

(see *Continental*).

Some time after her charter to Arnold Bernstein had ended, the *Continental* passed through the Suez Canal on an Australian voyage.

Laurence Dunn collection

Sources

Primary Sources

Files at Companies House, London; Lloyd's Confidential Index (London); Lloyd's Registers (London); Lloyd's Shipping Index (London).

Newspapers and Periodicals

Fairplay International Shipping Weekly (Coulsdon); Lloyd's List (London); Marine News (World Ship Society, Kendal); Palestine Post (Jerusalem) and, later, The Jerusalem Post; Sea Breezes (Liverpool); Shipping Today and Yesterday (Bournemouth); Ships Monthly (Burton on Trent); Steamboat Bill, the Journal of the Steamship Historical Society of America (Chatham, N.J.). (The work of Peter Eisele in this journal has been particularly informative); The Times (London); Travel Trade Gazette (London).

Books

N.R.P. Bonsor: North Atlantic Seaway (revised edition. Volume 1: David & Charles, Newton Abbot, 1975; Volumes 2-5: Brookside Publications, Jersey, 1978-80).

N.R.P. Bonsor: South Atlantic Seaway (Brookside Publications, Jersey, 1983).

Alan L. Cary: Liners of the Ocean Highway (Sampson Low Marston, London, 1938).

Sylvia and Peter Duncan: The Sea My Steed, the Personal Story of Captain Donald Sorrell (Robert Hale, London, 1960).

Frederick E. Emmons: American Passenger Ships, The Ocean Lines and Liners, 1873-1983 (University of Delaware Press, 1985).

Frederick Emmons: The Atlantic Liners, 1925-70 (David & Charles, Newton Abbot, 1972).

Frederick Emmons: Pacific Liners, 1927-72 (David & Charles, Newton Abbot, 1973).

T.K. Fitchett: The Long Haul: Ships On The England–Australia Run (Rigby Publishers, Adelaide, 1980).

Cmdr. C.R. Vernon Gibbs, R.N.: Western Ocean Passenger Lines and Liners, 1934-1969 (Brown, Son & Ferguson, Glasgow, 1970).

Duncan Haws: Merchant Fleets – 9. Anchor Line (TCL Publications, Burwash, 1986).

D. Hughes and P. Humphries: In South African Waters, Passenger Liners Since 1930 (Oxford University Press, Cape Town, 1977).

David F. Hutchings: RMS Queen Mary – 50 Years of Splendour (Kingfisher Publications, Southampton, 1986).

Francis E. Hyde: Cunard And The North Atlantic, 1840-1973 (Macmillan, London, 1975).

Richard P. de Kerbrech: Shaw Savill & Albion, The Post-War Fortunes Of A Shipping Empire (Conway Maritime Press, London, 1986).

Arnold Kludas: Die Grossen Passagierschiffe, Fähren und Cruise Liner Der Welt (Koehler, Herford, 1983).

Arnold Kludas: Great Passenger Ships of The World, Volumes 1-5 (translated by Charles Hodges. Patrick Stephens, Cambridge, 1975-77).

Clive Langmead: Worse Things Happen At Sea (Lion Publishing, Tring, 1984).

John M. Maber: North Star To Southern Cross, The Story Of The Australasian Seaways (T. Stephenson & Sons, Prescot, 1967).

Robert O. Maguglin: The Official Pictorial History, The Queen Mary (Oak Tree Publications, San Diego, 1985).

Michael Marus: The Unwanted, European Refugees In The Twentieth Century (Oxford University Press, New York, 1985).

Neil McCart: Passenger Ships Of The Orient Line (Patrick Stephens, Wellingborough, 1987).

R.S. McLellan: Anchor Line, 1856-1956 (Anchor Line, Glasgow, 1956).

William H. Miller: The Last Atlantic Liners (Conway Maritime Press, London, 1985).

William H. Miller: The Last Blue Water Liners (Conway Maritime Press, London, 1986).

William H. Miller: Transatlantic Liners, 1945-1980 (David & Charles, Newton Abbot, 1981).

W.H. Mitchell and L.A. Sawyer: The Cape Run (Terence Dalton, Lavenham, 1984).

Mitsui-OSK Lines: The First Century of Mitsui-OSK Lines, Ltd. (Tokyo, 1985).

George Musk: Canadian Pacific (David & Charles, Newton Abbot, 1989).

John Niven: The American President Line and Its Forebears, 1848-1984 (University of Delaware Press, 1986).

Francesco Ogliari, Achille Restelli, Giorgio Spazzapan and Alessandro Zenoni: Trasporti Marittimi di Linea, Volumi 5 and 6 (Cavallotti, Milan, 1986).

E.W. Paget-Tomlinson: Bibby Line, 175 Years Of Achievement (Bibby Line, Liverpool, 1982).

Peter Plowman: Passenger Ships Of Australia and New Zealand (2 volumes, Conway Maritime Press, London, 1981).

John Slader: The Red Duster At War (William Kimber, London, 1988).

Eugene W. Smith: Passenger Ships Of The World, Past and Present (George H. Dean, Boston, Massachusetts, 1978).

Milton H. Watson: US Passenger Liners Since 1945 (Patrick Stephens, Wellingborough, 1988).

Colin F. Worker: The World's Passenger Ships (Ian Allan, London, 1967).

Acknowledgements

A number of people have been of great assistance while I have been writing this book. I am particularly grateful to the staffs at the National Maritime Museum at Greenwich and the Guildhall Library in the City of London. John D. Henderson of Vancouver was most informative on the early careers of the Charlton sisters. Arie Langedijk resolved the mystery of the *Harpathian* and others. A conversation with Laurence Dunn yielded much interesting detail about some of the ships. I have enjoyed talking to Mrs. Isobel Sorell about the career of her late husband, Captain Donald Sorrell.

Index